SUMMER FEASTS

Molly Finn

Simon and Schuster
NEW YORK

OTHER PUBLICATIONS OF MOLLY FINN

Cooking for Carefree Weekends
by Molly Finn and Jeri Laber

Designed by Stanley S. Drate
Manufactured in the United States of America

1 2 3 4 5 6 7 8 9 10

Library of Congress Cataloging in Publication Data

Finn, Molly.
  Summer feasts.
  Includes index.
  1. Cookery. I. Title.
TX652.F48   641.5'6   78-31331

ISBN: 0-671-24056-0

*For my mother
and my children—Hannah, Becca,
Danny, Deirdre and Abby—
in celebration of our wonderful summers*

Contents

Acknowledgments

My thanks to all my summer cooking and eating comrades, to Hattie Mandelbaum for her arugula inspiration; to Rosemary Deen for many ideas, consultations and vegetables; to Mary Barnds, cooking soulmate; to Natalie Bowen for time and advice lovingly given; to Jeri Laber for all we did and learned together; and my most special and loving thanks to Jim, who willingly planted, weeded, picked, peeled, chopped, tasted, tested and never complained until I offered him three cucumber soups and five steamed custards for dinner one night.

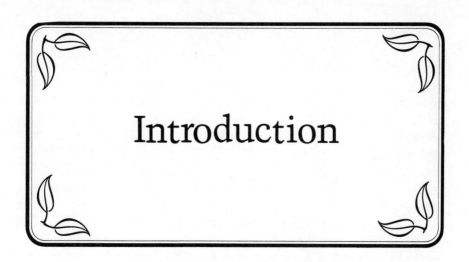

Introduction

A feast is what you make it. It can be a lavish spread served on rare china or a sun-warmed tomato, picked and eaten in a flourishing garden. This book is about the second kind of feast—the kind that's made out of the simplest elements, chosen with care, put together with attention, eaten with good appetite, appreciated with all the senses and received with joy and gratitude.

Summer brings an abundance of good things to feast upon. Beautiful vegetables, ripe fruit, fish and shellfish straight from the sea, fresh herbs in the kitchen garden—these are summer's best. Whether we eat them cold or hot, cooked or uncooked, plain or beautifully sauced, these gifts that are unique to summer will never be as good at any other time of year and should be enjoyed in their prime. They should also be treated with respect, eaten raw or very simply cooked, combined with only the purest butter or oil, fresh lemons, rich cream. In summer we want food that is light, colorful, piquant, as appealing to the eye as to the palate. We want food that is also easy to prepare, allowing the cook to serve leisurely and festive meals without spending a lot of time in a hot kitchen. This can be achieved—but only with good planning.

If you plan carefully, you can be as flexible as you like about when you actually cook a meal, free to spend an afternoon before a dinner party swimming, or to linger over a cool, before-dinner drink. Keep meals simple; it makes more sense in summer to extend a meal with lots of beautifully fresh, raw vegetables than to spend a lot of time fussing over them in the kitchen. Plan menus carefully so you never have to cook more than one last-minute dish at a time. Serve all-cold meals or combine hot and cold foods in a meal—and not just hot meat and cold salad. Cold meats and fish are excellent served with hot vegetable dishes. Study the menus on pp. 275-279. Each menu offers a variety of ways of putting together a colorful, delicious and interesting meal which can be prepared either entirely in advance or with a minimum of last-minute cooking.

To keep cool in summer—and to keep your cool—you should cook either very simply at the last minute, or well in advance. I try to use the oven as little as I can in summer; it makes the kitchen hot and the cook irritable. Use the oven only when you can be out of the kitchen when the oven is on and for an hour or two after as well. Baked pâtés, a fish loaf and quickly roasted beef can all be made a day or more in advance and are excellent if you are entertaining a lot and want to have a good supply of cooked food on hand. And I cannot resist baking fresh fruit pies and tarts—there is simply nothing to replace them.

But most of the recipes in this book call for cooking on top of the stove or on a charcoal grill. Many dishes can be prepared entirely or partially in advance. Dishes requiring long, slow simmering can be cooked at your convenience, in the cool of the morning or evening or whenever you can be out of the kitchen except for an occasional moment to stir, poke, taste and adjust. If you get in the habit of preparing the ingredients at your convenience and refrigerating them until it's time to cook, last minute steaming, poaching, sautéing or frying should never keep you in the kitchen for more than half an hour right before a meal.

Be as flexible as you can in your whole approach to food. When possible, plan your menus in the garden or market, centering a meal on what is freshest and most appealing on a given day. Cook more at one time than you need, so you'll have something on hand to take on a picnic, or the makings of another meal a day or two later when it's too hot to cook. While the charcoal grill is hot, broil an extra piece of meat; it won't be any more work and you can have both the basis of a second delicious dinner and the virtuous sense that you've made better-than-usual use of the glowing coals. If you can, steam extra fish or vegetables each time you cook. You will find many uses for both scattered through the recipes in this book. Make a big batch of chicken stock, freeze it in small containers to add to vegetable soups, and use the chicken cooked in the stock for salads, sandwiches, a mousse or a pâté.

Be flexible about the order of serving foods and be experimental about their temperatures. Anyone who has eaten little tidbits right out of the refrigerator knows how unexpectedly delicious they can be. While I don't happen to be a cold pasta addict, I *have* found that most foods that are very good hot are very good cold or, even better, at room temperature. If you serve foods at the "wrong" temperature with confidence, people will congratulate themselves on their discovery.

The same applies to the order in which foods are served. Almost anything can be a first course—or a main course—provided that it is served with style, assurance and a sense of appropriate quantities and combinations. A small piece of pumpernickel covered with fresh sweet butter, a thin slice of cold steak and a good grinding of pepper would make a delightful first course for a meal of fish soup. Tuna and Watercress Salad, p. 79, could equally well be the first or main course in a cold meal that included pâté, cheese, fresh bread and a fruit tart for dessert. Be bold and use your imagination; be guided by your own experience of what tastes good, and when.

Remember that freshness and simplicity are the keynotes of good summer food. All the recipes in this book call for fresh vegetables and fruits. No out-of-season, canned or frozen fruits or vegetables should be used. Herbs in all recipes are meant to be fresh unless a dried substitute is indicated. If you can't get a variety of fresh herbs, use the ones you can get instead of substituting inferior dried herbs. Experiment with new combinations of vegetables and herbs and invent your own repertoire of summer soups, salads and sauces.

Years of spring planting, summer harvests and feasts have gone into the making of this book. I hope it will heighten your enjoyment of summer, as it has mine.

SEASONINGS AND HERBS

All summer long we use fresh garlic and lemons, scallions, parsley and fresh herbs by the basketful. They find their way into almost every soup, sauce or sauté. They are beautiful, delicious, indespensible. Without them, summer cooking would be less colorful, less piquant, less ... well ... just *less!*

Fresh garlic and lemons are always easy to get in the market. No substitutions, please. Powdered garlic and bottled lemon juice will take away all the charm of the fresh fish and vegetables you make a point of buying. Think of fresh garlic and real lemons as staples; keep them on hand at all times and replace them when the supply is low.

Scallions, my favorite summer cooking onions, give a light but characteristic onion flavor and a pleasant dash of color with a minimum of cooking. You may, of course, substitute any other member of the onion family, including shallots, leeks or chives. (*But nothing dried!*) *Sweet red Italian onions* are the mildest and sweetest for eating raw. The best are imported from Italy, are longer than they are wide, and are available only in the summer. These onions are sold by the string at roadside stands. A string of red onions is a good investment—decorative and delicious.

Parsley is without a doubt the most useful of herbs and deserves a section to itself. Flat-leaved parsley, also called Italian, is much more flavorful than curly parsley. Use it when you can get it. Parsley is worth planting even if your garden is very small. Homegrown parsley has much more flavor than the store-bought. I plant my parsley in hedges, that is, in very thick rows. I sow a whole package of seed in a 1-by-4-foot row and it really does produce a hedge. What a joy it is to grab as large a handful as you can hold and just lop it off. Within a few weeks, it has grown back. Mix some chervil seed with the parsley in the last foot of your row—it seems to grow much better in the shade of the parsley than it ever does on its own.

Parsley has a strong, distinctive flavor and should be used when that flavor is what you want. A glance at the recipes in this book will convince anyone that I want it often, but not chopped and sprinkled indiscriminately over everything, frequently masking the subtle flavor of carefully prepared food. If you want to garnish a dish with parsley, put a few decorative sprigs on the plate, not on the food.

Fresh herbs. If you grow or can get fresh herbs, you know what a difference they make. Since I've been growing my own, there are very few dried herbs that seem worth using. The few that retain their flavor fairly well are thyme, oregano and marjoram. Dried basil, chervil, parsley, chives and dill are worthless. Dried tarragon is somewhere in between; it has a pleasant flavor, but not like the real thing. Dried rosemary has a convincing flavor but an awful texture. Tie it in cheesecloth and discard it before serving.

At their best, herbs should be, like any other vegetable, unblemished, fresh and moist; but even slightly wilted fresh herbs have a much better flavor than their dried versions.

Do not wash herbs before storing them. If you have to store them for a while, put them, perfectly dry, in a tightly covered plastic container in the refrigerator and wash just as much as you need at one time. Most herbs are quite perishable and should be used within two or three days, especially basil, dill, chives and chervil. Tarragon, savory and rosemary will keep up to a week if they are well protected.

The flavor of herbs can be preserved in vinegar, oil or wine. Rinse off several large sprigs of the herb you have chosen and dry them well. Put the herbs in a bottle of wine or vinegar and reseal the bottle. To make a flavored oil put the herbs in a clean, dry bottle; heat the oil but do not boil and pour the oil over the herbs. Seal each bottle tightly. Use the flavored wine, vinegar and oil in cooking and salads.

Recipes for *herb butters* may be found on pp. 235-36.

Coarse, kosher salt is the best kind to use. If you read the labels on most salt boxes, you will discover that most salt contains *sugar*. Coarse salt contains nothing but salt and it tastes that way. I also prefer its texture. Use it in cooking, too.

Unless a recipe calls for *whole peppercorns*, all the pepper you use should be *freshly ground*. Pepper doesn't just add sharpness to food; it has a real flavor of its own which disappears rapidly once the pepper is ground. Season foods with pepper toward the end of their cooking and keep a pepper mill on the table for last-minute additions.

THE CARE AND HANDLING OF FOOD IN SUMMER

It's not hard to keep food fresh, safe and appetizing in summer if you keep in mind a few general principles:

Always refrigerate milk products, eggs, meat and fish unless you are going to cook them immediately,

Cool cooked food in the refrigerator—don't leave it out to cool.

The warmer the air, the shorter the time it takes food to reach room temperature, the ideal temperature for serving most "cold" dishes. A large, deep bowl of food takes longer to come to room temperature than the same quantity spread out on a platter, but neither should be left out for more than an hour on a warm day (over 80°). Mayonnaise, custards and other foods containing a lot of eggs should not be left out of the refrigerator for more than 15 minutes before serving.

If food is left after a meal, refrigerate it as soon as possible.

Be sure to adjust the temperature of your refrigerator if the weather is very warm, if you are storing an unusually large amount of food or if you are cooling a lot of hot food.

PICNICS

If you're willing to go to the trouble of packing things properly, almost any food can be taken on a picnic. But some foods are especially easy to pack and easy to eat. Many of the foods in this book are suitable for picnics; here are some that do not spoil easily and are very easy to eat. Refrigerate cold foods until just before leaving for the picnic. Then pack the food in a well-insulated container and keep it cold with a few of those re-usuable cans of solidly frozen liquid sold for the purpose. Take some napkins, some buttered bread to use as edible plates and a plastic serving utensil or two.

*A thermos of cold soup to be drunk from paper cups, especially Gazpacho, p. 50, Green Bean, p. 51, or Spinach Soup, p. 59.

*Raw or cooked vegetables and cooked meats, cut in chunks, to dip into a jar of Arugula Dip, p. 12, Tapénade, p. 13, Onion-Vinegar Sauce, p. 246, or Horseradish Sauce, p. 240.

*A container of stuffing (Tuna-Cottage Cheese, p. 123, Rice Salad with Eggplant and Peppers, p. 96, or Zucchini Caviar, p. 150) and some prepared raw vegetables, large lettuce leaves or Basil Crêpes, p. 37.

*Rillettes, p. 21, or Fish Pâté, p. 17, packed in a plastic cup, and a box of crackers or Melba toast to spread it on.

*Cold Vegetable Meatballs, p. 181, Fried Chicken Balls, p. 193, or Stir-Fried Chicken Bits, p. 194, to eat with your fingers.

SIMPLE NO-COOK SUMMER FOODS

Here are some good things to eat that need *no cooking* at all:

*Sweet onion, cucumber or tomato sandwiches made with any kind of good fresh bread spread with sweet butter or homemade mayonnaise.

*Flat anchovy fillets on fresh Italian bread spread with sweet butter.

*Green pepper halves filled with cottage cheese.

*Canned salmon with chopped onions and vinegar.

*Chunks of tomato with sour cream.

*White Bean or Chick Pea Salad. You can make a very good salad using canned white beans or chick peas. Put the beans in a strainer and rinse them well under cold running water. Shake out all the liquid and put the beans in a bowl. For two 1-pound cans of beans, enough to serve 4–6, add a medium-sized sweet onion, sliced or diced, 3 or 4 tablespoons of chopped parsley and a double recipe of Vinaigrette Dressing, p. 251. Toss everything together and let it marinate for an hour or so before serving.

*Steak Tartare. It's wasteful to use fine fillet of beef for this dish. Use any fresh, lean beef with all fat and sinews removed, chopped in a food processor or twice by the butcher. Serves 4–6.

> 2 pounds ground lean beef
> 4–6 egg yolks
> 12 anchovy fillets
> 1 2-ounce jar capers, drained
> 1 large sweet onion, diced
> chopped parsley

Mound individual servings of chopped meat on plates and make an indentation in the top of each portion with the back of a spoon. Put a raw egg yolk in each indentation and garnish the plates with anchovy fillets and little piles of capers, onion and chopped parsley.

Here's a list of no-cook dishes in this book (omitting the many raw vegetable salads):
*Dips for Raw Vegetables, pp. 12-14.
*Cucumber Soup with Buttermilk, p. 49.
*Uncooked Tomato and Basil Sauce for pasta, p. 44.
*Gravlax, p. 168.
*Seviche, p. 170.
*Tuna and Watercress Salad, p. 79.
*Bulgur Salad, p. 81.
*Greek Salad, p. 86.
*Stuffed Raw Peppers, p. 122; Cucumbers, p. 85; and Tomatoes, p. 134.
*Tuna-Cottage Cheese Stuffing, p. 123.
*Bulgur-Basil Stuffing, p. 123.
*Greek Salad Stuffing, p. 124.

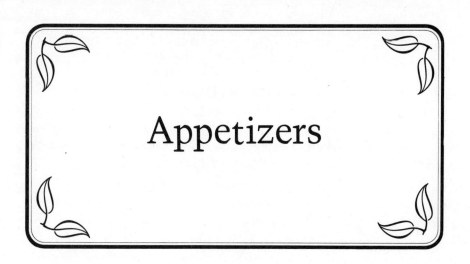

Appetizers

Summer, with its abundance of fresh, sweet, crisp vegetables, is the time to make the most of those sauces that have come to be known as "dips." It is easy to invent dips that are several light years beyond the ubiquitous sour cream–onion soup mixture. For starters, try mixing sour cream with some *fresh* chopped onion. Season with salt, freshly ground pepper and some chopped herbs and you have a spendid dip for raw vegetables of all kinds, and barely cooked vegetables, too. If you add some cooked shrimp or chunks of cold chicken or fish and some hot boiled potatoes, a good dip can serve as the center of an excellent meal—a perfect and easy way of entertaining a crowd.

In addition to the dips that follow, homemade mayonnaise in any of its variations, especially *Aioli*, p. 244, Basil Puree, p. 232, and Cucumber Sauce, p. 232, make good dips.

Ricotta Dip

(ABOUT 1½ CUPS)

This very bland dip is excellent for strong vegetables such as onion rings, hot peppers, and radishes. Vary the herbs to taste.

1 15-ounce container ricotta
2–4 tablespoons milk
1 clove garlic, minced
1 tablespoon each chopped dill and chives
salt and freshly ground pepper

Don't make this dip in the food processor—it gets too soupy. Beat the ricotta with the milk until it has the consistency you like. Add the garlic and herbs and season with salt and pepper.

Arugula Dip

(1 CUP)

Arugula (rocket, roquette, rucola are some of its many names) is a wonderful salad green when it is young, tender and mild. But there's no reason to scorn the abundant crop of tough old leaves that always follows the early salad cuttings. A few of these leaves, coarsely chopped, are enough to flavor a salad, but if you want to use arugula wholesale, here are three splendid ways: Arugula Sauce for Pasta, p. 41, Arugula Vinaigrette, p. 251 and this Arugula Dip:

2 cups coarsely chopped arugula leaves
½ cup olive oil
3 tablespoons wine vinegar
1 clove garlic, peeled
½ teaspoon salt

Put all the ingredients in the container of a blender or food processor and chop to a fine puree. Serve as a dip for raw vegetables. It is especially good with sliced kohlrabi and turnip, peeled broccoli stems, carrots and green peppers.

Sardine-Anchovy Dip

(ABOUT 1 ½ CUPS)

This is one of the best dips for raw vegetables and a good sauce for hard-cooked eggs. For an attractive antipasto, spread a thick layer of this mixture on a plate and arrange hard-cooked egg halves and an assortment of raw vegetables on top. Sprinkle with chopped chives and parsley.

1 can (3¾ ounces) skinless and boneless sardines with their oil
4 anchovies
1 8-ounce package cream cheese
sour cream
4 tablespoons chopped chives
lemon juice
salt and freshly ground pepper

To make the dip in a food processor. Chop the chives and remove them from the container. Replace the steel blade and add the sardines, the anchovies and the cream cheese, cut into small pieces. Process until everything is well blended. Transfer the mixture to a bowl and add sour cream until the mixture has the consistency of a dip or a thick sauce. Stir in the chives and season to taste with lemon juice, salt and freshly ground pepper.

To make the dip by hand. Mash the sardines and anchovies together well, then mash them with the cream cheese. Add some sour cream and if the mixture is still too thick, thin it with a little milk. Stir in the chives and season to taste with lemon juice, salt and pepper.

Tapénade

(ABOUT 1 CUP)

Tapénade is strong and salty—people usually love it or hate it. It is traditionally served with hard-cooked eggs, either as a sauce or mashed with the egg yolks. It's hard for me to think of a better summer lunch than a couple of hard-cooked eggs and a fresh green pepper with tapénade, a piece of good bread, and a glass of cold white wine.

Tapénade is an excellent dip for raw vegetables. Mixed with sour cream or mayonnaise, it makes a very good dressing for a fish salad. Mayonnaise flavored with tapénade is delicious with cold chicken, or spread on the bread for chicken sandwiches.

> *half of a 6½-ounce can tuna fish*
> *4 anchovies*
> *8–10 black, oil-cured olives, pitted*
> *1 large clove garlic*
> *1 tablespoon capers*
> *juice of ½ lemon*
> *½ cup olive oil*

Blend all the ingredients together in a blender or food processor. Put the sauce in a bowl, taste, and add more lemon juice if you like. The sauce will separate as it stands, so stir it just before serving. Tapénade will keep for 2 weeks in the refrigerator in a tightly closed container.

Chicken and Chicken Liver Pâté

(2 CUPS)

The green peppercorns give this pâté its very special flavor.

> *6 tablespoons rendered chicken fat or butter*
> *2 medium onions, finely chopped (about 1½ cups)*
> *½ pound raw, boneless chicken, cut in small pieces or 1 cup cooked*
> *   chicken*
> *½ pound chicken livers, trimmed and cut in half*
> *2 tablespoons bruised green peppercorns*
> *½ cup heavy cream*
> *salt*

Melt the chicken fat or butter in a large skillet. Add the onions and sauté them over medium-low heat for about 15 minutes, stirring from time to time until the onions are soft and golden brown. Add the chicken to the pan; cook the chicken with the onions for 5 minutes, then add the livers and cook for another 5–10 minutes, until both the chicken and the livers are cooked through.

To make the pâté in a food processor. Put the onions, the fat, the chicken, and the livers and 1 tablespoon of peppercorns in the container and process, using the steel blade, until the mixture is smooth. Add the cream and blend in. Then scrape the pâté into a bowl. Stir in the remaining peppercorns and add salt to taste.

To make the pâté in a blender. Remove the chicken from the pan. Put the cream in the blender container and add the onions, the melted fat or butter and the livers. Blend for a few seconds, then remove the cover and add 1 tablespoon of the peppercorns and the chicken a few pieces at a time. Blend until the pâté is smooth. Put it in a bowl, stir in the remaining peppercorns and add salt to taste.

Pack the pâté into a crock and refrigerate it for at least a day before serving.

If you wish, you can make this pâté using cooked chicken. Blend it with the livers after they are cooked.

Chicken-Liver Pâté with Fresh Herbs

(2 CUPS)

½ cup (1 stick) butter
1 small clove garlic, minced
1 pound chicken livers
salt and freshly ground pepper
2 tablespoons brandy
1 tablespoon chopped tarragon
2 tablespoons chopped chives
2 tablespoons chopped chervil or parsley
½ cup heavy cream

Melt the butter in a skillet, add the garlic and cook for a minute over medium heat. Add the chicken livers and cook them, stirring frequently, until they are just cooked through but still pink in the middle. Season the livers well with salt and freshly ground pepper. Remove the livers from the pan, add the brandy, turn up the heat and boil for a minute or so until the alcohol has evaporated.

Puree the livers with the pan juices in a blender or a food processor. Stir in the chopped tarragon, chives and chervil or parsley, taste and correct the seasoning with salt and pepper. (The flavor of the herbs will not be apparent until the pâté has had a chance to stand for a while. You can add plenty of salt and pepper, but do not destroy the delicacy of flavor by adding more herbs.) Whip the cream until stiff and fold it into the pâté. Scrape the pâté into a bowl or crock, cover and refrigerate for at least 4 hours, but preferably overnight.

Latin American Clam Cocktail

(SERVES 6)

You can buy glassfuls of clams and oysters prepared this way at street stalls in Colombia and other South American countries. The proportions of seasonings in the sauce are, of course, entirely a matter of taste. The sauce is wonderful with oysters when they are in season.

¼ cup olive oil
juice of 1 large lemon or 2 limes
1 large clove garlic, chopped
4 tablespoons chopped, fresh coriander or parsley
Hot Sauce for Meat, p. 240
3 dozen small hard-shelled clams, shucked with their juice reserved

Mix the oil, lemon or lime juice, garlic and coriander or parsley with the Hot Sauce. Add the clams and their juice and let the cocktail chill for about half an hour. Serve in small glasses and eat with a spoon.

Fish Pâté

This pâté is good made with any kind of fish. Leftover steamed, poached or broiled fish is just fine; so is fish taken from heads and bones that have been used for making fish stock. But it's worth cooking fish just for this pâté if you are having a cocktail party, a buffet or an elegant picnic. (One pound of boneless fish equals about 2 cups of cooked fish.)

4 tablespoons unsalted butter, at room temperature
1 ½ cups cold cooked fish, all skin and bones removed
1 tablespoon lemon juice
1 tablespoon finely chopped chives
1 tablespoon finely chopped dill
salt and freshly ground pepper

To make the pâté in a food processor. Put all the ingredients into the container and blend them with the steel blade until they are well combined.

To make the pâté by hand. Cream the butter until it is very soft. Mash the fish well, then mash it into the butter. Add the lemon juice, herbs and some salt and freshly ground pepper and combine well.

Taste the fish and correct the seasoning with lemon juice, salt and/or pepper. Pack it into a small bowl or crock and chill at least 6 hours, preferably overnight. Serve on toast or squares of dark pumpernickel or in sandwiches with plenty of watercress.

Variations. Thyme, parsley, chervil or fennel leaves are all good herbs to use in this pâté. Substitute any one of them, finely chopped, for the dill, but use the chives in any case. You can also mix in a few cut-up black Greek olives or some capers.

Pork, Liver and Bacon Pâté

(ONE 9 x 5-INCH LOAF)

The pâté can be made in the cool of the evening and enjoyed at a picnic or summer feast.

2 ½ pounds boneless pork
¾ pounds calves liver
1 pound sliced bacon
1 medium onion, minced
butter
4 cloves garlic, minced
½ cup dry white wine
¼ cup brandy
12 juniper berries, crushed
12 peppercorns, cracked
1 ½ teaspoons salt
6–8 bay leaves

Set aside 6 strips of bacon.

Put the pork, liver and the rest of the bacon through a meat grinder or chop (but do not pulverize) the meat in a food processor. Put the chopped meat in a large mixing bowl. Sauté the minced onion in a little butter until it is soft but not brown, and add it to the meat. Add the garlic, wine, brandy, juniper berries, peppercorns and salt and combine everything very thoroughly. (You can prepare this mixture and refrigerate it for several hours before baking it, if it is more convenient.)

Preheat the oven to 350°.

Sauté a little bit of the meat mixture and taste it. Correct the seasoning if necessary; the amount of salt needed depends upon the saltiness of the bacon. Place 3 or 4 bay leaves on the bottom of a 9 x 5-inch loaf pan or a deep, 1½-quart casserole. Line the pan with the reserved bacon strips, laying them crosswise side by side and allowing the ends of the bacon strips to hang over the edges. Put the pâté mixture in the pan, pack it down well, and pull the bacon ends over the top of the mixture until the ends meet. Arrange the 3 or 4 remaining bay leaves across the top of the pâté. Cover the pan tightly with a double layer of foil, set it in a pan of boiling water, and bake, covered, for an hour.

The pâté must be weighted down while it cools to give it the proper texture. Use another loaf pan filled with heavy cans of food as a weight, or put a brick on top of the foil covering and stand some heavy cans on it. Let the pâté cool for about half an hour, then refrigerate it. Leave the weights on until the pâté is completely cold. They may be left in place until the pâté is served, but this is not necessary.

Refrigerate the pâté for a least a day, preferably 2 or 3 days, before serving. It will keep in the refrigerator for about 10 days.

Veal and Pork Pâté

(ONE 9 x 5-INCH LOAF)

1 pound boneless veal
1 pound lean, boneless pork
½ pound calves or chicken liver
1 ½ pounds fresh pork fat
2 tablespoons brandy
¼ cup dry white wine
2 cloves garlic, peeled and crushed
2 teaspoons fresh thyme leaves or ½ teaspoon dried thyme
¼ teaspoon ground mace
1 tablespoon salt
lots of freshly ground pepper

Chop the veal, pork, liver and half the pork fat in a food processor or chop the liver by hand and put the rest of the meats through a meat grinder. Add all the other ingredients and combine thoroughly. Put the mixture in the refrigerator for several hours to allow the flavors to combine.

Preheat the oven to 350°. Cut the remaining pork fat into strips and line the bottom and sides of a 9 x 5-inch loaf pan, reserving enough fat to cover the top of the pâté. Pack the meat mixture well into the pan, cover it with strips of pork fat, then with a double layer of foil. Place the pan in a larger pan of boiling water and bake the pâté for an hour.

Let the pâté cool for half an hour or so, then weight it with a brick or with cans of food set into another loaf pan. Refrigerate the pâté for a day or 2 before serving. You may remove the weights after 6 hours or so.

Serve the pâté sliced, with bread, butter and tiny sour pickles.

Pitchah *(Calf's Foot Jelly)*

(SERVES 12 AS FIRST COURSE)

There's no way to make *pitchah* sound as good as it tastes—it sounds like a sneeze when correctly pronounced—P'tcháh. Those who are familiar with this kind of dish—brawn and head cheese are other examples—will recognize *pitchah* as a version of a classic. It's the Jewish version, so it is made with calf's feet rather than the more familiar pig's feet. The extremities of both these animals are full of gelatinous meat and, when they are simmered for hours with seasonings, they produce a richly flavored broth which sets, when cold, into aspic with a beautiful texture. A few slices of *pitchah* make a wonderful first course or light lunch. Molded in a ring mold and garnished with watercress, it makes an unusual, delicious and easy-to-serve summer buffet dish.

> *about 4 pounds calf's feet*
> *6–8 cups water*
> *5–6 bay leaves*
> *1 large onion, sliced*
> *1 tablespoon mixed pickling spice*
> *5 large cloves garlic, peeled*   *tied in cheesecloth*
> *2 sprigs dill*
> *12 peppercorns, bruised*
> *1 tablespoon salt*
> *4 hard-cooked eggs, sliced*
> *salt and freshly ground pepper*

Put the calf's feet in a soup pot or Dutch oven and add the cold water. If 6–8 cups of water do not cover the feet, transfer them to a smaller pot. *Do not add more water.* Bury the cheesecloth bag of seasonings in the pot, add the salt and bring the water to a boil. Skim the broth, lower the heat, cover the pot and simmer for 3–4 hours, or until the meat is very soft and falling from the bones. Strain the broth into a bowl. Taste it and correct the seasoning with salt and pepper. Don't be afraid to season the broth highly; it won't taste as strong when it is cold and jelled. Set the broth aside, over a pilot light or in a bowl of warm water so it will not jell.

Discard the bag of seasonings and remove all the meat and gristle from the bones while they are still warm. If you allow the bones to get cold, it will be very difficult to detach the meat. Scrape out any bits of marrow from the bones. Cut the meat, gristle and marrow into small pieces.

Put the slices of hard-cooked egg on the bottom and sides of a 9 x 5-inch loaf pan, a 2-quart ring mold or 2 smaller molds. Place the cut-up meat on top of the eggs. Ladle the broth gently over the meat, being careful not to disturb the arrangement of the eggs. If there is any extra broth, mold a couple of hard-cooked eggs in it or save it to use whenever you need a good, strong broth. Cover the mold with foil and refrigerate until set, at least 4 hours. If any fat has congealed on the surface, remove it with a spoon and wipe it off with paper towels.

To unmold the *pitchah*, run a knife around the edges of the mold, dip it briefly into hot water and invert a serving plate, face-down, over the mold. Invert the mold and serving dish; a smart rap on the mold should loosen the *pitchah*.

Pitchah can also be eaten hot as a soup. Chicken hearts, gizzards and necks are often added to the cooking meats. Heat the cut-up meats in the broth before serving.

Rillettes de Porc

(3–4 CUPS)

Rillettes, little pots filled with finely shredded pork cooked in its own seasoned fat, are delicious and quite easy to make. They keep well in the refrigerator for several weeks and can be served any time you would serve a pâté. With a salad and good bread, they make a fine lunch. They are perfect served as a first course at dinner or as a cocktail party spread, and are an ideal picnic food. I always pack some of each batch in plastic glasses to be taken on picnics and served on Melba toast.

There is some dispute about how to achieve *rillettes* with a perfect texture. Traditionally, the very soft meat is drained and pulled into fine shreds with two forks. I find the fingers extremely useful and somewhat faster in breaking up the pieces of meat into shreds without reducing it to a pulp. I'm sure purists would sneer at the idea of making *rillettes* from ground pork. I did, until I tried it once. It's not a perfect texture, but it *is* a perfect flavor and a very good spread. If you aren't up to that extra step of shredding the meat, try making the *rillettes* with ground pork. You might find them so delicious that you'll be willing to try the more traditional method the next time.

Any inexpensive cut of pork is fine for *rillettes*. I usually make it, using the trimmings, when I prepare a loin for stuffing or steaks, or when I bone a shoulder.

2 pounds boneless pork, cut into small chunks (or ground)
2 pounds fresh pork fat, cut into small pieces
½ cup water
1 clove garlic, minced
1 bay leaf
8–10 sprigs fresh thyme or ½ teaspoon dried thyme
1 ½ teaspoons salt
lots of freshly ground pepper

Put the pork, the fat and the seasonings in a heavy pot with a tight-fitting lid. Add half a cup of water to keep the meat from sticking, bring to a boil, lower the heat, cover the pot and cook *very slowly* for about 3 hours. The meat is done when it is very soft and swimming in the melted fat.

Drain the meat into a colander which has been set into a large bowl. Set the bowl of fat inside. When the meat is cool enough to handle, remove any small pieces of partially rendered fat and return them to the pot. Cook the fat over low heat, mashing it from time to time with a fork, until the fat has melted and the cracklings are crisp and brown. These are a delicious addition to the *rillettes,* chopped and mixed in with the meat after it is shredded.

Put the meat into a bowl and pull it apart into fine shreds, using 2 forks, your fingers or a combination of the two. Keep shredding the meat until it makes a fine paste and there are no solid bits left. (If you are using ground meat, mash it with a fork to break up any meat which is stuck together.) Add the chopped cracklings to the meat and blend in ½ cup or so of the melted fat. Taste the meat and add more salt and/or pepper if it is too bland. Remember that it will be eaten cold, so be sure it is well seasoned. Put the meat into small glazed pots (custard cups are good), mugs or glass jars (or plastic glasses, if you plan to take it on a picnic), filling them within ½-inch of the top. Fill the pots with the melted fat, being sure all the meat is well covered. Do not mix the fat with the meat juices in the bottom of the bowl; it is the pure fat that preserves the *rillettes.* Cover the pots tightly with foil and refrigerate them.

Bring the *rillettes* to room temperature before serving. This can take from ½ hour to 1½ hours, depending on the size of the container and the temperature of the air. Don't leave them out of the refrigerator too long on a very hot day. Serve on thin slices of French bread or toast.

Any extra fat, including the layer on top of the *rillettes*, is delicious and may be used either on toast or in cooking.

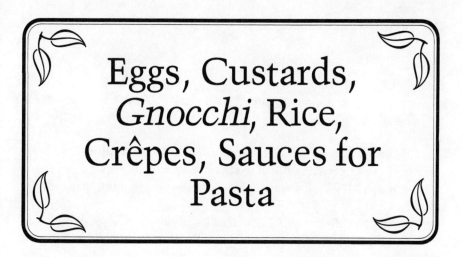

Eggs, Custards, *Gnocchi*, Rice, Crêpes, Sauces for Pasta

EGGS

Cottage Cheese Eggs

(SERVES 4)

6 eggs
3 tablespoons cottage cheese
salt and freshly ground pepper
2 tablespoons butter
1 tablespoon chopped chives, optional

Break the eggs in a bowl and beat them lightly with a fork. Add the cottage cheese and some salt and pepper and stir them into the eggs.

These eggs must be cooked in a 12-inch frying pan; only in a large pan can the liquid produced by the cottage cheese cook away, leaving creamy rather then watery eggs. If you want to cook more than 6 eggs, do it in 2 batches unless you have an enormous pan.

Melt the butter, stir in the eggs and cook over low heat, stirring constantly, until the eggs are lightly set and the curds of cottage cheese are soft and melting. Add the chives if you wish, and serve immediately.

Eggplant and Eggs

(SERVES 6)

This vegetable-egg mixture is good hot or cold. As a filling for a hero sandwich, with or without a few slices of ham, it makes an excellent picnic lunch. It is also good as a filling for eggplant, peppers or tomatoes.

This recipe calls for half a pound of eggplant—a very small eggplant indeed, or part of a larger one. I suggest making a double recipe and setting half of it aside before adding the eggs. The vegetables will keep for 3 or 4 days in the refrigerator. They can be eaten as they are or reheated and cooked with eggs a few days later.

½ pound eggplant
¼ cup olive oil
1 medium onion, coarsely chpped
1 large clove garlic, chopped
1 sweet red or green pepper, seeded and diced
1 tablespoon chopped basil or parsley, optional
salt and freshly ground pepper
4 eggs

Cut the eggplant into ½-inch dice, salt it and let it drain in a colander for 15–20 minutes, while you prepare the other vegetables. Heat the oil in an 8- or 9-inch frying pan. Add the onion and cook it over medium heat for about 5 minutes, until it is beginning to soften. Wipe the eggplant dry with paper towels. Stir the garlic into the onion, cook for another minute or 2 and add the eggplant and pepper, stirring to combine all the vegetables well. Lower the heat to medium low, cover the pan and cook the vegetables, stirring from time to time, until they are soft, 15–20 minutes. Taste and season with salt and freshly ground pepper. Add the herbs if you wish. This much can be done in advance; if you are cooking extra vegetables, set some aside at this point. Reheat the vegetables before proceeding with the recipe.

Beat the eggs lightly with a fork and stir them into the hot vegetables. Cook over medium heat, stirring constantly, only until the eggs have begun to set. Remove the pan from the heat. The heat of the vegetables will finish cooking the eggs; they should remain quite soft and creamy.

Here is an alternative and equally good method of cooking this dish. You will need 6 eggs. Use a 12-inch pan to cook the vegetables, watching carefully to be sure they do not stick to the pan. When they are soft, make 6 slight depressions in the vegetable mixture with a large spoon and break an egg into each one. Continuing to cook the vegetables over medium low heat, cover the pan and cook the eggs for 3–4 minutes. The whites should be set and the yolks still soft. Serve immediately.

This is an excellent brunch dish, especially good with ham or Canadian bacon. You can serve it on toast if you wish.

Poached Eggs on Anchovy Toast with Sautéed Cherry Tomatoes

(SERVES 6)

4 tablespoons sweet butter, at room temperature
1 2-ounce can flat anchovy fillets
1 recipe Sautéed Cherry Tomatoes, p. 135.
12 eggs
6 slices bread
buttered toast

Cut the anchovies into small pieces and mash them very thoroughly with the soft butter. Put water in a large skillet or saucepan to a depth of about 3 inches and start heating it. Prepare the Sautéed Cherry Tomatoes.

While the tomatoes are cooking, poach the eggs, a few at a time, in the simmering water. When they are done, keep them warm in a bowl of warm water. Toast the bread and spread each slice generously with the anchovy butter.

Have 6 plates ready. Remove the eggs from the water with a slotted spoon and put them on paper towels to drain. Put a slice of anchovy toast on each plate and place 2 poached eggs on each piece of toast. Add a large spoonful of cherry tomatoes and serve immediately.

Serve plenty of plain buttered toast to mop up the delicious juices.

Butter-Stuffed Hard-cooked Eggs

(FOR 6 EGGS)

As everyone knows, hard-cooked eggs can be stuffed with any number of things, and they are almost always good. I think the most delicious and the most delicate stuffing for hard-cooked eggs is lots of very soft herb butter mashed with the yolks. The combination brings out the flavors of egg, butter and herbs to perfection. If you can get it, chervil is the ideal herb to use.

6 hard-cooked eggs, shelled and cut in half lengthwise
4 tablespoons unsalted butter, at room temperature
1–2 tablespoons heavy cream
2–3 tablespoons chopped chervil, chives, parsley or mint

or

2–3 teaspoons chopped tarragon or dill
salt and freshly ground pepper

The butter must be quite soft. Room temperature in a warm room on a summer day is warm enough. If the room is cool, soften the butter by putting it in the sun or near the pilot light of the stove—but don't let it melt.

To use a food processor. Put the yolks, butter, cream and herbs in the container and blend them, using the steel blade, for 30–60 seconds, until the herbs are very finely chopped. Scrape the mixture into a bowl and season to taste with salt and freshly ground pepper.

To prepare the yolks by hand. Push them through a sieve and mash them into the butter. Chop the herbs as fine as possible and blend them in. Season to taste with salt and pepper.

Pile the mixture into the whites and garnish each half with an herb leaf. Serve at room temperature. If the eggs have been chilled, take them out of the refrigerator half an hour before serving.

Hard-cooked Eggs with Chicken Livers

(ENOUGH FOR 6)

4 tablespoons rendered chicken fat or butter
½ pound chicken livers, trimmed
salt and freshly ground pepper
1 large onion, coarsely chopped
6 hard-cooked eggs, coarsely chopped

Heat the chicken fat in a large skillet. Add the chicken livers and sauté them over medium heat until they are just cooked through, about 5 minutes. Remove them from the pan with a slotted spoon, season well with salt and pepper and set them aside. Add the onion to the fat in the pan. Cook it over low heat for about 15 minutes, stirring frequently, until it is soft and golden brown. While the onion is cooking, chop the eggs and cut the chicken livers into small pieces. When the onion is cooked, add the eggs and livers and combine everything gently. Taste and add salt and pepper if necessary. If the mixture is very crumbly, add another tablespoon or 2 of chicken fat or butter to bind it.

Serve warm with radishes and slices of raw kohlrabi and/or turnip, or use in sandwiches made with rye bread. Look in the index for a list of sauces to use on hard-cooked eggs.

STEAMED CUSTARDS

Steamed custards are among the most delicate foods in the world. Recipes follow for several different vegetable custards, two seafood custards and one made with chicken livers. All are ideal first courses for an otherwise cold meal, and are simplest to serve if you make them in individual custard cups or soufflé dishes. The vegetable custards also make an elegant accompaniment to a really good cut of simply grilled meat.

Steamed Lettuce Custard

(SERVES 8 AS FIRST COURSE)

Substitute any leafy vegetable (chard, spinach, sorrel or water cress) for the lettuce in this recipe, or add to the custard mixture about 2 cups of cooked vegetable puree such as broccoli or eggplant. This is a fine way to use cold, cooked vegetables, left over or specially cooked for this exquisite dish. Season each vegetable discreetly with a small amount of an appropriate seasoning (for example, a little grated cheese for eggplant, a sprig or 2 of chopped dill for spinach).

> *10 cups shredded lettuce leaves or 2 1-pound heads of lettuce, shredded*
> *1 bunch watercress or ¼ cup finely chopped chervil or parsley*
> *3 tablespoons butter*
> *4 scallions including green tops, thinly sliced*
> *3 eggs, lightly beaten* ⎫
> *1 cup heavy cream* ⎭ *beaten together with a fork*
> *salt and freshly ground pepper*

Wash the lettuce (and watercress, if you are using it) and steam it in the water clinging to the leaves until it is completely wilted. Drain the lettuce (save the juice for a soup), and chop it, by hand or in a food processor. Do not use a blender unless you can keep the lettuce from turning into a puree; it should be rather coarsely chopped. Put the chopped lettuce into a sieve to drain. Melt the butter in a small pan and sauté the scallions (and herbs, if you are using them) for 2 or 3 minutes. Press the lettuce down in the sieve and squeeze it to be sure it is as dry as possible. Add the lettuce and scallions to the egg-cream mixture and season it to taste with salt and freshly ground pepper.

To steam the custard. Spoon the mixture into 8 buttered 4-ounce custard cups or ramekins or pour it into a buttered 1½-quart soufflé or baking dish. Put a rack in a steamer (or improvise one, following the suggestions on p. 103), add 1 inch of boiling water and place the custard(s) on the rack. Cover the dish(es) lightly with waxed paper, cover the steamer and steam over medium high heat, 10–15 minutes for ramekins, 20–25 minutes for a soufflé dish. The custard is done when a knife inserted in the center comes out clean. Serve hot.

Scallion and Herb Custard
(SERVES 8 AS FIRST COURSE)

Use this as a model for herb-flavored custards. You can substitute a bunch of watercress, blanched, drained and chopped, for the scallions, if you prefer it.

6–8 scallions including green tops, finely chopped (about ½ cup)
2 tablespoons butter
2 tablespoons finely chopped parsley
2 tablespoons finely chopped tarragon
3 eggs
1 cup heavy cream
salt and freshly ground pepper

Sauté the scallions and herbs in the butter gently until they are soft but *still bright green*, about 5 minutes. Beat the eggs and cream together, add the vegetables and season to taste with salt and freshly ground pepper. Follow the directions for steaming the custard, above.

Fresh Corn Custard

(SERVES 8 AS FIRST COURSE)

The perfect way to use leftover corn on the cob. If you never have any, cook a couple of extras and hide them away. Also excellent with fresh peas.

3 eggs
1 cup heavy cream
2 cups fresh, cooked corn kernels
salt and freshly ground pepper
a pinch of nutmeg

Beat the eggs and cream together, add the corn and season the mixture with salt, pepper and a pinch of nutmeg. Follow the directions for steaming custard, p. 31.

Steamed Clam Custard

(SERVES 6)

This style of steamed custard is found in Oriental cookery. The custard itself has a beautifully delicate texture and is separated slightly from a very delicious broth. Serve hot, in individual custard cups or soufflé dishes.

1 dozen hard-shelled clams, shucked, with juice reserved
1–1⅔ cups chicken stock, preferably homemade, p. 72
4 eggs
2 teaspoons vegetable oil } *beaten together with a fork*
½ teaspoon salt

Put the clam juice in a measuring cup and add enough chicken stock to make 2 cups. Warm the mixture. Cut each clam into several pieces with a sharp knife and put the clams into 6 individual custard cups or soufflé dishes. Gradually beat the warm stock into the egg mixture and pour the mixture over the clams. Follow the directions for steaming the custard, p. 31.

Steamed Shrimp Custard

(SERVES 6)

½ pound shrimp
2 cups chicken stock
4 eggs
2 tablespoons vegetable oil   } beaten together with a fork
½ teaspoon salt

Rinse the shrimp. Put the chicken stock in a small saucepan over medium heat and, as you shell the shrimp, add the shells to the warming stock. When it comes to a boil, remove it from the heat and let it cool for a few minutes. Put the shrimp into 6 individual custard cups. Strain the warm stock and very gradually beat it into the egg mixture. Pour the mixture over the shrimp. Follow the directions for steaming the custard, p. 31.

Chicken Liver Custard

(SERVES 4)

For a really fancy lunch, turn this custard out of the molds and serve with Tomato Sauce with Cream and Tarragon, p. 249. It is equally good hot or cold.

¼ pound chicken livers (about 4 livers)
3 eggs
1 cup heavy cream
salt and freshly ground pepper

Puree the livers with the eggs in a blender or food processor. Add the cream and season with salt and freshly ground pepper. Pour the mixture into very well-buttered individual molds. Follow the directions for steaming custard, p. 31.

Basil Gnocchi

(SERVES 6 AS FIRST COURSE)

These very delicate dumplings are not always easy to make the first time. They require a little practice. If you really love basil, however, you will find it well worth learning to make them. Frozen Basil Puree, p. 232, is fine to use in this dish, so you can cook it any time in the year that you're longing for a whiff of summer.

1 ½ cups ricotta
2 eggs
6 tablespoons freshly grated Parmesan cheese
½ cup flour
salt and freshly ground pepper
3 tablespoons Basil Puree, p. 232 or 10 large leaves basil, pureed in
    a blender with 2 tablespoons olive oil
6 tablespoons (¾ stick) sweet butter
more grated Parmesan cheese

In a mixing bowl, combine the ricotta, the eggs and the Parmesan cheese, mixing them well with a whisk. Sprinkle the flour over the top, a bit at a time, and combine it thoroughly with the cheese mixture. Add about a teaspoon of salt, a few grinds of pepper and the basil puree and stir them in well. Taste and add more salt if necessary. Refrigerate the mixture for 3 or 4 hours.

Bring a lot of water to a boil in your spaghetti pot. Put a flameproof serving dish or pan on a Flame Tamer or asbestos pad over very low heat. Melt the butter in a small pot and pour a little of it into the serving dish.

When the water comes to a boil, turn heat down a little so it is boiling very gently. It will be necessary to adjust the heat under the water from time to time as you cook the gnocchi. It must be kept at a gentle boil. If it boils too vigorously, the gnocchi will fall apart; if it is not boiling, they will become soggy.

Take a teaspoonful of the cheese mixture and, using another teaspoon, push it into the boiling water. Cook about 12 or 15 gnocchi at a time. They will rise to the surface of the water when they are done, within 5 minutes. If they seem to be taking too long to rise to the surface, dislodge them gently from the bottom of the pot with a long-handled spoon. Remove the gnocchi from the water with a slotted spoon, shake them well over paper towels to drain away the water, and put them in the buttered dish. Cover the dish loosely by laying a piece of foil over it.

When all the gnocchi are cooked, pour the hot, melted butter over them. Pass a bowl of freshly grated Parmesan cheese to sprinkle over the gnocchi.

Rice with Zucchini and Ham

(SERVES 6)

This is a nice, light dish for lunch or supper. Serve it with a big green salad, followed by cheese and fruit for a quick and relatively effortless last-minute meal.

> 4 tablespoons butter
> 1 pound cooked ham, diced (about 2 cups) or ¾ pound Genoa
>   salami or mortadella sausage, cut into small pieces
> 1 large clove garlic, minced
> 2 medium zucchini, diced (1½–2 pounds)
> ½ cup chopped parsley
> salt and freshly ground pepper
> 2 cups raw rice (6 cups cooked)
> about ½ cup freshly grated Parmesan cheese

Melt the butter in a large skillet or shallow Dutch oven. Add the meat and cook it for 5 minutes or so over medium heat. Stir in the garlic and add the zucchini. Turn the heat to medium high, toss the zucchini to coat it all with butter, and sauté it, uncovered, stirring frequently, for about 10 minutes, until it is just cooked. Add the parsley and cook for another minute or 2. Season with salt and freshly ground pepper.

While the zucchini is cooking, cook the rice according to package directions or your usual method. Add the hot rice to the pan and carefully mix it with the zucchini and ham, over low heat, adding about 6 tablespoons of grated cheese. Taste and add more salt, pepper and/or cheese. Serve hot.

Tomato Soubise

Soubise is a puree of onions and rice cooked in chicken stock. It is delicious plain or mixed with other vegetables. Serve it with plain grilled meat or with Chicken Scallopine, p. 198.

3 large onions, sliced
4 tablespoons butter
1 cup rice
2 large or 3 medium-sized ripe tomatoes, peeled, seeded and
*   chopped (about 2 cups)*
2 cups chicken stock
½ cup half-and-half or cream

Blanch the onions in about 2 quarts of boiling water for 3 or 4 minutes to remove some of their sharpness. (If you use sweet onions, you may simply sauté them until soft in the melted butter before adding the rice.) Melt 2 tablespoons of the butter in a heavy saucepan and add the onions, rice, tomatoes and chicken stock. Cook, covered, over medium heat, until the rice is very soft, about 30 minutes. You can't overcook this rice; the softer the better.

Puree the vegetable-rice mixture in a food processor or put it through a food mill or a sieve. Melt the rest of the butter in the pot and add the soubise and the cream. Stir over medium heat until it is hot and serve immediately. The soubise can be prepared several hours in advance. Add the butter and cream just before reheating it gently.

Variation.
Spinach or Sorrel Soubise. Omit the tomatoes and add another cup of chicken stock when you cook the rice. When the rice is done but still hot, stir in 2 cups of blanched spinach or 2 cups of raw, chopped sorrel leaves (they will wilt immediately in the hot rice). Puree the vegetables and finish the soubise as described under Tomato Soubise, above.

Basil Crêpes

(16–18 CRÊPES)

These crêpes are so good that snackers in the kitchen can demolish a whole batch before they are ever filled. They are nice to take on a picnic or fill on the spot with Chicken Salad, p. 80 or Tuna-Cottage Cheese Stuffing, p. 123.

Use this recipe as a model for crêpes flavored with different herbs; allow one herb to dominate, and puree the herbs with a little olive oil before mixing them with the batter.

CRÊPES
3 eggs
½ cup milk mixed with ½ cup water
¾ cup flour mixed with ½ teaspoon salt
*3 tablespoons Basil Puree, p. 232 or a scant ½ cup chopped basil,
        pureed in a blender with 3 tablespoons olive oil*
butter

FILLINGS
freshly grated Parmesan cheese
Eggplant and Peppers, p. 114, warmed
Tomato Sauce, p. 248, warmed
ricotta
chopped parsley   } *mixed together*
salt and freshly ground pepper

Combine the eggs, milk and water, then gradually beat in the flour, using a blender or a hand beater. Beat until the batter is smooth and stir in the basil puree. Refrigerate the batter for an hour or 2. Pour the batter into a pitcher and spread a clean dish towel on the stove or any nearby surface.

Heat a little butter in a 6-inch frying pan. When the pan is hot, pour in enough batter to cover the bottom of the pan solidly, without leaving any holes. If there is too much batter in the pan, pour the excess back into the pitcher. When the bottom of the crêpe is golden brown, turn it over, brown it on the other side and turn it out of the pan onto the dish towel. Continue to make crêpes until all the batter is used. Spread the finished crêpes out on the towel.

To fill the crêpes. Melt a tablespoon of butter in a flameproof serving dish or pan and put the pan on a Flame Tamer or asbestos pad over low heat. Sprinkle about a teaspoonful of grated cheese over half the surface of each crêpe, add a scant tablespoon of one of the other fillings if you wish (they are very good with the grated cheese alone), fold the other half over it, and then fold the crêpe again to form a triangle. Put the folded crêpes in the heated pan, dot each one with a little butter and sprinkle them with a little more grated cheese. Cover the pan with foil and heat the crêpes until the butter on top has melted. Serve hot.

Summer's Best Basil Crêpes
(SERVES 6 AS FIRST COURSE, 4 AS MAIN COURSE)

Basil crêpes served this way, stacked into a sort of cake with different fillings between the layers, make a wonderful light summer meal . . . and a delightful brunch, lunch, supper or generous first course every month of the year, if you have remembered to freeze a good supply of Basil Puree, p. 232.

Folowing the recipe on the preceding page, make the batter for basil crêpes. Cook the batter in an 8-inch pan to make about 12 crêpes. For a 12-crêpe stack you will need:

a generous cup of Tomato Sauce, p. 248
a generous cup of ricotta
a generous cup of Eggplant and Peppers, p. 114 or some other cooked
    vegetable mixture such as Ratatouille, p. 153 or Peperonata, p. 128
½ cup freshly grated Parmesan cheese
3 or 4 tablespoons butter

Melt 2 tablespoons of butter in a heatproof serving dish, set it on a Flame Tamer or asbestos pad over low heat, and spread the pan with 3 tablespoons of tomato sauce. Put a crêpe in the pan, sprinkle it with Parmesan cheese, dot it with a little butter and lay another crêpe on top of it. Spread some eggplant and pepper on that crêpe, some ricotta on top of the next one. Continue adding crêpes and alternating fillings, leaving a few tablespoons of tomato sauce to use on the last crêpe. Cover the last crêpe with tomato sauce, dot it with butter and sprinkle it with cheese. Cover the pan with foil and heat it for about 10 minutes. Cut the stack of crêpes into wedge-shaped pieces and serve with a little of the tomato sauce spooned over it. Serve warm, not hot.

Cheese Blintzes

(16 BLINTZES)

These tender, eggy crêpes filled with cottage cheese are nothing like any frozen or restaurant version I've ever tasted. Blintzes make a wonderful summer breakfast, brunch, lunch or dessert. They can be made in advance and refrigerated for a day or so; then they take only 10 minutes from refrigerator to table. They can also be frozen and need only be partially thawed before their final cooking.

Plain cheese blintzes are delicious with sliced strawberries and sour cream. You can make a slightly sweet, spicy filling and add raisins; you can make a savory filling with chopped herbs. Add a little chopped ham to the cottage cheese filling, or a bit of grated lemon rind, or half a cup of blueberries. But remember—this is a light dish. Just a touch of this or a dash of that will do the trick. Always top blintzes with a dollop of sour cream.

CRÊPES
3 eggs
½ cup milk mixed with ½ cup water
¾ cup flour mixed with a dash of salt
2 tablespoons melted butter
butter for frying

FILLING
1 pound cottage cheese or pot cheese ⎫
1 egg, lightly beaten ⎬ mixed together
⎭

Variations. Add to the cheese mixture:

*1 scallion, finely chopped, mixed with a tablespoon finely chopped
    parsley, a pinch of salt and a little freshly ground pepper*
2 tablespoons chopped ham and 1 tablespoon chopped dill
*1 tablespoon sugar mixed with a pinch each of cinnamon and
    nutmeg*
*1 tablespoon sugar, 1 teaspoon grated lemon rind and 2 tablespoons
    raisins*

Combine the eggs, milk and water, then gradually beat in the flour, using a beater or blender. Beat until the batter is smooth and stir in the melted butter. Pour the batter into a pitcher and spread a clean dish towel on the stove or any nearby surface.

Heat a little butter in a 6-inch frying pan. When the pan is hot, pour in enough batter to cover the bottom of the pan solidly, without leaving any holes. If there is too much batter in the pan, pour the excess back into the pitcher. When the bottom of the crêpe is golden brown, turn it out onto the dish towel, cooked-side up. Continue to make crêpes until all the batter is used, adding a little butter to the pan from time to time only if the crêpes are sticking. Spread the crêpes out on the towel as they are cooked.

To fill the blintzes, put a tablespoon of filling in the center of the cooked side of a crêpe. Fold opposite edges of the crêpe over the filling four times to form a small, square package, and put the blintzes on a platter. At this point you may cover and refrigerate the blintzes up to 24 hours, or wrap them well in foil and freeze them.

Ten minutes before serving, melt 2 or 3 tablespoons of butter in a large skillet. Put the blintzes in the butter, seam-side down, and cook over moderately low heat until they are golden brown. Turn them carefully with a spatula and brown the other side. Cook the blintzes in 2 pans if you can, so they will all be done at the same time. Otherwise, cook them in 2 batches, adding more butter to the pan if necessary. Serve hot with sour cream.

SAUCES FOR PASTA

Arugula Sauce for Pasta
(ENOUGH FOR 1 POUND PASTA)

This is a very distinctive and delicious sauce, quite unlike anything else. It is a beautiful color and tastes like the essence of green.

1 cup coarsely chopped arugula leaves, tightly packed
¼ cup olive oil
1 large clove garlic, peeled
1 teaspoon salt
lemon juice to taste
1 pound pasta
4 tablespoons butter, at room temperature
freshly grated Parmesan cheese, optional

Puree the arugula with the oil and garlic in a blender or food processor. Season to taste with salt and lemon juice.

Cook the pasta according to package directions. Put a colander into the bowl in which you intend to serve the pasta and put the bowl in the kitchen sink. When the pasta is cooked, drain it into the colander. Empty the bowl, dry it and put the butter in the bowl (you now have a nice hot serving bowl). Shake all the water out of the pasta and toss it with the butter in the bowl. Add the arugula sauce and toss again. Some people prefer this pasta with grated cheese, some without. Pass a bowl of grated cheese for those who like it, and a peppermill for everybody to use.

The arugula puree freezes very well and it is a very pleasant surprise to come upon it in mid-winter. To freeze, puree just the arugula and oil. Add the other ingredients after the puree has thawed.

Clam and Parsley Sauce

(FOR 1 POUND OF PASTA)

2 dozen large clams, well scrubbed
3 large cloves garlic
2 cups chopped parsley
¾ cup olive oil
salt and freshly ground pepper

Put the clams in a large pot with ¼ cup water, cover the pot and steam the clams over high heat *just until* the shells have opened, about 5 minutes. Uncover the pot and remove it from the heat. Do not cook the clams any longer than this or they will be tough. While the clams are cooling, chop the garlic and parsley. Remove the clams from the shells and cut each one into several pieces. Discard the shells and strain the broth through several layers of cheesecloth or paper towels.

Heat the oil in a large skillet. Add the garlic and cook it very slowly for a minute or 2—do not let it brown. Add the parsley, stir it in well, add the clam broth and simmer for 3 or 4 minutes. Taste the sauce and add salt and freshly ground pepper to taste. Make the sauce to this point before you cook the pasta. When the pasta is almost done, gently reheat the sauce. Put the clams in the sauce only when you drain the pasta, and pour the sauce over the pasta as soon as the clams are heated through.

Ham and Herb Sauce for Pasta

(ENOUGH FOR 1½ POUNDS OF PASTA)

¾ cup olive oil
¼ pound country ham, Canadian bacon or proscuitto, coarsely
  chopped or ½ pound of a milder, cooked ham
2 cloves garlic, minced
½ cup chopped parsley
1 tablespoon chopped fresh marjoram or ½ teaspoon dried marjoram
6–8 leaves fresh basil, chopped or 1 teaspoon fresh thyme leaves
salt and freshly ground pepper
1½ pounds pasta

Heat the oil in a frying pan, add the ham and garlic and sauté them very gently, without browning, for 4 or 5 minutes. Add all the herbs, stir them in well, sauté them very gently for 2 or 3 minutes more and turn off the heat. Let the herbs steep in the oil while the pasta is cooking.

Cook the pasta until it is done, drain it, put it in a hot serving dish and pour the sauce over it. Toss thoroughly and serve immediately.

Ham and Tomato Sauce

(FOR 1½ POUNDS OF PASTA)

This sauce is excellent on pasta or rice. Mixed with rice, it makes a good stuffing for zucchini or eggplant.

4 tablespoons olive oil
¾ pound cooked ham, diced (about 1 ½ cups)
1 medium onion, coarsely chopped
1 large clove garlic, minced
2 pounds plum tomatoes, peeled
 and coarsely chopped
6 large leaves basil, chopped
 (1 heaping tablespoon)   or 3 cups fresh Tomato
2 tablespoons chopped parsley   Sauce, p. 248.
1 teaspoon salt
lots of freshly ground pepper
½ teaspoon sugar
1 ½ pounds pasta, cooked or 6 cups cooked rice (2 cups raw)

Heat the oil in a large skillet. Add the ham and cook it gently for 5 minutes or so, until it is lightly browned. Add the onion and continue to cook for 5–10 minutes, until the onion is soft. Stir in the garlic and cook for another minute or 2. If you are using already prepared tomato sauce, add it now and simmer for 10 minutes.

If you are using raw tomatoes, add them, with the herbs, to the pan, stir well and cook over medium heat for about 20 minutes, until most of the liquid from the tomatoes has cooked away. Add the salt and sugar, taste the sauce and adjust the seasoning.

Pour the sauce over freshly cooked, buttered pasta or rice and serve immediately.

Pesto

(ENOUGH FOR 1 POUND PASTA)

Please use only the best ingredients when you make this sauce. The olive oil must be of good quality and the cheese must be real Parmesan cheese, freshly grated, not that white powder that comes in a jar.

½ cup Basil Puree, p. 232
2 tablespoons olive oil
2 cloves garlic, minced
2 teaspoons salt
lots of freshly ground pepper
3 tablespoons butter
1½ cups freshly grated Parmesan cheese
1 pound spaghetti or other pasta

Put the basil puree in a small bowl and mix it with the oil, the garlic, the salt and plenty of freshly ground pepper.

Cook the pasta according to package directions. Put a colander into the bowl in which you intend to serve the pasta and put the bowl in the kitchen sink. When the pasta is cooked, drain it into the colander. Empty the bowl, dry it and put the butter in the bowl (you now have a nice hot serving bowl). Shake all the water out of the pasta and toss it with the butter in the bowl. Add the basil mixture and toss again, then sprinkle in about ½ cup of cheese and toss to combine well. Serve immediately. Pass the rest of the grated cheese in a bowl.

Uncooked Tomato and Basil Sauce

(ENOUGH FOR 1½ POUNDS PASTA)

This delicate sauce is very easy to make. Be sure not to turn the tomatoes into a puree; little chunks of raw tomato give the sauce a lovely texture.

3 cloves garlic, peeled
about 1 cup finely chopped basil leaves

6–8 large, very ripe tomatoes, peeled and cut in quarters
½ cup olive oil
salt and freshly ground pepper to taste
freshly grated Parmesan cheese

To make the sauce in a food processor. Put the garlic and basil in the bowl and chop with the steel blade until they are finely chopped. Add the tomatoes and process for a few seconds only, turning the motor on and off once or twice, until the tomatoes are coarsely chopped. Pour the mixture into a bowl, stir in the olive oil and season to taste with salt and pepper.

To make the sauce in a blender. Put the olive oil, basil and garlic in the container, blend for a few seconds and then gradually blend in 3 or 4 pieces of tomato. Coarsely chop the remaining tomatoes and pour the blended mixture over them. Season to taste with salt and pepper.

To make the sauce by hand. Mince the garlic and basil, coarsely chop the tomatoes, and combine them with the oil. Season to taste with salt and pepper.

Let the sauce stand for a couple of hours before serving, so the flavors have a chance to combine. Stir the sauce, taste it again and adjust the seasoning before pouring it over freshly cooked pasta. Pass around a bowl of grated cheese to sprinkle over the pasta.

All of the following tomato sauces are good on pasta:
*Tomato Sauce with Butter, p. 247.
*Tomato Sauce with Olive Oil, p. 248.
*Tomato Sauce with Cream and Tarragon, p. 249.

Noodles with Cottage Cheese and Sour Cream
(SERVES 4 AS A MAIN COURSE,
6 AS A SIDE DISH)

This dish, with a salad and some fruit for dessert, makes a very cheap and satisfying lunch or quick supper. It is at its best, though, as a rich, bland accompaniment to salty or spicy meat. Serve it hot with thin slices of cold ham or tongue.

12 ounces broad egg noodles
1 ½ cups cottage cheese
1 cup sour cream
salt and freshly ground pepper
2 tablespoons chopped chives, optional

Cook the noodles in lots of boiling, salted water until they are done. Drain them and return them to the pot. Over very low heat, stir in the cottage cheese and sour cream. When they are thoroughly mixed in, season to taste with salt and plenty of freshly ground pepper, and some chives if you wish. Serve immediately.

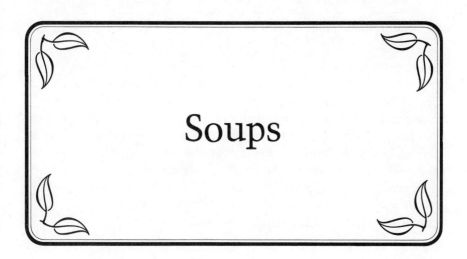

Soups

Beet Borsch

4 or 5 medium beets with their greens
1 large onion
2 teaspoons salt
juice of 1 large lemon (3–4 tablespoons) or more, or a few crystals of
     sour salt (available on the spice shelf of most supermarkets)
2–3 tablespoons brown sugar

GARNISH
sour cream
boiled new potatoes, optional
chopped dill, optional

Scrub the beets well (their cooking water will be used in the soup) and cut off the leaves. Cover the beets with water, partially cover the pot and cook the beets briskly for 30–40 minutes or until they are tender when pierced with a sharp knife.

Meanwhile, trim the stems from the beet greens, chop the leaves fine and set them aside. Peel the onion and grate or finely chop it. When the beets are done, remove them from the water and let them cool a bit. Slip off the skins and grate the beets by hand or in a food processor.

47

Measure the beet juice and add enough boiling water to make 5 cups. Bring the liquid to the boil and add the grated beets and the onion. Simmer the soup for 5 minutes more. Add the salt, a tablespoon or so of brown sugar and 3 or 4 tablespoons of lemon juice or a few crystals of sour salt and stir well. Taste the soup and adjust the balance of sweet, sour and salty to your taste. Remember that when the soup is cold, the flavor will not be as strong, so add plenty of seasoning.

Serve the soup ice cold with a dollop of sour cream. To make a more substantial (and very delicious) dish, add a hot boiled potato and a sprinkling of fresh dill to each plate as well.

Carrot Soup

(SERVES 6)

This carrot soup thickened with rice is a French classic. It would be a shame to waste the early, small, tender carrots from the garden by turning them into soup, however good it is. Save this for the end-of-season harvest of big carrots, usually very sweet but not always very tender.

4 tablespoons butter
8–10 carrots (about 1 pound), scraped and cut up, chopped or
    shredded
1 leek, white part only, sliced or 1 small onion, chopped
3 tablespoons raw rice or ½ cup cooked rice
4 cups dilute chicken stock (2 cups chicken stock mixed with 2 cups
    water)
1½–2 cups milk, heated to boiling point
salt and freshly ground pepper

Melt the butter in a 3-quart pot. Add the carrots, leek and the rice and cook them in the butter until the vegetables are soft. Since the rice is used as a thickening and should be very soft, you can add either raw or cooked rice at this point. Add the broth, bring to a boil, turn the heat down, cover the pot and simmer the soup until the rice is soft and the vegetables are done, at least 20 minutes.

Puree the soup in a food processor, a blender or a food mill. Return it to the pot, add the hot milk gradually until the soup is the proper consistency, and season the soup with salt and freshly ground pepper.

Cucumber Soup with Buttermilk

(SERVES 4–6)

2 medium cucumbers or 1 very large one
2 cups buttermilk
2 cups chicken stock, preferably homemade, p. 72
2 teaspoons salt
freshly ground pepper
2 tablespoons chopped chives
a little chopped dill, optional

Peel the cucumbers and remove the seeds if they are woody. Shred the cucumbers in a food processor or with a grater. Mix the cucumbers in a bowl with the buttermilk and the chicken stock and add the salt, pepper, and chives. Refrigerate the soup for several hours before serving. If you use homemade jellied chicken stock, the flavor and texture of this soup will be especially appealing.

Sprinkle each serving with a little chopped dill.

Cold Eggplant Soup

(SERVES 6)

This is an unusual and delicious soup. A sprinkling of bright-green parsley adds a lovely touch of color.

½ the recipe for Eggplant and Peppers (2 cups), p. 114
2 cups plain yogurt
2 small cloves garlic, crushed
milk
salt
chopped parsley

Puree the eggplant and peppers in a food processor, a food mill or a blender. Add a little milk if some liquid is needed. Beat the yogurt with the garlic and about ½ teaspoon salt; it will liquefy slightly. Combine the yogurt mixture thoroughly with the eggplant puree and cautiously thin it with milk until it has the consistency of a very thick soup. This soup has, and should have, a concentrated flavor that will be lost if too much milk is added. Adjust the seasoning with more salt and chill until serving time. You can make this soup a day or two in advance. Sprinkle each serving with parsley.

Gazpacho

Lots of people claim to have the recipe for *the* gazpacho, either the "authentic" gazpacho or the "best." Of course, there's no such thing. There are countless authentic gazpachos, and the best is the one you like best. This is the version I like best.

2 pounds (6 large) ripe tomatoes
1 pound (2 medium) cucumbers, peeled
½ pound (3 medium) green peppers, seeded
¼ pound (1 small) sweet onion, peeled
1 large clove garlic, peeled
¼ cup olive oil ⎫
¼ cup wine vinegar ⎬ *combined*
2 teaspoons salt ⎭

Cut all the vegetables into chunks. Chop or puree all the ingredients together.

If you are using a food processor. This proportion of vegetables should make a nice, thick, slightly crunchy soup. If you want the soup a bit more liquid, add another large tomato.

If you are using a blender. Always put some tomatoes in first, with a bit of oil and vinegar to provide the necessary liquid. Puree the vegetables in several batches, leaving a little liquid in the blender container to start each batch. Set aside several pieces of cucumber and pepper to add, diced, as a garnish when you serve the soup. Serve the gazpacho cold, with lots of Garlic Croutons, p. 73.

Variations. Add:
3–4 tablespoons chopped hot peppers
                  or

3–4 tablespoons chopped parsley
              or
2 tablespoons chopped basil

For a more filling but somewhat blander soup, beat in 3 or 4 raw eggs while you puree the vegetables.

Green Bean Soup

(SERVES 6)

This soup is equally delicate thickened with rice or potato. It is good hot or cold. It is a fine way to use green beans that have gotten big, but that are still fresh and sweet. As with most soups, it seems to taste better after it has rested a few hours after cooking. If you reheat it, be careful not to overcook it, or the fresh taste of the beans will be lost.

Fresh summer savory combines particularly well with green beans; add it to the beans as they cook. If all you have is dried savory, forget it.

3 tablespoons butter
6 scallions including green part thinly sliced (scant ½ cup)
2 tablespoons uncooked rice or ½ cup peeled, diced potato
4 cups dilute chicken stock or vegetable stock (2 cups stock mixed
    with two cups water)
1 pound green beans, stem ends removed
1 tablespoon chopped fresh summer savory, optional
2 cups milk, heated to boiling point
salt and freshly ground pepper

Melt the butter in a 3-quart pot. Add the scallions and cook them gently, without browning, for a few minutes. Add the rice or potato, stir it into the butter, and add the stock. Bring it to a boil, turn the heat to medium and cook until the rice or potato is done, 20 minutes, or more if necessary. Add the beans and savory, if you have it, and cook briskly for about 10 minutes more, until the beans are just tender and are still bright green. Remove the soup from the heat and puree it in a food processor, a blender, or a food mill. Return the soup to the pot and add the hot milk. Season with salt and freshly ground pepper. Serve hot or cold.

Lettuce Soup

(SERVES 8 HOT, 6 COLD)

This is one of the simplest of soups and one of the best.

*2 heads lettuce or enough leaf lettuce to make 6–8 cups, washed and
    shredded
3 cups good chicken stock, homemade if possible, p. 72*

FOR COLD SOUP
*½ cup half-and-half or light cream
salt and freshly ground pepper*

FOR HOT SOUP
*3 cups milk
salt and freshly ground pepper
Parsley Butter, p. 236*

You will need a large pot for this soup because the lettuce is very bulky before it is cooked. Bring the stock to a boil and add as much lettuce as you can. When each batch of the lettuce has wilted, add some more, continuing to cook it over high heat and pushing the leaves into the boiling liquid. Once all the lettuce has been added, cook the soup for about 10 minutes. Strain the soup and return the liquid to the pot. Puree the wilted lettuce with a little of the stock, using a food processor, a blender or a food mill. The puree shouldn't be too smooth—leave it a bit crunchy. Combine the puree and the stock.

If you are serving the soup cold. Refrigerate it at this point. Just before serving, stir in the cream and season it with salt and a few grinds of pepper.

If you are serving the soup hot. Add the milk and heat the soup until it just comes to a boil. Taste and add salt and a little freshly ground pepper. Put a piece of the Parsley Butter in each soup bowl and ladle the soup over it.

Pea Soup

(SERVES 6)

You can puree this soup or not, as you wish. For a puree, there is no need to cut up the vegetables before cooking.

4 tablespoons butter
8 scallions including green tops, thinly sliced
1 small carrot, scraped and cut in 2-inch matchsticks
1 cup finely shredded lettuce leaves
3 cups chicken stock, preferably homemade, p. 72
2 pounds fresh peas, shelled (2½–3 cups)
1 cup half-and-half
salt and freshly ground pepper
a little sugar if necessary
2 egg yolks, only if you are not pureeing the soup

Melt the butter in a 3-quart pot. Add the scallions, carrot and lettuce and cook them gently for about 5 minutes. Add the chicken stock, bring it to a boil and add the peas. Cover the pot and cook over medium heat for 10–15 minutes, until the peas are just cooked (and still very bright green).

If you are pureeing the soup. Process it in the blender or food processor until it is a smooth puree. Return it to the pot, through a strainer if necessary. Add the cream, salt, pepper and a little sugar to taste, and heat gently until the soup is hot. Serve with Butter Croutons, p. 73.

If you are not pureeing the soup. Mix the half-and-half with the egg yolks. Ladle a little hot soup into the mixture to warm it, then pour it into the soup pot. Season the soup with salt, pepper and a little sugar to taste. Heat the soup very gently for a few minutes, but keep it below the boiling point.

Pistou

(SERVES 8–10)

This is one of the great summer meals. This recipe makes a lot of pistou. Plan to serve it as the main dish of a lunch or supper. Follow it with a platter of good cheese, a crusty loaf and a bowl of choice summer fruit.

3 tablespoons olive oil
1 large onion, sliced
3 large ripe tomatoes, peeled and cut in chunks
10 cups boiling water
1 tablespoon salt
½ cup freshly shelled beans (cranberry or romano beans) or 1 cup
    cooked dried white beans
1 large potato, peeled and diced (about 1 cup)
1½ pounds zucchini, cut in ½-inch dice (4 cups)
1 pound green beans, broken in 1-inch lengths (4 cups)
¼ cup small pasta
12 large leaves basil, finely chopped or 3 tablespoons Basil Puree,
    p. 232
3 cloves garlic, minced
salt and freshly ground pepper
freshly grated Parmesan cheese

Have all the vegetables ready before starting to cook the soup. Heat the oil in a big soup pot, add the onion and cook it gently, without browning, for about 10 minutes. Add the tomatoes, stir them into the onion and cook for about 10 minutes more. Add the hot water and a tablespoon of salt, turn up the heat and bring the soup to a boil. Add the shelled beans (only if they are fresh; if you are using cooked beans, add them later), bring the soup back to the boil, cover the pot, turn down the heat and simmer for 20 minutes. Bring the soup back to the boil and add each vegetable, in the order given, bringing the soup to a full boil after each addition, and stirring well each time. After the green beans have been added and the soup is boiling, add the pasta (and the cooked beans, if you are using them), stir it in very well, and turn the heat to low. Stir in the basil or basil puree and garlic, season to taste with more salt and some freshly ground pepper, and simmer the soup for 4 or 5 minutes, until the pasta is just cooked. Serve the soup with freshly grated Parmesan cheese.

You can make *pistou* ahead of time but be sure to undercook it if possible so the vegetables will retain their firm texture. Remove the soup from the heat and stir in the pasta; the heat of the soup will cook it. Add the basil or basil puree and garlic only at the last minute, or their fragrance will be greatly diminished. If you plan to freeze the soup, omit the potato and the pasta. You can add them after thawing or leave them out. Season the thawed soup with basil or thawed Basil Puree, p. 232.

Pistou is as good cold as it is hot and, with less water, becomes a delicious vegetable stew.

Cold Potato and Herb Soup

(SERVES 6)

2 tablespoons butter
6–8 scallions including green tops, sliced
1 tablespoon chopped tarragon or 3 tablespoons chopped dill or 2
    tablespoons chopped mixed herbs
2 large potatoes, peeled and diced small
6 cups strong, homemade chicken stock, p. 72
2 cups half-and-half
salt and freshly ground pepper
chopped herbs, whichever ones you have used in the soup
½ cup heavy cream, optional

Melt the butter in a 3-quart pot and sauté the scallions until they are soft but not brown. Add the herbs and potatoes and cook for 3 or 4 minutes more over low heat. Add the stock, bring to a boil and simmer the vegetables until the potatoes are soft, about 20–25 minutes. Add the half-and-half, bring the soup back to the boil and turn off the heat. Puree the soup in a blender or food processor until it is smooth and season it to taste with salt and freshly ground pepper. Taste the soup again when it is cold and adjust the seasoning.

Serve the soup cold, sprinkled with chopped herbs. Stir in some heavy cream if you like a richer soup.

Red, White and Green Vegetable Soup

(SERVES 6–8)

This is one of the loveliest, most delicate and summery of soups, and can include a little bit of almost every vegetable that's ripe in my mid-July garden. Put in as much variety as you can, but only a little bit of each vegetable, so no one flavor will dominate. The garnish of cooked shrimp is a touch common in Scandinavian and Russian soups, and well worth the expense.

1 pound peas, shelled (1 generous cup)
2 small new potatoes, peeled and cut in ¼-inch dice (about ½ cup)
1 small turnip or kohlrabi, peeled and cut in ¼-inch dice
¼ pound green beans, cut in ½-inch pieces (about 1 cup)
1 cup broccoli flowerets
2 teaspoons salt
¼ pound spinach leaves, finely shredded (2 tightly packed cups)
8–10 red radishes, thinly sliced
2 tablespoons butter
2 tablespoons flour
1 cup milk or ¾ cup milk and ¼ cup cream
freshly ground pepper

GARNISH
½ pound cooked shrimp, cut in ½-inch pieces
chopped dill

Put the peas, potatoes, turnip, beans and broccoli in a soup pot and add the salt and enough water just to cover the vegetables, about 5 or 6 cups. Bring the water to a boil, cover the pot and cook the vegetables for 5 minutes. Add the spinach, bring back to a boil and cook 5 minutes more. Add the radishes, stir them in and remove the pot from the heat. You may prepare the soup in advance to this point.

Melt the butter in a small saucepan over low heat. Add the flour, stir it well and cook, *without browning,* for 2 or 3 minutes. Whisk in the milk and cook, stirring constantly, until the sauce is thick and smooth. Continue to cook over low heat, stirring from time to time, for about 10 minutes. Add to the sauce about a cup of the stock in which the vegetables were cooked, mix it in well and then pour the thinned sauce into the soup. Heat the soup, let it simmer for a couple of minutes, adjust the seasoning with salt and pepper, and serve hot. Put some shrimp in each bowl and sprinkle the soup with chopped dill.

Sorrel and Potato Soup

(SERVES 6)

8–10 scallions including green tops, sliced
3 tablespoons butter
2 large potatoes, peeled and diced
about ¼ pound sorrel leaves (2–3 cups shredded) or 1 large bunch
    watercress, coarsely chopped
3 cups chicken stock, preferably homemade, p. 72
salt and freshly ground pepper

Sauté the scallions in the butter in a 3-quart pot. When they are soft but not brown, add the potatoes and the sorrel and toss them in the butter over low heat until the sorrel leaves have wilted. Add the stock, bring it to a boil, turn down the heat and simmer the soup for 20–30 minutes, until the potatoes are done (taste one to be sure). (If you are using watercress instead of sorrel, add it *after* the potatoes are almost cooked and simmer it for only 5–10 minutes.)

Season the soup to taste with salt and pepper.

Cream of Sorrel Soup

(SERVES 6)

2 tablespoons butter
3 scallions including green tops, sliced
1 pound sorrel leaves, shredded (8–10 cups)
4 cups strong chicken stock, preferably homemade, p. 72
2 cups hot milk
2 egg yolks
½ cup heavy cream
salt and freshly ground pepper

Melt the butter in a 3–4 quart soup pot. Sauté the scallions gently, without browning, for 5 minutes. Stir in the sorrel and when it is wilted, add the chicken stock, bring it to a boil, turn down the heat and let the soup simmer for 10 minutes. Add the hot milk, simmer for 5 minutes more, and puree the soup in a blender or food processor. Return the soup to the pot, over low heat. Combine the egg yolks and heavy cream. Add a little of the hot soup to the yolk-cream mixture, then pour the mixture into the soup and continue to heat it, stirring constantly, for 5 minutes or so. Remove the soup from the heat and season it with salt and freshly ground pepper. The soup is equally good hot or cold.

Sorrel Puree. You can make an excellent sorrel puree to serve with fish by following this recipe but omitting the chicken stock and milk. There's no need to put the sorrel in the blender. Add a little of the cooked sorrel to the yolk-cream mixture, then stir the mixture into the sorrel over low heat. Do not let it boil or the egg yolks will scramble.

Schav

(SERVES 6–8)

This recipe comes from a dear old friend and a wonderful cook. It will be hard to buy the bottled version in the supermarket after tasting this *schav*, the famous Jewish "sour grass" soup. A perfect lunch, with rye bread spread with sweet butter.

> *1 pound sorrel*
> *6 scallions, chopped*
> *1–2 teaspoons salt*
> *a few crystals sour salt (available on the spice shelf in your super-*
> *   market), optional*
> *1 egg, beaten in a large bowl*
> *1½ cups sour cream*
>
> GARNISH
> *4 or 5 hard-cooked eggs, cut in pieces*
> *2 large cucumbers, peeled and diced*

Wash the sorrel well, trim off the tough stems and stew them in a little water. Chop the leaves and put them, with the scallions, into a 3–4-

quart pot. Add 8 cups of water and the salt, bring it to a boil, turn down the heat and simmer, partially covered, for 20 minutes. Strain the juice from the stems into the soup and taste the mixture. It should be very tart; if it is not, add 2 or 3 crystals of sour salt and simmer the soup for 10 minutes more. Taste again and add salt and/or sour salt to taste. The soup should be highly seasoned; it will taste much less sour when it is cold and has been mixed with sour cream. Ladle a little soup into the beaten egg, beating constantly. Add more hot soup, then stir the egg mixture into the pot of soup and turn off the heat.

Chill the soup and stir in the sour cream. You may add the eggs and cucumbers to the soup at this point, or put them in bowls on the table and let people help themselves. Serve the soup ice cold.

Spinach Soup

(SERVES 6)

2 tablespoons butter
1 medium potato, peeled and diced (about ¾ cup)
4 cups dilute chicken stock (2 cups chicken stock mixed with 2 cups
       of water or one can full-strength chicken stock mixed with
       enough water to make 4 cups)
1 pound spinach
2 cups hot milk
½ cup heavy cream

Melt the butter in a large soup pot, add the potato, stir it around to coat it with butter and sauté it gently for 2 or 3 minutes. Add the stock, bring it to a boil, turn the heat to medium and cook, uncovered, until the potato is done, about 15–20 minutes. Meanwhile, trim the spinach of tough stems and wilted leaves and wash it very carefully in several changes of water. When the potato is soft, add the spinach to the pot. Because raw spinach is so bulky you may not be able to add it all at once. Keep adding spinach, pushing it into the hot liquid in the bottom of the pot, until it is all wilted. Cook the spinach for another minute or two, not more, until it is tender but retains its bright green color. Remove the pot from the heat and let the soup cool for a little while. Puree the vegetables in a food processor or blender, or put them through a food mill. Return the puree to the pot, stir in the hot milk, add salt and freshly ground pepper to taste, and simmer the soup very gently for about 5 minutes. Stir in the cream just before serving. This soup is equally good hot or cold. If you serve it cold, taste it before serving and add more salt and/or pepper if necessary.

Tomato and Pepper Soup

(SERVES 6)

3 tablespoons olive oil
1 large onion (about ½ pound), sliced
3 medium green peppers, seeded and coarsely chopped
1 medium or 2 small fresh hot peppers, seeded and coarsely
    chopped, optional
6–8 ripe tomatoes (about 2 pounds), peeled and cut into chunks
4 cups stock (2 cups chicken stock mixed with 2 cups water or 4 cups
    vegetable stock, saved from steaming vegetables)
2 teaspoons salt
½ teaspoon sugar
1 medium zucchini (about 1 pound), diced
½ cups cooked rice (½ cup raw), optional but very good

Heat the oil in a 3–4-quart pot. Add the onion and cook it gently until it is wilted, 5–10 minutes. Add the peppers and continue to cook gently, stirring frequently, for another 5–10 minutes. Add the tomatoes, stir them into the other vegetables and cook until the juices begin to boil. Add the stock and the salt, bring to a boil, lower the heat and let the soup simmer uncovered for about 15 minutes. Taste the soup and adjust the seasoning with salt and/or sugar. Bring the soup back to the boil, add the zucchini, cover the pot and cook fairly rapidly for 10 minutes or until the zucchini is just tender. Put a spoonful of rice in each bowl before serving.

If you are making this soup in advance, or to freeze, turn off the heat before adding the zucchini. It will cook just enough when the soup is reheated.

This soup is very good cold, too, either just as it is or pureed.

Tomato Soup with Swiss Chard

(SERVES 6)

3 tablespoons olive oil
1 large onion (about ½ pound), finely chopped
6–8 ripe tomatoes (about 2 pounds), peeled and finely chopped
4 cups dilute stock (2 cups chicken stock mixed with 2 cups water or
    4 cups stock saved from steaming vegetables)
2 teaspoons salt
freshly ground pepper
½ teaspoon sugar
about 1 pound Swiss chard leaves, shredded (3–4 cups tightly
    packed)

Heat the oil in a 3–4-quart pot, add the onion and cook it, without browning, for 10 minutes. Add the chopped tomatoes and cook the mixture, stirring from time to time, for about 10 minutes. Add the stock, bring to a boil, add salt, pepper and a little sugar to taste, turn down the heat and simmer the soup, uncovered, for 15 minutes. Bring the soup to a full boil, add the Swiss chard, cover the pot and cook briskly for 10 more minutes. Serve hot or cold with Garlic Croutons, p. 73.

Spinach is a fairly good substitute for Swiss chard in this soup. If you use spinach, cook it for only 3 or 4 minutes.

Variation.
Puree the soup after it is cooked and add a cup of half-and-half.
Serve chilled.

Cream of Tomato Soup

(SERVES 6)

2 tablespoons butter
1 small onion, chopped
¼ cup (4 tablespoons) raw rice or ¾ cup cooked rice
3 or 4 sprigs fresh thyme or a pinch of dried thyme
6–8 ripe tomatoes (about 2 pounds), coarsely chopped
3 cups chicken broth, preferably homemade, p. 72
about 1 teaspoon salt
½ cup heavy cream
freshly ground pepper
a little sugar
chopped chives

Melt the butter in a 2–3-quart pot. Add the onion and cook until it is wilted, 5–10 minutes. Stir in the rice, the thyme, the tomatoes, the chicken broth and the salt, bring it to a boil and cook, covered, over low heat, until the rice is very soft, about 30 minutes (15 minutes if you start with cooked rice). Rub the soup through a fine sieve or puree it in a food processor or blender, then rub it through a fine sieve to make a perfectly smooth puree. Return the soup to the pot, gently heat it and stir in the cream. Taste and adjust the seasoning with salt, pepper, and sugar if the tomatoes give the soup an acid taste. Garnish each serving with chopped chives.

Cream of Tomato with Tarragon

(SERVES 6)

6 cups strong, homemade chicken stock, p. 72
1 cup Tomato Sauce with Cream and Tarragon, p. 249
salt and freshly ground pepper
a few tablespoons of cooked pasta or rice, optional

Bring the stock to a boil in a 2-quart saucepan. Turn down the heat, stir in the tomato sauce and simmer gently for 5 minutes. Taste the soup and season with salt and pepper. If you happen to have some, put a tablespoon of cooked pasta or rice in each bowl. Good hot or cold.

Vegetable Minestra

(SERVES 6–8)

This is an Italian version of *pistou*, flavored with parsley instead of basil.

> 2 tablespoons olive oil
> 1 large sweet onion, chopped
> 1 small carrot, diced
> 1 medium potato, peeled and diced
> 4 large tomatoes, peeled and coarsely chopped
> ¼ pound green beans, cut in ½-inch pieces (about 1 cup)
> 2 or 3 small zucchini, diced
> 2 cups shredded lettuce or spinach or chard
> 2 cloves garlic
> about 1 cup chopped parsley
> salt and freshly ground pepper
> freshly grated Parmesan cheese

Heat the olive oil in a 4- or 5-quart soup pot. Add the onion, carrot and potato and cook them, without browning, for about 10 minutes. Add the tomatoes and 4 cups of boiling water and simmer the soup for 10 minutes. Add the beans, the zucchini and the shredded greens and cook the soup for another 10–15 minutes, until the potatoes, beans and zucchini are done. Chop the garlic and parsley together until they are a very fine puree. Season the soup with salt and freshly ground pepper. Turn off the heat and stir in the parsley mixture. Serve the soup hot, with freshly grated Parmesan cheese.

Zucchini Soup Base

This all-purpose vegetable soup base comes to the rescue of the victim of zucchini overproduction, a condition that afflicts most amateur gardeners for a month or two each year. The principle is this: you can drink more of a vegetable than you can eat. Vast quantities of zucchini can be consumed in near-liquid form. While zucchini's harsh critics claim that it is bland, those of us who truly appreciate this mainstay of the garden refer to it as having a delicate flavor, one that blends well with almost anything you can think of. And so this soup base, frozen in 1-quart containers, is blended throughout the year with tomatoes, spinach, chard, pureed green beans, eggplant, peppers, chicken, turkey, duck, beef, veal, pork and vegetable stocks, bits of leftover gravies and sauces, and that extra tablespoonful of cooked rice or pasta. Everything you mix with it seems to taste better, and it's never the same twice. Zucchini Soup Base makes a good, nonfattening thickening for all kinds of soups.

For 1 Quart of Soup Base

(ENOUGH TO MAKE 6 CUPS OF SOUP)

2 tablespoons butter
¼ of a small onion, sliced
3 medium zucchini (about 2 pounds), sliced, diced or coarsely
    chopped
½ cup chicken or vegetable stock

Melt the butter in a pan and sauté the onion, without browning, for a minute or 2. Add the zucchini and cook it in the butter for a couple of minutes. Add the stock, bring it to a boil, lower the heat, cover the pan and cook the zucchini until it is very tender, 10–15 minutes. Puree the zucchini in a blender, a food processor or a food mill.

To serve, add about 2 cups of pureed vegetables and/or stock. Season the soup with salt and pepper after the additions have been made.

For a good, pure zucchini soup. Heat the base with one cup of good chicken stock and 1 cup of milk. This soup, and the combinations of zucchini with other pureed vegetables, are all equally good hot or cold.

This recipe is meant only as the most approximate guide. Once you get the idea, it certainly is not necessary to measure the butter or liquid you add to the zucchini; it should be just enough to give a bit of accent to the flavor and to make it easy to puree. Be cautious with the onions; too much spoils the flavor. This is an ideal way to use those monstrous squash that take you by surprise several times during every season. If the seeds are woody, remove them before you cook the squash.

New England Clam Chowder

(SERVES 6)

This is a somewhat unorthodox way of making a classic soup, but I do believe it is the best clam chowder I have ever tasted.

18 large chowder clams or 2 dozen smaller hard-shelled clams
bottled clam juice
2 large potatoes, peeled and diced
2 medium onions, diced
4 tablespoons butter
1 tablespoon flour
2 cups milk
freshly ground pepper

Bring some water to a boil in a kettle. Wash the clams in several changes of water and scrub them under running water with a stiff brush. Put the clams in your largest pot, pour in 2 cups of boiling water, turn the heat high, cover the pot and steam the clams only until they open, 5–10 minutes. Remove the clams from the pot and from their shells and set them aside. Discard the shells and strain the broth through a double layer of cheesecloth. Measure it—there should be about 4 cups. If less, add bottled clam juice and/or water to make 4 cups. If a bit more, don't worry. Rinse out the pot, pour the broth back into it and bring it to a boil. Add the potatoes and onions and cook them, partially covered, over medium heat, until they are tender, about 20 minutes.

While the vegetables are cooking, chop the clams in a food processor, by hand, or put them through a grinder. I think you get the best chowder by chopping some of the clams very fine and leaving some rather coarsely chopped. Melt the butter in a saucepan, add the flour and cook gently, without browning, for 2 or 3 minutes, stirring with a wire whisk. Add ½ cup of the milk and cook, stirring, over medium heat until the sauce is thick and smooth. Whisk in the rest of the milk, bring it to the boil and pour it into the soup. Season the soup with freshly ground pepper. It probably will need no salt. Simmer for 5 minutes, turn off the heat, stir in the chopped clams and serve.

Manhattan Clam Chowder

(SERVES 6)

For reasons I have never been able to fathom, people who love the French and Italian tomato-based fish soups are very snobbish about Manhattan clam chowder. The idea seems to be that this is some sort of upstart, trying to horn in on the only legitimate chowder territory, New England. There's no reason to compare a good Manhattan clam chowder with the pasty orange stuff served in restaurants. I've been served plenty of pasty white stuff called New England clam chowder. Maybe what this much maligned soup needs is a new name!

18 large chowder clams or 2 dozen smaller hard-shelled clams
bottled clam juice
2 pounds ripe tomatoes, peeled, seeded and coarsely chopped
1 large potato, peeled and diced
1 large onion, diced
2 teaspoons fresh thyme leaves or ½ teaspoon dried thyme
2 stalks celery with leaves, thinly sliced
1 medium carrot, scraped and diced
4 tablespoons butter
1 tablespoon flour
freshly ground pepper

Bring some water to a boil in a kettle. Wash the clams in several changes of water and scrub them under running water with a stiff brush. Put the clams in your largest pot, pour in 2 cups of boiling water, turn the heat high, cover the pot and steam the clams only until they open, 5–10 minutes. Remove the clams from the pot and from their shells and set them aside. Discard the shells and strain the broth through a double layer of cheesecloth. Measure it—there should be about 4 cups. If less, add bottled clam juice and/or water to make 4 cups. If a bit more, don't worry. Rinse out the pot, pour the broth back into it and bring it to a boil. Add the tomatoes, potato, onion and thyme and cook them, partially covered, over medium heat, for 10 minutes. Add the celery and carrot and continue cooking for 10–15 minutes more, until the vegetables are done.

While the vegetables are cooking, chop the clams in a food processor or by hand or put them through a grinder. I think you get the best chowder by chopping some very fine and leaving some rather coarsely chopped. Melt the butter in a saucepan, add the flour and cook gently, without browning, for 2 or 3 minutes, stirring with a wire whisk. Add ½ cup of the soup and cook, stirring, over medium heat, until the sauce is thick and smooth. Add another ½ cup of soup, stir well, then add the sauce to the soup in the pot. Taste the soup and season it with freshly ground pepper and more thyme if necessary. Simmer the soup for 5 minutes or so, turn off the heat, stir in the chopped clams and serve.

Clam or Mussel Soup
(SERVES 6 AS FIRST COURSE, 4 AS MAIN COURSE)

4 dozen small, hard-shelled clams
                    or   } *or a combination*
2 quarts (4 pounds) mussels
½ cup olive oil
1 small onion, chopped (about ½ cup)
1 large clove garlic, minced
2 pounds ripe tomatoes, peeled, seeded and coarsely chopped
½ cup chopped parsley and 1 or 2 sprigs of thyme, and/or 2 or 3
    leaves of basil and/or a little fresh or dried oregano or marjoram
½ cup dry white wine mixed with ½ cup water
salt and freshly ground pepper

Scrub the clams thoroughly with a stiff brush under running water. Clean the mussels according to the directions, p. 172. Heat the olive oil in a pot large enough to hold all the clams and/or mussels when they are open. Add the onion to the oil and cook it slowly for 5 or 6 minutes, until it is transparent but not browned. Add the garlic and cook for another minute or 2. Stir in the tomatoes and the herbs and when they are boiling, add the wine and water. Bring to a boil, turn down the heat and simmer for 10 minutes. Add a little salt (the shellfish will supply some) and a few grinds of pepper. Turn the heat to high, add the clams and/or mussels, cover the pot tightly and steam over high heat for 5–10 minutes, or until all the shells have opened. It will probably be necessary to redistribute the clams in the pot, moving the open shells gently from the bottom to the top of the pile to allow them all to steam in the shortest possible time. Discard any mussels which have not opened by this time—they may simply be shells full of sand and can ruin the whole potful if they fall open by accident.

Spoon the clams and/or mussels into soup bowls and ladle the soup over them. Serve with plenty of crusty bread to mop up the sauce.

White Fish Soup
(SERVES 8 AS FIRST COURSE, 6 AS MAIN COURSE)

This soup makes a delicate and satisfying main course, especially when the fish is freshly caught, the potatoes are new and the herbs are right out of the garden. If you serve it as a first course, omit the potatoes altogether or use just a cup or so of diced potatoes. Use the fish trimmings to make the stock.

3 tablespoons butter
1 large onion, chopped
about 8 cups Fish Stock, p. 69
*12 small new potatoes, scrubbed or 6 medium potatoes, peeled and
    cut in half*
*3 pounds boneless fish (preferably a mixture of several kinds such as
    bass, halibut, cod, tile, pike, eel)*
3 tablespoons chopped parsley ⎫
3 tablespoons chopped dill   ⎬ *mixed together*
3 tablespoons chopped chives   ⎭
salt and freshly ground pepper
sour cream

Melt the butter in a 4–5-quart soup pot. Add the onion and cook it gently until it is transparent but not brown, about 5 minutes. Add the stock and bring it to a boil. Add the potatoes, bring the soup back to the boil, turn down the heat and simmer the potatoes, partially covered, until they are almost done, about 20 minutes. Add the fish, making sure it is covered by the broth, and cook gently until it is done, 5–10 minutes, depending on the thickness of the pieces. Stir in half the chopped herbs and adjust the seasoning with salt and freshly ground pepper. Put the rest of the herbs in a bowl and pass them, along with a bowl of sour cream, to garnish the soup.

Fish Stock

(ABOUT 8 CUPS)

2–3 pounds fish heads and trimmings from mild, white fish
1 onion, peeled
1 carrot
1 stalk celery with leaves
4 sprigs parsley
1 bay leaf
4 peppercorns, bruised
1 tablespoon salt
3 cups dry white wine
1 8-ounce bottle clam juice
4 cups water

Put all the ingredients in a large soup pot. Bring to a boil, skim off the foam and cook over moderate heat, uncovered, for 20–30 minutes, not more. Strain and use the stock to poach fish or to make soups or sauces.

Sometimes it is possible to buy large fish heads, wings or collars very cheaply. They make wonderful stock and usually have enough meat on them to make fish soup a very inexpensive dish. If you intend to use the meat in a soup or salad, remove the heads, etc., from the pot after 5–10 minutes. Let them cool a little, remove the meat from the bones and set it aside. Return the skin and bones to the stock pot and cook them for another 20 minutes. This is a rather messy business, but if you don't mind plunging into fish up to your wrists, you will be rewarded with several cups of excellent fish. Add cooked fish to soup just before serving.

Red Fish Soup

(SERVES 6–8)

This soup is really a main course dish. You could serve a small bowl of it as a first course, especially if you have some left after serving it as a meal, but it's both good and substantial enough to serve as the principal part of a lunch or dinner. It can be served first, followed by a salad and cheese course and then dessert, or equally well, preceded by a first course of pâté, *rillettes* or stuffed eggs.

The quantities given here indicate good proportions of ingredients. If you add all the suggested ingredients, this soup will probably be enough for 12; it certainly will if you add a few more clams or mussels, another ½ pound of fish or scallops and a bottle of clam juice. Use the fish trimmings to make the stock.

¼ cup olive oil
1 large onion, chopped
4 large cloves garlic, chopped
1 bulb fennel (about ½ pound) with leaves, thinly sliced
or
4 stalks celery with leaves, thinly sliced
2 pounds ripe tomatoes (6–8 tomatoes), peeled and coarsely chopped
1 tablespoon chopped basil
2 tablespoons chopped parsley
4–6 cups Fish Stock made with heads and trimmings, p. 69
¼ teaspoon saffron, dissolved in a little water
3 pounds boneless fish (preferably a mixture of several different
    kinds, cut into large chunks)
1 ½ dozen small clams or mussels, well scrubbed, optional
½ pound scallops (whole bay scallops or sea scallops cut in
    quarters), optional
salt and freshly ground pepper
chopped parsley

Heat the olive oil in a large soup pot. Add the onion, garlic and fennel or celery, stir well and cook without browning for about 10 minutes. Stir in the tomatoes, basil and parsley, bring to a boil and add the fish stock. When the soup comes back to a boil, taste and add salt, stir in the saffron, turn down the heat and simmer for 15–20 minutes. The soup may be prepared up to this point as much as a day in advance. It may also be frozen. Proceed with the recipe 20 minutes before serving.

Bring the soup back to a boil, turn down the heat and add the fish, making sure that all of it is covered with soup. Cover the pot and simmer the soup for 5–10 minutes, until the fish is just cooked. Taste the soup and correct the seasoning with salt and freshly ground pepper. If you are adding scallops to the soup, stir them in as you remove the pot from the burner; the heat of the soup will cook them.

If you are adding clams and/or mussels to the soup, scrub them well and steam them open in ½ cup of water. Put them, in their shells, into the soup when the fish is done. Strain their juice into the soup through several layers of cheesecloth, and stir it in.

Sprinkle some chopped parsley over all and serve with plenty of warm, crusty bread.

Cream of Mussel Soup (Billi Bi)

(SERVES 6)

This rich, delicate soup is made from the winy broth of *Moules Marinière*. Plan to serve the mussels another time, another way, p. 174.

broth from 1 recipe Moules Marinière, p. 172
4 egg yolks
1 cup heavy cream
chopped chervil or parsley

Strain the broth through several layers of cheesecloth, add enough water to make 4 cups, and bring it to a boil in a 2-quart pot. Turn the heat very low. Beat the egg yolks and cream together with a fork and whisk in 1 cup of the hot broth, beating all the time. Add the yolk-cream mixture to the broth in the pot and continue to whisk over low heat for 5 minutes or so, until the soup is very hot and has thickened slightly. Don't let it boil or the eggs will scramble. Garnish each bowl with a sprinkling of chervil or parsley. Good hot or cold.

Jellied Chicken Soup (and Boiled Chicken)
(ABOUT 8 CUPS)

This is a wonderful soup to have in summer. It is excellent as is; it can be garnished in many ways or flavored with herbs. If you use this stock as the basis of a cold vegetable soup (Sorrel, Lettuce or Tomato with Cream and Tarragon) the soup will have a perfect texture with no additional thickening. At the same time, if you wish, you can cook plain chicken to use in sandwiches, salads, a mousse, or a pâté.

Three pounds of necks, backs and giblets (what I call "chicken junk") will produce about 4 cups of a fine-flavored, well-jelled stock. Add another cup or so of water for each additional pound of chicken. Meaty pieces will produce less gelatinous stock than bony ones. Three pounds of chicken junk and a 3½ pound chicken will give you 8 cups of excellent soup and 3–4 cups of chicken meat. A fowl produces the best-flavored stock, but the meat is rather tough and takes a long time to cook, 1½–2 hours for a small fowl.

If the stock is skimmed when it comes to the boil and simmered slowly from that point on, the soup will be clear. Boiling makes it cloudy.

3 pounds chicken backs, necks, giblets ("chicken junk")
a 3–3½ pound chicken in 1 piece or a small fowl (3–4 pounds)
1 small onion
1 small carrot
2 sprigs parsley
1 tablespoon salt

Rinse off the chicken junk and put it and the chicken in a 4–5-quart pot with 10 cups of water, the onion, carrot and parsley (no need to peel the onion or carrot) and salt. Bring it to a boil, skim the soup well, turn down the heat, partially cover the pot and simmer slowly for about 2 hours. Remove the chicken after an hour or so. If you want a really strong stock, remove the meat from the chicken and put the skin and bones back in the pot to cook for another hour.

Strain the soup and measure it. If you have more than 8 cups, boil it until it is reduced to 8 cups. Taste and season the soup with salt. Chill the soup and remove the fat which congeals on the surface.

Jellied soup should be served in a cup, topped with a sprinkling of chopped herbs and a dollop of plain whipped cream or a squeeze of lemon juice.

Herb Consommé. If you want a strong flavor of some particular herb, steep it in the soup while it is still hot. Use 1 teaspoon of chopped herb for each 2 cups of soup. Strain the soup when it is cool and chill it.

Consommé Madrilène. While the soup is cooking, cut up 3 large tomatoes and cook them in a small saucepan until they are reduced to 1 cup. Add the concentrated tomatoes to the soup during the last 15 minutes of cooking. There's no need to peel or seed the tomatoes if you add them to the soup before it is strained.

Butter Croutons

(2–3 CUPS)

6 slices white bread
4 tablespoons butter

Stack the bread, cut it into half-inch cubes and put it in a bowl. Melt the butter in a large frying pan, pour it over the bread cubes and toss them thoroughly to butter them all. Put the bread in the frying pan and toast it, over low heat, turning and turning it until the cubes are crisp and golden brown. Serve with hot vegetable soup, especially Lettuce Soup, p. 52, Green Bean Soup, p. 51 or Pea Soup, p. 53.

Garlic Croutons

(2–3 CUPS)

2–3 cups French or Italian bread, cut in large dice
½ cup olive oil
2 large cloves garlic, peeled and cut into several pieces

Heat the oil with the garlic in a large pan, preferably one with high sides, over low heat, until the garlic is golden. Press it down in the oil to extract its flavor, remove and discard the garlic. Raise the heat to medium, add the bread, toss it to coat each piece with oil and continue to cook, tossing very frequently, until the bread is well toasted and crisp.

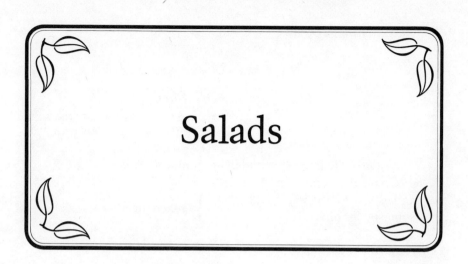

Salads

FISH SALADS

Fish salads are very good eaten as a first course or lunch, but I think they are at their best when used as a filling for raw vegetables. Green peppers, tomatoes, cucumbers and large, firm lettuce leaves (especially Romaine) are all excellent cases for fish salad; when you serve it this way, you can make a little leftover fish go a long way. These recipes call for 2 cups of cooked fish, enough salad to feed 8 for lunch when it is stuffed into raw vegetables and extended, perhaps, with some hard-cooked eggs and a good loaf of bread. This is wonderful finger food for a party and easy to take on a picnic. Put the fish salad in a plastic container and the prepared vegetables in a plastic bag and combine them at the picnic.

Fish Salad with Olives

(ENOUGH FOR 4 FOR LUNCH OR
TO FILL 8 VEGETABLE HALVES)

2 cups cooked fish, all skin and bones removed
6–8 Greek olives, pitted and cut up
4 tablespoons Tapénade, p. 13
4 tablespoons olive oil   } mixed together
            or
½ cup Anchovy Sauce, p. 231

Combine all the ingredients and chill until serving time. Garnish the salad with red and green pepper strips or use it to fill raw vegetables.

Fish Salad with Garlicky Mayonnaise

(ENOUGH FOR 4 FOR LUNCH
OR TO FILL 8 VEGETABLE HALVES)

2 cups cooked fish, all skin and bones removed
10–12 radishes, cut in quarters or ½ cup diced fennel stalks
2 tablespoons chopped dill or fennel leaves
2 tablespoons chopped chives
1 cup Garlicky Mayonnaise Dressing, p. 252
salt and freshly ground pepper
lemon juice to taste

Combine the fish, vegetables and herbs with the mayonnaise dressing. Season to taste with salt, pepper and lemon juice and let the salad stand in the refrigerator for at least half an hour. Garnish the salad with radishes and fennel stalks or use it to fill raw vegetable cases or lettuce leaves.

Fish Salad with Horseradish Dressing

(ENOUGH FOR 6 FOR LUNCH
OR TO FILL 12 VEGETABLE HALVES)

2 cups cooked fish, all skin and bones removed
2 or 3 new potatoes, boiled, peeled and diced (about 1 cup)
4 scallions including green tops, thickly sliced
1 cup Horseradish Sauce, p. 240
salt

Combine the fish, potatoes and scallions with half the horseradish dressing and add salt to taste. Let the salad stand in the refrigerator for an hour or two. About twenty minutes before serving, remove it from the refrigerator and add the rest of the dressing. Mix well. Serve the salad garnished with watercress or use it to fill raw vegetables.

Mussel Salad with Rice

(SERVES 6 AS A FIRST COURSE)

You can make this salad beautifully with leftover *Moules Marinière*, p. 172, if you are lucky enough to have any.

2 quarts mussels, cleaned according to the directions, p. 172
1 cup dry white wine
¼ teaspoon saffron, optional but good
¼ cup olive oil
2 or 3 scallions, chopped
1 large clove garlic, chopped
1 ½ cups raw rice, preferably converted rice
1 sweet red pepper, seeded and cut into small dice
2 tablespoons chopped parsley
salt and freshly ground pepper

Steam the cleaned mussels open in the wine. Remove the mussels from their shells, cover and refrigerate them. Strain the juice through several layers of cheesecloth (to eliminate sand) and measure it. Add the saffron and enough water to make 3 cups. You can make the dish up to a day in advance to this point. Heat the liquid before proceeding with the recipe.

Heat the oil in a 1½–2-quart saucepan. Sauté the scallions and garlic for a minute or two, then add the rice and stir until it has absorbed the oil. Pour in the hot liquid, add a teaspoon of salt and bring it to a boil. Stir, turn the heat to low, cover the pot and cook the rice for 15–20 minutes, until it is tender and all the liquid has been absorbed. If the rice looks too moist, fold a clean dish towel in half and place it between the pot and the lid. Turn off the heat under the rice and leave it covered for 15 minutes or so.

Add the chopped pepper and parsley to the rice, taste it and season with salt and freshly ground pepper. When it is cool, stir in the mussels. Add a little more olive oil if you think the salad is too dry. Serve at room temperature.

Tuna Salad with Kohlrabi

(SERVES 6)

This is a very good combination. Turnip greens, broccoli rabe or kale are all good substitutes for the kohlrabi greens, but they don't replace the sweet, crunchy bulb. Add some diced cucumber to the salad if you don't have kohlrabi.

DRESSING
⅔ cup olive oil
juice of 2 lemons (4–6 tablespoons)
2 cloves garlic, minced   } mixed together with a fork
1 teaspoon salt
freshly ground pepper

2 10-ounce cans tuna fish, drained
1 sweet red onion, thinly sliced
3 medium bulbs kohlrabi with leaves

Bring 3 or 4 quarts of water to a boil in a large pot. Make the dressing in a salad bowl. Stir in the tuna and onion and let them marinate while you prepare the kohlrabi.

Cut the leaves from the kohlrabi and blanch them in the boiling water for about 5 minutes. Drain the leaves in a colander and rinse them with cold water to stop the cooking. Dry the leaves in paper towels, shred them coarsely and add them to the salad bowl. Peel the kohlrabi bulbs and cut them into ½-inch dice. Toss the kohlrabi into the salad and let it marinate for half an hour or so before serving.

Salade Niçoise

Salade Niçoise is a glorified—a truly glorified—tuna fish salad. It should be arranged beautifully on a platter rather than tossed in a bowl, each element separate but all brought together with plenty of good, garlicky vinaigrette sauce. The usual ingredients are tuna fish, anchovies, hard-cooked eggs, olives, lettuce, tomatoes, green peppers, cold boiled potatoes and cold, barely cooked green beans. Good additions to the salad are scallions or sweet onions, cucumbers and tiny artichokes. Needless to say, the vegetables should be perfect and perfectly fresh.

Arrange your selection of ingredients on a bed of crisp lettuce. Pour Vinaigrette, p.251, over everything about 15 minutes before serving, and serve an extra pitcher of it on the side. Quantities, of course, depend entirely on how many people are eating and how hungry they are—this salad is a great lunch for 2 or 20.

Tuna and Watercress Salad

(SERVES 6)

Make a lot of this salad—it's hard to stop eating it.

2 or 3 large bunches watercress
2 10-ounce cans tuna, drained
3 or 4 large green or red peppers, seeded and cut into bite-sized
*   pieces*
Anchovy Sauce, p.231

Wash the bunches of watercress and cut them in half crosswise. Put the watercress in a large salad bowl with the tuna and the peppers. Pour the Anchovy Sauce over the salad and toss well.

Chicken Salad

(SERVES 6)

4 cups cooked chicken, cut into bite-sized pieces
2 medium green peppers, seeded and diced
½ cup diced sweet onion (½ large onion)
2 tablespoons chopped basil
Garlicky Mayonnaise Dressing, p. 252

Combine all the ingredients at least half an hour before serving. If you chill the salad, let it come to room temperature for half an hour. Fill raw tomatoes with the salad and serve them on a bed of watercress. Pass around some more dressing in a bowl.

Chicken and Egg Salad with Anchovy Sauce

(SERVES 6)

3 cups cooked chicken, cut into bite-sized pieces
4–6 hard-cooked eggs, cut in pieces, not chopped
Anchovy Sauce, p. 231
watercress
tomatoes

Mix the chicken and the eggs with the Anchovy Sauce and let it marinate for half an hour. Put a bed of watercress in a bowl or on a platter and put the salad on top of it. Garnish the salad with lots of tomato wedges.

Chicken and Spinach Salad

(SERVES 6)

DRESSING
3 scallions including green tops, finely chopped
2 large cloves garlic, minced
juice of 1 large lemon (3–4 tablespoons)
½ cup olive oil
salt and freshly ground pepper
4 tablespoons chopped fresh dill

} beaten together with a fork

3–4 cups cooked chicken, cut in bite-sized pieces
1–2 pounds fresh spinach
2 small zucchini, diced

Make the dressing. Combine it with the chicken and let it marinate in the refrigerator for an hour or so. Trim the stems from the spinach and wash it carefully by swishing it around in several changes of cold water. Shake off as much water as possible and dry the spinach in a salad spinner or on towels. Just before serving, put the spinach and raw zucchini in a salad bowl, add the chicken and toss until the leaves are well coated with dressing. Taste and adjust the seasoning.

Bulgur Salad

(SERVES 6)

Bulgur, a staple food in the Middle East, is a delicious grain and an especially good one to use in summer because it needs no cooking. Simply soak it in water; it will more than triple in bulk and have exactly the right texture for a salad, even if it soaks all day. Bulgur can also be cooked. It takes a very short time and is a good substitute for rice. If you have trouble finding it, look in a health food store or one that specializes in Middle Eastern foods.

1 ½ *cups bulgur*
½ *cup olive oil*
¼ *cup wine vinegar or fresh lemon juice*
4 *tablespoons chopped parsley and/or chopped fresh mint*
4 *tablespoons chopped chives*
1 *teaspoon salt*
freshly ground pepper
2 *large tomatoes, cut into bite-size chunks*
2 *large cucumbers, peeled and cut into bite-size chunks*

Put the bulgur in a large bowl and cover it with 6 cups of warm water. Let it stand at room temperature for at least 2 hours. Drain it in a strainer and press it down to get out as much moisture as possible. Put the oil, vinegar, herbs, salt and pepper in a salad bowl and mix well with a fork. Add the bulgur and combine it with the dressing. Refrigerate, for several hours if you wish. Toss the tomatoes and cucumbers into the salad just before serving or their juice will make the salad too watery. Taste and add more salt and freshly ground pepper if you wish.

Cooked Cabbage Salad

(SERVES 8)

This makes a nice change from coleslaw. Use the sour cream dressing given below, or Arugula Vinaigrette, p. 251.

a firm cabbage (about 2 pounds), quartered and cut into ½-inch
    slices
salt

Bring a large pot of salted water to a rolling boil. Add the shredded cabbage, bring the water back to the boil and cook rapidly for 5 minutes, not more. Drain the cabbage into a colander and run cold water over it, tossing it with your fingers, until the cabbage is cool. Leave it in the colander to drain while you make the dressing (or refrigerate it and use it the next day.)

SOUR CREAM AND CARAWAY SEED DRESSING
2 scallions including green tops, coarsely chopped ⎫
1 cup sour cream   ⎬ *mixed together*
½ teaspoon caraway seeds   ⎭
salt and freshly ground pepper

Combine the cooked cabbage with the dressing and let it stand at least ½ hour before serving. Toss well, taste and correct the seasoning before serving the salad.

Carrot and Radish Salad

(SERVES 6–8)

4–6 large carrots, scraped and thinly sliced
2 cups red radishes, thinly sliced

DRESSING
juice of 1 large lemon   ⎫
1 large clove garlic, minced   ⎬ *mixed together*
1 teaspoon salt   ⎭

Combine the vegetables with the dressing and chill for at least an hour before serving. Toss the salad and correct the seasoning with salt and/or lemon juice before serving.

Cucumbers in Vinegar and Cucumbers in Sour Cream

(SERVES 6)

For the best cucumber salads, the cucumbers should be peeled, thinly sliced, sprinkled with a teaspoon or so of salt and allowed to drain in a colander for at least half an hour. Pat the cucumbers dry and marinate them in one of the following dressings before serving. Cucumbers in vinegar should marinate for at least 2 hours, but are still good after 24. Cucumbers in sour cream should be made within 2 hours of serving. If you don't presalt the cucumbers, be sure to add salt to the dressings.

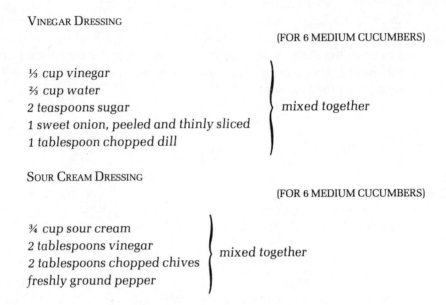

VINEGAR DRESSING

(FOR 6 MEDIUM CUCUMBERS)

⅓ cup vinegar
⅔ cup water
2 teaspoons sugar   } mixed together
1 sweet onion, peeled and thinly sliced
1 tablespoon chopped dill

SOUR CREAM DRESSING

(FOR 6 MEDIUM CUCUMBERS)

¾ cup sour cream
2 tablespoons vinegar
2 tablespoons chopped chives   } mixed together
freshly ground pepper

Cucumbers or Cucumber Soup with Yogurt

(SERVES 6)

Some combination of these two occurs in every yogurt-eating country. Here's a version that can be either soup or salad, depending on how much yogurt you add.

2 large cucumbers
4 scallions, finely chopped
2–3 large cloves garlic, crushed
2–4 cups plain yogurt, preferably homemade, p. 253
salt and freshly ground pepper
chopped mint to taste

Peel the cucumbers. Remove the seeds only if they are woody, and shred the cucumbers in a food processor or with a grater.

For salad. Combine the cucumbers, the scallions and 2 cloves of garlic with 2 cups of yogurt, season well with salt, freshly ground pepper and chopped mint and refrigerate for 2 hours before serving. If any liquid accumulates around the edges, pour it off. Mix the salad well and sprinkle on some chopped mint before serving.

For soup. Follow the directions for the salad but add an extra clove of garlic and use 4 cups of yogurt. Beat the yogurt vigorously with the salt before adding it to the cucumbers. This will liquefy it slightly. Add some pepper and chopped mint and refrigerate the soup for 2 hours. If any liquid accumulates around the edges, stir it into the soup. The soup is good thick, but if you wish you may thin it with a little milk before serving. Adjust the seasoning and serve cold, sprinkled with chopped mint.

Cucumber Salad with Fennel and Radishes

(SERVES 6–8)

This salad is a snap to make if you have a food processor: everything will be in neat, even slices in about 2 minutes. But it's an unusual and good combination, even worth slicing by hand.

> *2 cups sliced fennel stalks and leaves*
> *3 scallions including green tops, sliced*
> *2 large cucumbers, peeled and sliced*
> *1 cup radishes, sliced*
> *Vinaigrette Dressing, p. 251*

Toss everything together and let it marinate for an hour in the refrigerator before serving.

Stuffed Raw Cucumbers

Choose large cucumbers. Peel them, trim the ends and cut them in half lengthwise. Scoop out the seeds, using a grapefruit knife or spoon, and salt the cucumbers generously inside and out. Put them in a colander and let them drain for at least half an hour. Pat the cucumber shells dry with paper towels and stuff them with:

Tuna-Cottage Cheese Stuffing, p. 123
Shrimp Salad, p. 176
Fish Salads, pp. 76-79
Ricotta Dip, p. 12
Sardine-Anchovy Dip, p. 13

Fennel and Red Pepper Salad

(SERVES 6–8)

This is a beautiful and delicious late summer salad.

3 cups sliced fennel stalks and leaves
3 large sweet red peppers, seeded and cut in bite-sized pieces
Vinaigrette Dressing, p. 251

Mix the vegetables with the dressing and let the salad marinate in the refrigerator for an hour before serving.

Greek Salad

(SERVES 6)

6 good handfuls lettuce, prepared for salad
1 cup (about ½ pound) feta cheese, crumbled
2 large, ripe tomatoes, cut in wedges
1 sweet red onion, thinly sliced
1 large cucumber, peeled and sliced
¼ pound (12–15) black Greek olives
1 can (2 ounce) anchovy fillets

DRESSING
6 tablespoons olive oil
2 tablespoons wine vinegar
1 large clove garlic, minced
2 teaspoons chopped fresh oregano   } mixed together with a fork
   or marjoram or ½ teaspoon
   dried oregano or marjoram
salt and freshly ground pepper

Put the lettuce in a large salad bowl or on a large platter. Sprinkle the cheese over it. Arrange the tomatoes, onion rings, olives and anchovies in an attractive pattern. Pour the dressing over the salad and allow it to be admired before tossing and serving it.

Green Bean Salad with Yogurt

(SERVES 6)

1 ½ pounds green beans, stem ends removed

DRESSING
1 cup plain yogurt, preferably homemade, p.253
2 cloves garlic, crushed
2–3 tablespoons finely chopped dill } mixed together
1 teaspoon salt
plenty of freshly ground pepper

Snap the beans in half or leave them whole. Cook them slightly by blanching them in lots of boiling water, or steam them in a little water for about 5 minutes until they are barely tender. Cool the beans rapidly in cold water to prevent further cooking, drain them thoroughly and let them cool completely. Combine the beans with the dressing several hours before serving. Let the salad come to room temperature for 20–30 minutes before serving, if it has been refrigerated. Taste it and adjust the seasoning.

Variation.
Green Bean and Potato Salad. You can make this a potato salad with green beans, a green bean salad with potatoes, or a combination of equal amounts of each. For 6 servings, cook 3 medium potatoes, peel them and slice them into the dressing while they are still warm. Carefully stir in 1 pound of cooked green beans and let the salad stand for several hours before serving. If the dressing is a bit skimpy, add a little more yogurt and adjust the seasoning.

Rosemary's Green Bean Salad

(SERVES 6)

This salad has a very subtle flavor. You will notice that it has no vinegar or lemon in it. The flavor of the cracklings or bacon permeates the salad if you let it marinate for an hour or 2 before serving.

This is an excellent way to use oversized green beans, but only if you have a food processor.

2 pounds green beans
¼ cup chopped sweet onion, white or red
2 tablespoons olive oil
½ cup chopped crisp pork cracklings or 4 slices bacon, fried until crisp and crumbled
salt and freshly ground pepper

Following the directions on p. 100, blanch the beans until they are just tender. Chop the beans, *but do not puree them,* in the food processor, using the metal blade. The beans should be very coarsely chopped and have a crunchy texture. Mix in the onion, the oil and the cracklings or bacon. Taste and season with salt and freshly ground pepper.

LETTUCE

Lettuce is as satisfying a crop as a gardener can grow; it is delicious, productive and pretty enough to use as an edging for a flower bed. It comes up early, when our hunger for vegetables fresh from the garden is at its peak. I grow only leaf lettuce and I sow it very thickly in wide rows. When the leaves are large enough to eat, I cut them off about 2 inches from the ground and within a couple of weeks they have grown a second crop. In a good year (not too hot and plenty of rain) I get 3 or 4 cuttings from each row. I sow several different varieties, sometimes mixing the seeds together so I can pick mixed greens for a salad all at once. The lettuce plants last until the other vegetables are producing in overwhelming abundance. Then they gracefully die and we can concentrate on the beans, squash and tomatoes. But if you remember to sow it again in August, lettuce will grow in cool, early fall weather and you can once again have delicate, fresh greens until it gets really cold.

The very earliest, tenderest lettuce is best dressed with just a few tablespoons of good olive oil, a few drops of lemon juice, a little salt, a grind or 2 of pepper and a very discreet sprinkling of a delicate herb such as chervil, or a leaf or 2 of sorrel. Only fresh herbs will do; if you don't have them, use no herbs. New lettuce should definitely be underdressed. Young lettuce combines beautifully with early leaves of spinach or arugula, and especially with fresh peas.

As it matures and has a stronger and even slightly bitter taste, lettuce can be used in a variety of ways, all very good. Late lettuce and coarser members of the family, such as escarole and chicory and especially dandelion greens, are at their best with a somewhat stronger dressing. When lettuce is abundant, make it into a beautiful soup. Sauté finely shredded lettuce for a minute or 2 in butter, sprinkle it with lemon and parsley and you have a lovely vegetable to serve with broiled meat or fish. Steamed Lettuce Custard, p. 30 , is delicate and fresh tasting, an elegant first course or brunch dish. Small heads of lettuce are delicious braised with chicken stock and herbs.

The best way to wash leaf lettuce from the garden is to put the leaves in a sinkful of cold water and swish them around vigorously. The dirt and sand will sink to the bottom. The leaves will float and you can easily remove any yellow leaves or bits of garden debris. Shake the leaves to remove as much water as possible, tear them into bite-size pieces and dry them by your favorite method. Three equally good methods are to spin the lettuce in a salad dryer, to lay it on layers of toweling or to wrap it in a dish towel, take it outdoors and spin it vigorously in a large circle. The important thing is to get the lettuce as dry as possible. When it has been properly dried, lettuce will keep for a surprisingly long time in the refrigerator, wrapped in a plastic bag or a very slightly damp dish towel. Estimate quantities of salad by the handful; a good handful of torn-up salad greens is an average serving.

Delicate Dressing for New Lettuce

(SALAD FOR 6)

4 tablespoons good olive oil
1 clove garlic, peeled and cut, optional
a small squeeze of lemon juice (about 1 teaspoon) or 1 teaspoon wine
    vinegar
salt and a little freshly ground pepper
1–2 teaspoons chopped fresh chervil, parsley, chives or thyme
6 good handfuls young salad greens, washed and dried

If you think, as I do, that a salad isn't a salad without garlic, let a cut clove steep in the oil for a little while (15 or 20 minutes should be enough) before you dress the salad—the usual crushed or minced garlic would overpower the lettuce. Remove the garlic, combine all the ingredients and toss with the lettuce immediately before serving.

Pungent Dressing for Mature Lettuce, Escarole, Chicory or Dandelion Greens

(SALAD FOR 6)

¼ cup olive oil
¼ pound bacon, thickly sliced or very lean salt pork, cut into small
    strips
3 tablespoons wine vinegar
2 large cloves garlic, minced
salt and freshly ground pepper
6 good handfuls torn-up greens, washed and dried

Put the greens in a salad bowl. Heat the oil in a frying pan, add the bacon or salt pork and cook over medium heat until it is crisp and brown. Add the vinegar and minced garlic and bring to a quick boil, swirling the pan to combine the oil and vinegar. Remove the pan from the heat and grind in some pepper. Pour the dressing over the greens while it is still warm *but not hot*—this is not a recipe for wilted lettuce. Toss the salad and add a little salt and some more pepper if necessary.

Hot and Sweet Pepper Salad

(SERVES 6–8)

1 large, sweet red onion, thinly sliced
2 hot peppers, finely chopped (4–6 tablespoons)
1 teaspoon salt
¼ cup wine vinegar
¼ cup olive oil
6 large sweet red or green peppers, seeded and sliced

Put the onion and the hot peppers in a large salad bowl. Sprinkle them with the salt and pour the vinegar over them. Toss the vegetables and leave them to marinate for at least 2 hours.

About an hour before serving, add the oil to the bowl and mix it in well. Add the sweet peppers. Toss the salad and refrigerate it until serving time. Toss the salad again before serving.

POTATO SALADS

Digging little, round potatoes, especially the red ones, makes you feel like a miner discovering precious stones. Little new potatoes should be boiled or steamed and eaten with lots of butter, salt and freshly ground pepper and chopped fresh herbs. Aside from that, the best way to eat potatoes in summer is in salads. *Use any kind but Idaho or baking potatoes for salad.* The very quality we prize them for—their mealy dryness—makes for a mushy salad. Potatoes combine beautifully with meat, fish, other vegetables and almost any salad dressing. Peel, slice and dress them while they are warm so they will absorb the flavors of the seasonings.

Pesto Potato Salad

(SERVES 8-10)

6 *large potatoes (not Idaho) or 12–15 new potatoes*
4 *large green peppers, seeded and cut into 1-inch chunks*
1 *large sweet onion, peeled and cut in very large dice*

DRESSING
⅓ *cup olive oil*
⅓ *cup wine vinegar*
1 *large clove garlic, minced*
1 *heaping tablespoon Basil Puree, p. 232* } *beaten together with a fork*
   or 8–10 large leaves basil,
   finely chopped
1 *teaspoon salt*
lots of freshly ground pepper

Boil the potatoes in their skins until they are tender when pierced with a sharp knife, about 30 minutes. Combine the peppers and onion with the dressing in a large bowl.

Drain the potatoes as soon as they are done. When they are cool enough to handle, peel them and slice them into the bowl. Toss them gently in the dressing while they are still warm. Serve at room temperature.

Potato Salad with Ham or Tongue

(SERVES 6–8)

6 medium potatoes (not Idaho)
1 cup diced cooked ham or smoked tongue
1 cup diced fennel or celery with plenty of the fennel or celery
    leaves, chopped
Garlicky Mayonnaise Dressing, p. 252

Cook the potatoes until they are done and drain them. Put the dressing in a salad bowl. As soon as the potatoes are cool enough to handle, peel them and slice them into the bowl. Add the meat and fennel or celery and toss gently in the dressing until they are well combined. Let the salad cool and serve it at room temperature. If it has been refrigerated, let it come to room temperature for about half an hour before serving.

Watercress and Potato Salad

(SERVES 6–8)

2 pounds potatoes, old or new (not Idaho)

DRESSING
4 scallions including green tops, finely chopped
1 large clove garlic, finely chopped
2 teaspoons fresh thyme and/or 2 tablespoons chopped parsley
⅓ cup olive oil   } mixed together
⅓ cup wine vinegar, preferably a mild, white wine or rice wine
    vinegar
salt and freshly ground pepper

2 large bunches watercress, cut in thirds crosswise

Boil the potatoes. Make the dressing while they are cooking. When the potatoes are done, peel and slice them while they are still hot and toss them with half the dressing. Set them aside, for several hours if you wish.

Just before serving, put the watercress in a large salad bowl and pour the rest of the dressing over it. Add the potatoes and, using your hands, mix the two thoroughly together. Taste and correct the seasoning if necessary. Serve the salad before the watercress has a chance to wilt.

Potato Salad with Horseradish

(SERVES 6)

6 medium potatoes (not Idaho)
½ small sweet red Italian or Bermuda onion, diced
2 or 3 tablespoons chopped parsley
1 cup Horseradish Sauce, p. 240
salt and freshly ground pepper

Boil the potatoes, peel and slice them. Combine them with the onions, half the horseradish dressing and the seasonings while they are still warm. Chill for 2 hours. Twenty minutes before serving, remove the salad from the refrigerator and mix in the rest of the dressing. This salad is an excellent filling for raw green peppers.

Hot Potato Salad

(SERVES 6–8)

6 large potatoes (2–3 pounds) old or new (not Idaho)
½ pound bacon, sliced
1 large onion, chopped
½ cup beef broth
½ cup wine vinegar
salt and freshly ground pepper   } mixed together
a pinch or 2 of sugar

Boil the potatoes until they are done. Drain them and peel and slice them as soon as they are cool enough to handle. While the potatoes are boiling, cook the bacon in a large skillet until it is crisp. Drain it, leaving the fat in the pan, crumble it into small pieces and set it aside. Sauté the onion in the bacon fat until it is transparent.

Put the warm, sliced potatoes in a serving bowl. Add the vinegar-broth mixture to the onion in the pan and bring it to a boil. Pour it over the potatoes and mix it in well. Add the crumbled bacon. If the salad is not to be served immediately, put it in the pan and cover it. Put the pan on an asbestos pad or a Flame Tamer over *very* low heat. Taste before serving and add more salt and/or pepper to taste. Delicious with grilled sausages of any kind.

Rice Salad with Rosemary

(SERVES 6–8)

Use this as a model for other rice salads; it will give you the proper proportions of rice to dressing. The variations are infinite, ranging from simply using different herbs through the addition of substantial quantities of cut-up crisp vegetables and cold cooked meat, fish or poultry. You can cautiously add a little vinegar or lemon juice if you like.

⅔ cup olive oil
1 large clove garlic, cut into several pieces
1½ teaspoons chopped fresh rosemary
6 cups cooked rice (2 cups uncooked)
salt and freshly ground pepper
4 tablespoons chopped chives

Pour the oil into a large skillet or Dutch oven. Add the garlic and heat the oil over low heat until the garlic begins to turn golden. Press it in the oil to extract the flavor, remove the garlic and discard it. Stir the rosemary into the oil and add the rice. When it is well combined with the seasoned oil, add the salt, pepper and chives and stir until the herbs are well distributed, the rice is warm and all the oil has been absorbed. Taste the rice when it has reached room temperature, and adjust the seasoning. Serve at room temperature.

Rice Salad with Eggplant and Peppers

(SERVES 6–8)

This rice salad uses mixed, sautéed vegetables as a dressing; it's a very good way to extend small quantities of Eggplant and Peppers, p. 114, Ratatouille, p. 153 or Peperonata, p. 128 which you may have left after serving them at a meal.

1½–2 cups Eggplant and Peppers, p.114
6 cups cooked rice (2 cups uncooked)
a clove of garlic, crushed
salt and freshly ground pepper
2 or 3 tablespoons chopped parsley or basil

Mix the vegetables into the cooked rice, preferably but not necessarily while it is still warm. Taste and reseason the mixture with any or all the seasonings listed.

Serve at room temperature. If the salad has been refrigerated, leave it out for an hour before serving.

Spinach and Parsley Salad

(SERVES 6)

2 pounds spinach, thoroughly washed and trimmed of tough stems
1 cup chopped parsley
2 tablespoons lemon juice
6 tablespoons olive oil   } *mixed together*
1 small clove garlic, crushed
salt and freshly ground pepper

Blanch the spinach according to the directions on p. 100. Chop it coarse and mix it with the parsley. Add the dressing, mix well and allow the salad to stand for an hour or 2 before serving.

Summer Salad

(SERVES 6)

This is our favorite summer salad when all the vegetables are sweet, crisp and freshly picked. It is like a solid gazpacho. Drink the juice left in the bottom of the bowl when the salad is gone—it's delicious.

> *2 large cucumbers or 3 medium cucumbers, peeled and cut in large dice*
> *1 large sweet red onion, cut in large dice*
> *3 large green or red peppers, seeded and cut into bite-sized pieces*
> *2 or 3 large ripe tomatoes, cut in chunks*

DRESSING
> *½ cup olive oil*
> *½ cup wine vinegar* } *mixed together*
> *lots of salt and freshly ground pepper*

Combine all the ingredients in a big bowl and refrigerate for an hour or so before serving. Toss several times, if you get the chance.

Swiss Chard Salad

(SERVES 6)

> *2 pounds Swiss chard (about 2 cups after cooking)*
> *1 teaspoon salt*

DRESSING
> *1 tablespoon lemon juice*
> *4 tablespoons olive oil* } *beaten together with a fork*
> *salt and freshly ground pepper*

Wash the Swiss chard well and cut the stems into 1-inch lengths. Put them in a large pot with about ½ inch of water and a teaspoon of salt, cover the pot and bring it to a boil. Cut the leaves into 1-inch strips and put them in the pot on top of the stems. As the chard cooks, turn it in the pot so that the cooked chard at the bottom is replaced by the raw chard on top. When it is all wilted, cover the pot and cook another 5 minutes—*not more.* Drain the chard in a colander and rinse it with cold water to keep it from cooking more. Press the chard down in the colander to remove as much water as possible and pat it dry with paper towels. When the chard is cool, mix it with the dressing. Taste and correct the seasoning. Serve at room temperature.

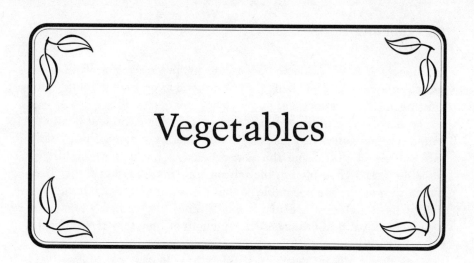

Vegetables

ON COOKING VEGETABLES

There are 3 basic ways to cook fresh summer vegetables: blanching, steaming, and sautéing or stir-frying. Each method has its advantages, but there is one cardinal rule to remember, no matter which method you choose: Do Not Overcook.

There is no summer vegetable that does not taste better raw than overcooked. As soon as a vegetable loses its fresh, bright color it is overcooked. As a matter of fact, properly cooked green vegetables are brighter green than raw ones. This is an excellent gauge to use in cooking spinach, broccoli, green beans, peas, both shelled and edible pods, asparagus and cabbage. Remove them from the pot before their bright color fades. If they are a bit underdone, remember to cook them half a minute longer the next time. Summer squash and zucchini are properly cooked as soon as their flesh becomes slightly transparent— not mushy. Peas and corn must still be very sweet; when they are over-cooked, their sugar turns to starch and they are not worth eating.

Color, texture and flavor all go together. Properly cooked vegetables have a pleasantly firm texture and look and taste beautiful.

Blanching is the best method to use for precooking vegetables, to remove excess juice from leafy vegetables and to prepare vegetables for stuffing and further cooking.

To blanch vegetables, plunge them into a large amount of lightly salted boiling water, 6–8 quarts, if you have a big enough pot, and 2 tablespoons of salt. Bring the water back to the boil as rapidly as possible. It is a good idea to blanch several small batches rather than one large amount of a vegetable so that the water can return to the boil before the vegetables are overcooked. Since you may be blanching vegetables for different purposes, the length of time they remain in the water will vary.

To blanch leafy vegetables. Blanch spinach and other leafy vegetables (such as chard, cabbage and lettuce) only long enough to wilt them. Remove the leaves immediately to a colander and rinse them with cold water to stop the cooking. Drain the leaves and press them down in the colander or squeeze them gently to remove as much moisture as possible.

To prepare zucchini and summer squash and eggplant for stuffing. Wash the vegetables thoroughly and trim off the stem ends. Add no more than 3 medium squash or 2 medium eggplants to the pot at one time. If you are preparing lots of vegetables, do it in several batches. Plunge the whole, unpeeled squash or eggplant into a large quantity of rapidly boiling, lightly salted water (6–8 quarts, if you have a big enough pot, and 2 tablespoons of salt). Cover the pot and boil the vegetables for 10–15 minutes. Remove the vegetables from the water and let them cool. If you want to stuff very large zucchini (and it's a very good use for them), blanch them one at a time and let them cook for 15–20 minutes.

To prepare green beans, broccoli, cauliflower, celery and fennel either for salads or for further cooking, put them in the big pot of boiling water until they are barely cooked or just tender, depending upon what use will be made of them. Cool the vegetables rapidly to stop the cooking, by spreading them out or rinsing them in cold water.

Blanched vegetables can be prepared hours in advance, reheated in butter or a sauce or used cold.

Vegetables cooked in a steamer are perhaps the purest and most beautiful; they seem to retain all their natural flavor and color and have a perfect texture.

Steaming can be done either in a steamer or by cooking vegetables in a very small amount of rapidly boiling water in a large pot or one with a domed lid, so that most of the vegetables in the pot are above the level of the water and are actually cooked by the steam.

Put 1–1½ inches of water in the steamer and bring it to a boil. Put the vegetables in the steaming basket or a colander or lay them on a rack, cover the pan and steam the vegetables until they are just done. It's impossible to tell exactly how long vegetables will take to cook; it depends on their condition, maturity and how large or small the pieces are. Test and taste frequently during cooking; you will soon get a sense of how long each vegetable takes to cook. Do not overcook! It is very easy to improvise a steamer. If you don't have one (I don't, as a matter of fact) see the suggestions on p. 103 . Save the water left in the steamer and use it when making soups.

To prepare butter-steamed vegetables. When you steam vegetables in a very small amount of water in a covered pot, you can enhance the flavor beautifully by adding a good lump of butter to the steaming water. The vegetables must be tossed a couple of times during the steaming so they will cook evenly. With a little experience, you will learn to put in just enough water so that it will have evaporated by the time the vegetables are cooked, leaving a lovely, buttery flavor. This is the best method for the last-minute cooking of very delicately flavored vegetables such as snow peas (edible pea pods), yellow summer squash, young turnips and the first tiny green beans from the garden.

For about 2 pounds of vegetables, put about half an inch of water in a 4-quart pot. Add half a teaspoon of salt and about 2 tablespoons of butter. Bring the water to a boil, drop in the vegetables and cover the pot. After about 2 minutes, bring the vegetables from the bottom of the pot to the top, using a slotted spoon, and cover the pot again. After another 2 minutes, toss the vegetables again and taste one. Continue steaming the vegetables until they are just cooked, remove them immediately from the heat and serve. Save the juice left in the pan to use in making soups.

Sautéed Vegetables are cooked in fat or oil, without liquid. This is the best method to use for cooking several vegetables together. Let the vegetables make their own sauce, using the juice of tomatoes as they cook, for example, or flavoring the oil with garlic or hot peppers and creating the wonderful blended vegetable flavors of such dishes as

Ratatouille, p. 153, Peperonata, p. 128, or Zucchini with Hot and Sweet Peppers, p. 151. Sautéed vegetables can almost always be reheated, are usually good either hot or cold, and keep for several days in the refrigerator.

Stir-frying is rapid sautéing in very hot oil, and a very good way of cooking vegetables quickly. The hot oil sears in their juices.

To sauté vegetables. Heat 1–2 tablespoons butter or olive oil per pound of vegetables in a large frying pan. Cook a little chopped onion, garlic or pepper in the oil to season it, then add the vegetable(s) and toss them to coat them with the oil. Cook over medium heat, stirring from time to time, until the vegetables are done. Add the vegetables that need the longest cooking first; then add the others in sequence so they will all be done at the same time. You may cover the pan for part of the time to speed up the cooking, but remove the cover for several minutes at the end so any excess liquid can evaporate. If you are using tomatoes, it may be necessary to boil the vegetables rapidly for a minute or two at the end of the cooking to concentrate their juices. Use butter only if the vegetables are to be eaten hot.

TO IMPROVISE A STEAMER

The principle of steaming is very simple: food is placed above—*not in*—boiling liquid in a covered pot. The steam cooks the food and little or none of its own juice and flavor are lost. Steamers are simply deep pots with tight-fitting lids into which a perforated basket can be set. An inexpensive, collapsible steaming basket can be found in most housewares shops. The Chinese steam food in lattice-bottomed straw baskets placed above boiling water; you can buy a steamer in any well-stocked Chinese market. But it is very easy to improvise a steamer, using equipment which is standard in most kitchens.

Look over your kitchen equipment. If you have a 4–6-quart pot with a tight-fitting lid, a large roasting pan with a domed lid, a metal colander, 2 or 3 heatproof custard cups and a cake-cooling rack, you can improvise a steamer with no difficulty. You will also need a plate or platter at least one inch smaller in diameter than the steaming pot. A glass pie plate is an excellent steaming platter to use in a round pot; a good-sized oval platter fits nicely into a roasting pan. Put the Pyrex cups in the pot and place the rack on top of them to raise it well above the level of the water. Be sure to protect your hands from steam burns—they can be serious. Wear rubber gloves or mitts when putting food into or removing it from the steam, or take the pot off the heat for a minute to allow the steam to subside. To facilitate removing a hot platter from a steamy pot, put a long strip of aluminum foil, folded lengthwise several times, under and around the narrow circumference of the platter like a belt. To remove the platter, grasp the two ends of the foil belt and gently lift it out of the pot.

To use a colander. Put 1½–2 inches of water in the pot and bring it to the boil. Put the food to be steamed into the colander and lower it into the pot. Cover the pot and steam the food until it is done (see individual listings for timing).

To use a rack. Bring plenty of water to a boil in a kettle. Put 2 or 3 custard cups in the pan and fill them with water to keep them from floating. Put the rack on top of the cups and pour 1–1½ inches of boiling water into the pan. Cover the pan and steam the food according to the directions in the recipes until it is done (see individual listings for specific instructions).

ON FREEZING VEGETABLES

After years of vegetable gardening and many experiments with the freezing of vegetables, I have concluded that it's hardly worth freezing vegetables in the usual way—cut up, blanched and packaged. Freezing can preserve the flavor, but it destroys the texture of vegetables. My procedure, therefore, is to change the texture of the vegetables in my own way, before freezing them, by turning them into soups, sauces and purees. This serves several purposes: vegetables in this form take up much less room than conventionally frozen ones, they need only to be thawed and heated before using, and they can be seasoned with all the aromatic herbs of summer while they are fresh and fragrant.

Unless you have unlimited freezer space, it's a good idea to freeze soups before adding stock. A well-flavored tomato puree (Tomato Sauce with Olive Oil, p. 248, made with only 1 or 2 tablespoons of olive oil) can provide the basis for vegetable, meat or fish soups and stews all year. Homemade tomato soups and sauces, frozen in summer, have a much better flavor than any made with even the best canned tomatoes; those made with fresh, out-of-season tomatoes have little flavor of any kind. If you are very pressed for time when the bulk of the tomato crop comes in, cut up raw tomatoes, freeze them in plastic bags and cook them later.

Zucchini Soup Base, p. 63, can provide the model for other vegetable mixtures to be frozen and used later in soups. I have frozen mixed purees of most garden vegetables and find that excellent soups can be made from all of them. Frozen vegetable purees are also good to use in Vegetable Meatballs, p. 181 and steamed vegetable custards, p. 30. Be sure to drain the vegetables well after they have thawed. Surprisingly, gazpacho freezes extremely well and provides a quick and easy way of using late summer oversupplies of cucumbers, tomatoes and peppers.

I prefer frozen to dried herbs, and with a few exceptions, I freeze all the herbs that grow in my garden. Chervil, that most delicate summer herb, loses its flavor in either freezing or drying. Parsley and dill are readily available in most vegetable markets year round and chopped scallion tops make an excellent substitute for fresh chives.

I usually freeze tarragon, thyme, marjoram, oregano, basil, savory and rosemary. There's no need to wash the herbs unless they are muddy or sandy. Strip the leaves from the stems and chop them. Freeze the chopped leaves in clearly labeled baby food jars or small plastic containers with tight lids. When you use the herbs, take out as much as you need and immediately put the jar back in the freezer. Chopped herbs thaw very rapidly. They should be added toward the end of cooking, when possible. Herb Butters, p. 235, can be frozen but lose their fresh taste if they are kept for more than a couple of months.

ON STORING VEGETABLES

Ideally, summer vegetables should go from the garden to the table in as short a time as possible. If the vegetables must be stored, whether in a shop, on a farm stand or in your kitchen, they should be handled with care to preserve their crispness and sweetness.

Vegetables should be stored dry. They should not be washed until just before they are used.

Except for tomatoes (and peppers which are turning red), *vegetables should be kept cold* to prevent their sugar from turning to starch. Corn should be refrigerated, unshucked, until just before it is cooked. Peas should be shelled just before cooking, if possible, or shelled and refrigerated, covered, for not more than an hour or so.

Unless you plan to cook them within a few hours, *put vegetables in plastic bags* so none of the moisture can evaporate.

The longer you store vegetables, the less fresh they will be and the less fresh they will taste.

The flavor and texture of tomatoes deteriorates rapidly when they are refrigerated. Even ripe tomatoes will keep for several days at room temperature if they are stored in one layer, preferably in baskets so that air can circulate around the fruit. Keep them out of the sun and away from the heat of the stove if the kitchen is hot. If you are lucky enough to have more tomatoes than you can eat, make soups and sauces and freeze them.

Beets with Their Greens

(SERVES 6)

An outstandingly beautiful dish—and very good, too.

6 medium-sized beets with fresh tops
1 tablespoon butter
salt
3 tablespoons sour cream
2 tablespoons chopped fresh dill

Cut the tops off the beets, scrub them well and boil them in water to cover until they are tender, 40–50 minutes. Let the beets cool a bit and slip them out of their skins. Shred the beets in a food processor or chop them fine.

While the beets are cooking, wash the beet greens and stems and cut them into 1-inch lengths. Melt the butter in 3 tablespoons of water, add a little salt and the greens. Cover the pan and steam the greens over high heat, stirring once or twice, until they are just cooked, about 5 minutes. The dish can be prepared several hours in advance to this point.

Shortly before serving, reheat the beet greens and toss the shredded beets with the sour cream and 1 tablespoon of the dill in a small pot until they are just heated through. Pile the beets in the center of a serving dish and surround them with their greens. Sprinkle the remaining dill over the beets.

To serve this dish cold, steam the beet greens as directed but omit the butter. Drain the greens and, when they are cool, dress them with 2 tablespoons of olive oil and some salt.

Broccoli

Because it doesn't have to be eaten the minute it is picked, broccoli has become one of the green vegetables we can eat all year round. Nevertheless, fresh broccoli in the summer is especially good. Eat it *raw* with almost any good dip, p.12. Eat it *cold*, dressed with a lemony, garlicky Vinaigrette Dressing, p. 251. Best of all, eat it simply *steamed*, p. 101, with a Hollandaise Sauce or Mousseline Sauce, pp. 237-238.

Broccoli is also very good in Red, White and Green Vegetable Soup, p. 56, or in Broccoli Soup, made exactly like Green Bean Soup, p. 51, substituting 1 pound of broccoli for the green beans and omitting the savory.

Corn

Freshly picked, freshly shucked, just-cooked corn is a delicacy we can enjoy for only a few weeks in the year. Unless we're having Indiana Succotash, below, I think the best way to eat corn is plain, boiled, on the cob, with plenty of sweet butter and salt. The next best way is to eat it cold, if any is left, on the cob, with salt, or in a Fresh Corn Custard, p. 32.

To boil corn on the cob. Bring lots of water to a boil in a pot large enough to hold the corn. Leave about 20 minutes for the water to come to the boil. Shuck the corn just before cooking it. Drop the ears into the rapidly boiling water and cover the pot. When the water returns to a rapid boil, the corn is done. Drain off the water and leave the corn in the covered pot to keep it hot.

Indiana Succotash

(SERVES 6)

To me, this is the ultimate summer dish. It can be eaten only in summer, and only at that point in summer when all its ingredients are in the perfection of their ripeness. It is best eaten outdoors, in a leisurely way, on a mild summer day or a warm, moonlit night. You can't just sit down and gobble succotash. Each person prepares his own bowlful, so there's a certain amount of ceremony, as befits this great dish with its beautiful colors and its unique contrasts of flavor and texture. All the vegetables have the sweetness of summer, but at the same time they are also crisp, tart, succulent, creamy, cold, hot and unctuous with butter.

We learned about succotash from a friend whose family ate it on their farm. We all feel very possessive of this treasure and a bit fearful of casting it out into the great world. Please treat it with respect. Don't try to make succotash unless you have fresh shell beans, absolutely ripe, delicious, juicy tomatoes, sweet, sweet onions and just-picked corn. We always use cranberry beans (also called horticultural beans) which are widely available in Italian markets. They have long, light-green pods speckled with pink. If you have a garden and can't get cranberry beans, there is every reason to grow them solely for use in Indiana Succotash.

5 pounds cranberry beans, shelled
at least 12 ears sweet corn, shucked just before cooking
8–10 large ripe, juicy tomatoes
2 large, very sweet onions, preferably red Italian onions
lots of butter
coarse salt

The beans can be cooked in advance or can be started 2 hours before you eat. Cover the beans by 1 inch with water and bring them to a boil. Turn down the heat, partially cover the pot and simmer the beans for about an hour. Cooking time will vary, depending on the age and freshness of the beans and upon how mushy you like them. Some people like very soft, creamy beans, others prefer a thoroughly cooked but firmer texture. Be sure to use enough water so that there will be some juice left when the beans are cooked. Watch the beans carefully while they are cooking and add a little more water if necessary. If they stick to the bottom of the pot and burn, they will have to be thrown away. You can cook the beans a few hours in advance and reheat them carefully in their juice—it's a good idea to put the pot over a Flame Tamer.

When the beans are cooked and hot, bring a lot of water to a boil in a pot large enough to hold the corn. Dice the onions and put them in a bowl on the table. Put a plate of tomatoes and a couple of dishes of butter on the table and make sure that some coarse salt is within everybody's easy reach. Each person should have a large soup bowl, a soup spoon, a sharp knife and several napkins.

Just before serving, put the corn in the boiling water. As soon as the water returns to the boil, take out the corn, put it on a platter and cover it with a clean dish towel to keep it hot. Put the hot beans into a serving bowl.

To prepare the succotash, put a large spoonful of the beans and their juice in your soup bowl. Next, stand an ear of corn on end in the bowl and cut the kernels into the bowl. Add a large piece of butter and let it melt while you cut a tomato into chunks and add it to the bowl. Sprinkle on plenty of chopped onion and salt and gently mix everything together.

The first spoonful will taste heavenly, the next, sublime; then you will notice that you need a little more tomato or another dab of beans. Soon the proportion of corn will be all out of balance. The readjustment of ingredients continues as long as they last. Then, with happy sighs, everyone looks forward to the next opportunity to continue the search for that elusive formula—the perfectly balanced dish of succotash.

Day Lily Buds

This may sound outlandish—or not worth the trouble. Neither is the case. Day lilies (those hosts of orange flowers that line country roads in early summer)—bud, flower, root—have for ages been food for many peoples, most notably the Chinese. Take a plastic bag along when you go for a walk, and pick buds that are tightly closed, about 1½–2 inches long and just beginning to show a hint of orange mixed with the green. A word of caution: don't eat too many of these at one time. Sometimes it takes a while to get used to wild foods.

To cook the buds, bring a little water to a boil in a skillet, throw in the buds, cover the pan and steam for 3–5 minutes. That's all. Serve hot, with butter and salt, or cold, as an exotic garnish for a cold chicken or fish mousse.

Green Beans

Very fresh green beans need only to have the stem-ends snapped off and a quick rinse before cooking. They seem to taste best when left whole and eaten with the fingers, but there's no reason not to snap them in half or thirds before cooking, if you prefer. Follow the directions on p. 100 for steaming or blanching beans to be eaten hot or cold. Please,

please do not overcook them. Properly cooked green beans should be bright green and just a little bit crunchy.

Hot Steamed Green Beans. Thyme and savory are delicious with green beans; put a few sprigs of either herb in the water when you steam or butter-steam green beans, p. 101 . Hot green beans are good with Egg-Lemon Sauce, p. 233, or Sour Cream Hollandaise with dill, p. 238.

Cold Steamed Green Beans should be dressed about ½ hour before serving with Vinaigrette Dressing, p. 251 , to which a little chopped thyme or savory has been added, or used in one of the green bean salads, p. 87-88.

Less-than-perfect green beans are more useful than most vegetables in questionable condition. If you must use beans that are too mature or are wilted or limp, use them in Green Bean Puree, below, Rosemary's Green Bean Salad, p. 88, or Green Bean Soup, p. 51.

Green Bean Puree

(SERVES 6)

A puree of green beans is delicious and is, in my opinion, the only acceptable way to freeze green beans. It is an ideal way to use slightly oversized beans when the crop gets ahead of you.

2 pounds green beans
butter
salt and freshly ground pepper

Following the directions on p. 100 , blanch the beans until they are just tender. Chop them to a puree in a food processor or puree them in a blender, using a little of the water in which they were blanched if you need liquid. Before serving, add a good lump of butter and some salt and freshly ground pepper to the puree and heat it over boiling water to prevent further cooking.

Frozen green bean puree should be thawed and drained before being heated over boiling water with butter. It will taste almost exactly like the fresh puree. (One pound of green beans makes 2 cups of puree.)

Stuffed Eggplant

(SERVES 4–6)

This is as much a method or an approach as it is a recipe. Eggplant can be stuffed with many different good things; be guided by what is in your refrigerator, your garden or your favorite roadside stand. This is not to say that it should be stuffed with everything at once; each time, let one flavor dominate, accentuated with herbs or some surprising, crunchy nut or vegetable.

2 small or 1 large eggplant (about 2 pounds)
6 tablespoons olive oil
4 scallions including green tops, sliced
2 medium zucchini, coarsely chopped
½ cup chopped parsley
2 teaspoons chopped fresh marjoram
chopped flesh of the eggplant
1 large clove garlic, crushed
1 cup cooked rice (about ⅓ cup raw)
4 large ripe tomatoes, peeled, seeded and chopped
salt and freshly ground pepper

Blanch the eggplant as directed on p. 100. When it is cool enough to handle, cut it in half lengthwise and scoop out the flesh, leaving a shell about ½-inch thick. Invert the shells to drain while you prepare the stuffing. Chop the flesh of the eggplant to add to the stuffing.

Heat 2 tablespoons of the oil in a flameproof casserole or Dutch oven large enough to hold the stuffed eggplant halves. Sauté the scallions for a minute or so, add the zucchini, half the parsley and 1 teaspoon of the marjoram and cook the mixture over medium-high heat, stirring frequently, until the zucchini is tender, about 8–10 minutes. Remove the pot from the heat and stir in the chopped eggplant, the crushed garlic, the rice, and 1 cup of the chopped tomatoes. Season with salt and freshly ground pepper. Mix the rest of the tomatoes with the remaining ½ cup of parsley and teaspoon of marjoram and season them well with salt and freshly ground pepper.

Put 2 or 3 tablespoons of the tomatoes in each eggplant half and fill the halves with the zucchini mixture. Heat 4 tablespoons of oil in the Dutch oven and stir in the seasoned chopped tomatoes. Set the stuffed eggplant halves in the pot, cover and cook over medium heat for 20 minutes. Remove the eggplant to a platter and pour the tomato sauce over them. Serve at room temperature.

Variations.

Reversing proportions, stuff zucchini halves with an eggplant mixture.

The Hot Sausage Stuffing, p. 127, and the Zucchini and Rice Stuffing, p. 128, are both excellent with eggplant.

Make a half-recipe of Eggplant and Eggs, p. 26, and substitute it for the zucchini mixture in the recipe. The eggs will set into a delicious custard. Serve at room temperature.

Eggplant and Peppers

(ABOUT 4 CUPS)

This simple dish, very good either hot or cold, has an amazing variety of uses and is nice to have on hand, especially if you are entertaining. It makes an excellent filling for Basil Crêpes, p. 37, for raw tomatoes, p. 134 , and for omelettes. Mix it with ground meat to make meatballs, p. 182 or with rice to make a cold salad. And it forms the basis for one of the best of the cold, summer soups, Cold Eggplant Soup, p. 49 .

about 2 pounds eggplant
salt
¼ cup olive oil
3 medium green peppers, seeded and diced

Peel the eggplant and cut it into ½-inch cubes. Sprinkle it with salt and put it in a colander to drain for about half an hour. Heat the oil in a large skillet, pat the eggplant dry with paper towels and stir it into the oil. For the first few minutes, cook the eggplant over medium-high heat, stirring it frequently and scraping it off the bottom of the pot if it sticks. Then turn the heat down, cover the pan and cook the eggplant for 15–20 minutes, until it is quite soft. Add the green peppers, stir to combine well, cover the pan and cook about 10 minutes more, until the eggplant is very soft and the green peppers are cooked through but still firm. The dish will probably not need any more salt, but taste it and add some if necessary.

Serve hot or cold or use in any of the recipes mentioned above. It is easy to double these quantities in order to have a good supply on hand; the eggplant and peppers will keep for a week or so in the refrigerator.

Eggplant a Funghetti
(SERVES 6–8 AS FIRST COURSE)

2–3 pounds eggplant (1 very large or 2 medium)
salt
about ½ cup olive oil
2 cloves garlic, minced
2 tablespoons chopped parsley
freshly grated Parmesan cheese

Wash and trim the eggplant but do not peel it. Cut it into ½-inch cubes, sprinkle it generously with salt and put it in a colander to drain for about half an hour. Pat the eggplant dry with paper towels.

Heat the oil in a deep frying pan or Dutch oven and cook the eggplant in it over medium heat, stirring and tossing it frequently to keep it from sticking, until it is quite soft, 20–30 minutes. Add the garlic and cook for 2 or 3 minutes more. Turn off the heat and stir in the parsley.

Serve the eggplant at room temperature, sprinkled with Parmesan cheese. If it has been refrigerated, let it come to room temperature before serving, 1–2 hours.

Eggplant Puree with Yogurt
(5–6 CUPS)

This delicious mixture can be used as a dip for raw vegetables, breadsticks or crackers, or as a filling for raw tomatoes or green peppers.

3 pounds eggplant
1 cup yogurt, preferably homemade, p. 253
3 cloves garlic, minced
salt and freshly ground pepper

Trim the stem end of the eggplant(s) and cut them in half lengthwise. Steam the eggplant in a steamer or a colander, p. 101 , for about 20 minutes or until it is very tender. Mash the eggplant, skin and all, or chop it fine in a food processor. Mix it with the yogurt and garlic and season to taste with salt and pepper.

Eggplant with Yogurt

(SERVES 6–8)

This version of the classic Middle Eastern combination is one everybody seems to love. It can be made with sautéed or with broiled eggplant. Broiling is easier and hotter. Sautéing is a bit more time consuming, but worth it if your kitchen gets very hot. The flavor is equally good either way, so take your pick.

2–3 pounds eggplant
salt
½ cup olive oil
1 large clove garlic, peeled
2 cups plain yogurt, preferably homemade, p. 253
about 1 teaspoon salt
1 small clove garlic, minced, optional

To sauté. Cut the eggplant into ½-inch dice, toss it with some salt and put it in a colander to drain for about ½ hour. Rinse off the salt and shake the eggplant in a dish towel to dry it. Put the olive oil in a deep sauté pan or Dutch oven and add a large clove of garlic, sliced. Heat the garlic in the oil until it browns, then remove and discard it. Add the eggplant and toss it several times to distribute the oil. Cook it over moderate heat for 15–20 minutes, stirring and tossing it frequently, until it is soft.

To broil. Cut the eggplant into ½-inch slices, salt the slices on both sides and put them in a colander to drain for about ½ hour. Rinse the slices and dry them on paper towels. Mince the garlic and mix it with the olive oil. Pour the oil onto 1 or 2 cookie sheets, dip the eggplant slices rapidly in the oil and broil them, turning once. They will take 5–10 minutes on each side. They should be tender and lightly browned.

Beat the yogurt well with the salt and, if you like a strong garlic flavor, add the additional clove of garlic. Allow the eggplant to come to room temperature. Put a few spoonsful of the yogurt mixture in a deep serving dish. Add a layer of eggplant, cover with yogurt and continue to alternate layers of eggplant and yogurt, ending with a layer of yogurt. Refrigerate, but be sure to bring the dish to room temperature before serving. This dish may be made a day or 2 in advance.

Sautéed Lettuce

(SERVES 6)

1 medium-size head lettuce for each serving
4 tablespoons butter
salt and freshly ground pepper
juice of ½ lemon or 4 tablespoons heavy cream
2 tablespoons finely chopped chervil or parsley

Wash the lettuce thoroughly, shake it dry and shred it. It will look like an enormous amount, but it will wilt away to very little as soon as it cooks. Melt the butter in large pot and put in as much lettuce as you can. Toss it in the butter and, as it wilts, continue to toss in more lettuce until it is all cooked. Add the lemon juice or cream and the salt and pepper and continue to toss the lettuce in the pot for another 2 or 3 minutes. Remove it to a serving bowl with a slotted spoon, bring the pan juices to a rapid boil to reduce them by at least half. Pour the juices over the lettuce, sprinkle with the chervil or parsley and serve.

Braised Lettuce

(SERVES 6)

3 large or 6 small heads lettuce
4 tablespoons butter
3 scallions including green tops, finely chopped
½ cup mixed chopped herbs (combine parsley, chervil and thyme
     with either basil or rosemary or tarragon)
salt and freshly ground pepper
1 cup chicken stock

Wash the heads of lettuce carefully by dunking them upside-down several times in a big basin of cold water. Shake the heads well and cut them in half, or even in quarters, if they are large. Melt the butter in a Dutch oven. Add the scallions and cook for 2 or 3 minutes, stir in the herbs and some salt and pepper. Turn the lettuce over and over in this mixture, add the chicken stock and when it comes to a boil, cover the pot and cook over low heat for 15–20 minutes. Turn the lettuce with tongs and continue to cook, uncovered, until most of the liquid has evaporated. Serve hot.

PEAS

Like corn, peas must be eaten as soon as possible after they are picked. There is nothing to compare with sweet, juicy fresh peas; they are so good raw that it's hard to get a proper potful to the table. Frozen tiny peas are very good and could be used in these recipes, but there's no excuse for this in summer, when fresh vegetables abound.

Peas can be steamed in a colander or in butter, p. 101, or cooked with lettuce, French-style, to make a delicious, early summer treat. Use large peas in a puree.

Peas Cooked with Lettuce

(SERVES 6)

4 tablespoons butter
4–5 cups finely shredded lettuce
6 scallions, including green tops, sliced
2 tablespoons chopped fresh mint
4 cups shelled peas (3–4 pounds unshelled)
salt and freshly ground pepper

Melt 3 tablespoons of the butter in a large, deep frying pan or Dutch oven. Turn off the heat. Spread half the lettuce on the butter, sprinkle it with the scallions and mint and put the peas in an even layer on top. Sprinkle on about a teaspoon of salt and a few grinds of pepper, dot the peas with the remaining butter and cover them with the rest of the lettuce. (The peas can be prepared in advance to this point. Put the pan in the refrigerator if you intend to leave it for more than half an hour before cooking.)

Put a tight-fitting cover on the pan and put it over fairly high heat until you hear it beginning to cook. Turn down the heat so that the peas steam without danger of burning. If the pan seems too dry after 5 minutes or so (lettuce varies in its water content), add a few tablespoons of water to the pan. Steam the peas for 15 minutes or so. Start tasting after 10 minutes and remove them from the heat the minute they are done. They should be sweet, tender, juicy and bright green.

Puree of Peas

(SERVES 6)

4 cups shelled peas
4 tablespoons butter
½ cup heavy cream
salt and freshly ground pepper
a little sugar

Steam the peas in a colander, p. 101 , until they are tender. Puree them in a food processor or blender until they are smooth. Stir the butter and cream into the hot puree, or reheat it very gently, over boiling water, until the butter has melted and the peas are hot. Season to taste with salt, pepper and a little sugar.

PEPPERS

Do we prize them most for their flavor, their crispness, their versatility—or their beauty? The variety of shape, color and flavor is unmatched in any other vegetable. Peppers can be deep-green cubes or long, skinny dark-red spikes, red and green cherries, yellow cones. Their color is most remarkable when they are in the process of turning from green to red and for a week or so may be one of nature's ineffable colors, neither green nor brown nor rust, mysteriously hinting of orange and purple. Peppers come in all temperatures: sweet green ones may seem cool as watermelon; the hottest can literally blister your lips. The hardest to find are those medium-hot ones, described in the seed catalogue as having "sweet flesh and hot ribs."

Stuffed peppers are usually assumed to be filled with a rice-meat mixture and baked in the oven. How sad that the most stuffable vegetable there is should lead so limited a life. A perfect lunch: a great big deep-red crisp sweet juicy pepper, split open, seeded and filled with very fresh cottage cheese or ricotta. Recipes and suggestions for other raw-pepper stuffings follow.

Slightly cooked pepper quarters are delectable stuffed with something fishy or salty, Stuffed Pepper Boats, p.124. Cooked stuffed whole peppers are juicy, sweet and delicate when they are steamed in olive oil and tomatoes on top of the stove. The flavors of hot and sweet peppers complement each other; you will find them combined in several recipes, especially Hot and Sweet Pepper Salad, p.91 and Zucchini with Hot and Sweet Peppers, p. 151. A bit of chopped hot pepper is a good addition to almost any of the stuffing recipes or suggestions given here, and half-hot peppers are marvelous stuffed—but do warn people. Tolerance and taste for hot pepper varies greatly from one person to another. A few words of warning: the seeds of hot peppers are considerably hotter than the flesh; be careful to discard them unless you like your peppers very hot. Protect your hands (or more accurately, protect yourself from your hands) when you have been cutting hot peppers. You can burn your eyes or mouth by merely brushing them with a peppery hand. Hot pepper juice can take several days to wash off. I usually wear an old pair of white cotton gloves when I cut up hot peppers.

Stuffed Raw Peppers

The best way to seed a pepper for stuffing raw or for cutting up is to turn it stem-end down and cut halfway through the pepper. Break it apart; one half will come clean of seeds. Grasp the core and the top of the pepper and break it off. Brush out any few remaining seeds and trim away the pithy ribs.

A medium-sized pepper-half holds about ½ cup of stuffing. All the following are delicious stuffings for raw peppers. Improvise, experiment, and you will soon find as many more.

Tuna-Cottage Cheese Stuffing, p. 123
Bulgur-Basil Stuffing, p. 123
Greek Salad Stuffing, p. 124
Seviche, p. 170
Fish Salads, pp. 76–79
Stir-Fried Chicken Bits, p. 194
Zucchini Caviar, p. 150
Eggplant Puree with Yogurt, p. 115
Lentils with Sorrel, p. 131

STUFFINGS FOR RAW VEGETABLES

Tuna-Cottage Cheese Stuffing
(ENOUGH FOR: 6–8 PEPPERS OR 8–10 TOMATOES OR
4–6 CUCUMBERS)

1 6½-ounce can tuna fish
1 pound cottage cheese
about ½ cup chopped chives
1 medium clove garlic, crushed
lemon juice to taste
salt and freshly ground pepper
about 20 radishes, sliced or cut in quarters
1 large cucumber, peeled, seeded and diced

Break up the tuna with a fork, mash it and combine it well with the cottage cheese. Season the mixture with the chives, garlic, lemon juice, salt and pepper. Fold in the radishes and cucumbers.

Bulgur-Basil Stuffing
(FOR 6 MEDIUM PEPPERS, 8–10 TOMATOES)

1 cup bulgur
2–3 tablespoons Basil Puree, p. 232 or about ½ cup finely chopped
    basil
1 clove garlic, crushed
3 tablespoons olive oil
salt and freshly ground pepper

Soak the bulgur in 3 cups of water for 2 hours. Drain it well and pat it dry with paper towels. Stir in the basil, garlic, oil, salt and pepper and be sure they are well combined. Taste and adjust the seasoning—you may want to add a good bit more basil.

Greek Salad Stuffing
(FOR 6 GREEN PEPPERS, 8–10 TOMATOES)

1 6½-ounce can tuna fish
½ pound feta cheese, crumbled (about 1 cup)
1 can (2 ounces) anchovy fillets, cut into pieces
12 black Greek olives, pitted and cut in pieces
½ sweet red onion, diced

DRESSING
6 tablespoons olive oil
2 tablespoons wine vinegar
1 large clove garlic, crushed
lots of freshly ground pepper
} mixed together with a fork

Combine the tuna, cheese, anchovies, olives and onion in a bowl. Toss them with the dressing until they are thoroughly mixed.

Stuffed Pepper Boats
(SERVES 12 AS A FIRST COURSE)

6 medium peppers
1 6½-ounce can tuna fish
1 large clove garlic, crushed
juice of 1 small lemon (2–3 tablespoons)
salt and lots of freshly ground pepper
2 tablespoons capers, optional
¼ cup olive oil

Seed the peppers and cut them into quarters lengthwise to form boatlike shells. Mash the tuna fish well and combine it with the garlic, lemon juice, salt, pepper and capers. Adjust the seasoning to taste; the fish should be very highly seasoned. Put a tablespoon or so of filling in each shell. Heat the oil in a large skillet. When it is warm, set the pepper boats carefully in the oil. Cover the pan and cook over medium heat for

5–8 minutes, until the peppers have just begun to cook. Remove the peppers from the pan with tongs, put them on a platter and pour the oil over them. Serve at room temperature.

Variations.
Put 1 tablespoon Tapénade, p. 13 , on each piece of pepper. Cook as
  directed above.

Put 1 or 2 anchovy fillets in each piece of pepper. Add 1 or 2 finely
  chopped cloves of garlic to the warm oil when you add the
  peppers, and pour it over them after they have cooked.

Cooked Stuffed Peppers

(6 PEPPERS)

6 large green or red peppers
1 recipe stuffing, pp. 126–128
½ cup olive oil
1 or 2 ripe tomatoes, cut in chunks

Cut the tops off the peppers and remove the seeds. Fill each pepper *loosely* with stuffing; do not pack it down or it will be soggy. Put the olive oil and the tomatoes in a Dutch oven or a flameproof casserole with a tight lid, and arrange the peppers, open-side up, in the pan. Cover the pan, turn the heat up high until the oil is bubbling hot, then turn the heat low and stew the peppers, covered, for 20–25 minutes. Put the peppers on a platter. Mix the pan juice well and pour it around the peppers. Spoon some of this sauce over and around each pepper when serving. Serve at room temperature.

STUFFINGS FOR COOKED PEPPERS

Cook the stuffing in the pot in which you intend to cook the peppers; if there is any left, it will add seasoning to the sauce.

All of these stuffings are good in eggplant and zucchini, too. Check the eggplant and zucchini listings in the Index to find directions on how to prepare them for stuffing.

Tomato and Herb Stuffing

(ENOUGH FOR 6 PEPPERS)

½ cup olive oil
1 large onion, finely chopped
2 cloves garlic, minced
1 large ripe tomato, cut in ½-inch dice
10–12 leaves basil, finely chopped
½ cup finely chopped parsley
salt and freshly ground pepper
2 cups unseasoned bread crumbs, preferably freshly made from
    stale bread

Heat the olive oil in a large frying pan. Add the onion and cook it, without browning, for 5 minutes. Add the garlic, cook it for a minute or 2 and add the tomato, herbs, salt and pepper. When they are well mixed, add the bread crumbs and combine thoroughly. Cook the stuffing over low heat, stirring frequently, for 10–15 minutes, until the bread crumbs are lightly toasted.

Anchovy and Caper Stuffing

(ENOUGH FOR 6 PEPPERS)

½ cup olive oil
6 scallions with green part, thinly sliced
2 cloves garlic, minced
6–8 anchovies, cut in small pieces
2 tablespoons capers
½ cup finely chopped parsley
freshly ground pepper
grated rind of ½ lemon
2 cups unseasoned bread crumbs, preferably freshly made from
    stale bread

Heat the olive oil in a large frying pan. Add the scallions and cook them over low heat, without browning, for 2 or 3 minutes. Add the garlic, cook it for a minute or two and add the anchovies, capers, parsley, lemon rind and several grinds of pepper. When these are well combined, add the bread crumbs and mix well to distribute all the seasonings. Cook the stuffing over low heat, stirring frequently, until the bread crumbs are lightly toasted, 10–15 minutes.

Hot Sausage Stuffing

(ENOUGH FOR 6 PEPPERS)

2 or 3 hot Italian sausages
½ cup olive oil
1 large onion, finely chopped
½ cup finely chopped parsley
2 cups unseasoned bread crumbs, preferably freshly made from
    stale bread
2 tablespoons freshly grated Parmesan cheese
salt and freshly ground pepper

Remove the sausage meat from its skin and cook it over medium heat until it is cooked through, crumbly and nicely browned. Remove it with a slotted spoon and set it aside. Pour off the fat in the pan and add the olive oil. Cook the onion gently in the oil until it is soft, about 10 minutes, then stir in the bread crumbs and the cooked sausage. Mix them well with the onions and oil and cook the stuffing over low heat for about 10 minutes, until the bread crumbs are lightly toasted. Add the parsley and cheese, combine well and season to taste with salt and pepper.

Zucchini and Rice Stuffing
(ENOUGH FOR 6 PEPPERS)

1 medium zucchini (about 1 pound), cut into ½-inch dice
salt
½ pound lean ground beef
½ cup olive oil
1 large onion, finely chopped
1 cup cooked rice (⅓ cup raw)
2 pinches cinnamon
freshly ground pepper

Put the zucchini in a colander and sprinkle it with a teaspoon or so of salt. Let it drain while you prepare the stuffing.

Brown the meat in a large frying pan, turning it with a fork until it is cooked through and crumbly. Remove the meat from the pan and set it aside. Pour off any fat left in the pan, add the olive oil, heat it and cook the onion for about 5 minutes. Pat the zucchini dry with paper towels, add it to the onion in the pan and cook for 5 minutes. Add the meat, rice and seasonings, combine well, and cook, stirring frequently, until the zucchini is just tender, 5–10 minutes. Taste and correct the seasoning.

Peperonata
(3–4 CUPS)

This superb Italian concoction is probably best described as an essence rather than as an ordinary vegetable dish. It is delicious hot or cold; as an accompaniment to meat, fish or poultry; as a filling for omelets or a bed for poached eggs; as a sauce for pasta; as a relish on hero sandwiches or hamburgers; or as part of an antipasto platter. It could even substitute beautifully for dessert, served with an assortment of cheeses, good fresh bread and wine.

At its purest, peperonata is a glorious, intense red, made only with onion, red peppers and tomatoes. It is also good, if not quite as beautiful, made with green peppers. Garlic and/or a couple of leaves of fresh basil are sometimes added. Peperonata keeps for a long time in a jar in the refrigerator and, along with tomato sauce, can ensure that you will always have on hand the makings of a very good meal.

2 tablespoons butter
4 tablespoons olive oil
2 large onions, peeled and chopped
8 large red or green peppers, seeded and cut into strips
3 pounds plum tomatoes, peeled and coarsely chopped
salt

Melt the butter in the olive oil in a large frying pan. Add the onions and cook, stirring frequently, over medium heat, until the onions are soft. Add the peppers, stir well, cover the pan and cook for 10 or 15 minutes. Add the tomatoes, stir them in well, cover the pan again and cook for another 15 or 20 minutes. Uncover the pan and, stirring very frequently, continue to cook the peperonata until all the liquid in the pan has evaporated. Be very careful not to burn the vegetables. Serve immediately, reheat carefully over low heat, or serve at room temperature.

Sautéed Scallions

(SERVES 6)

3 large bunches (about 3 dozen) scallions
4 tablespoons butter
salt and freshly ground pepper

Trim the roots and any wilted leaves from the scallions and cut them to a uniform length to fit in a large skillet. Wash the scallions well, shake out the water and pat them dry. Melt the butter in a large, heavy skillet, turn the heat low and lay the scallions in the pan with all the bottom ends on the same side. Keep the pan a little off-center on the burner, so that the white ends of the scallions will cook faster than the green. Let them cook gently in the butter for about 5 minutes, then turn them over in bunches, using tongs, and cook for 3 or 4 minutes on the other side, until the white ends are tender when pierced with a knife and the green ends are still a bright color. Serve hot, as a garnish for grilled meat.

It is easier to cook this dish if you cut the scallions into 1-inch lengths and sauté them in the butter, stirring frequently, for 6 or 7 minutes. They will not look as impressive, but they will taste just as good.

Snow Peas (Sugar Peas)

A great delicacy, usually both very hard to find and very expensive, an abundance of snow peas is one of the vegetable gardener's greatest rewards. Eat them raw, steam them in a colander or butter-steam them, p. 101, just until their bright green color intensifies a little, their sweetness reaches an almost unbearable peak, and they are still crunchy.

Sorrel

Sorrel, one of the few perennial vegetables, is a pleasure to have in the garden from earliest spring until frost. Its tender leaves are a pleasant addition to an early salad and it gives a distinctive tang to soups and sauces of all kinds. I always freeze a little sorrel to get me through the winter months—and I always end up throwing it away because it lacks that fresh sharpness that's the reason for loving it. Sorrel is good as a substitute for, or mixed half-and-half with spinach in most recipes.

Sorrel stars in these recipes:

Cream of Sorrel Soup, p. 57
Sorrel and Potato Soup, p. 57
Schav, p. 58

Sorrel and Fish Rolls, p. 165
Lentils with Sorrel, p. 131
Sorrel Puree, p. 58
Sorrel Sauce for Fish, p. 161

Lentils with Sorrel

(SERVES 6–8)

This is a substantial and excellent vegetable dish to serve with simply prepared cold or grilled meat. It's also good on an hors d'oeuvre plate with a couple of slices of good salami, a hard-cooked egg, and some raw radishes or fennel. If you must, substitute spinach for sorrel and add a good squeeze of lemon to compensate for the sorrel's tartness.

½ cup olive oil
1 medium, sweet onion, diced
1 pound lentils (2 cups)
½–1 pound shredded sorrel leaves (4 or 5 cups)
salt

Heat the oil in a heavy 2-quart saucepan and cook the onion gently for about 5 minutes, until it is transparent but not browned. Add the lentils to the pan and turn them in the oil for a minute or so, then add 3½ cups hot water. Bring the liquid to a boil, turn down the heat, cover the pot and cook over medium-low heat, turning from time to time, until the lentils are tender but not mushy. You will have to watch them carefully after about 20 minutes. They will absorb all the water and it may be necessary to add a little more. Do not let the lentils stick to the bottom of the pan, and do not overcook them. As soon as the lentils are tender, stir in the sorrel and continue cooking until it is wilted, 5 minutes at the most. Season to taste with salt. Serve at room temperature.

Sautéed Radishes

(SERVES 4–6)

Radishes are best known as a garnish—a crunchy accent to soft, bland foods. Fresh radishes are a delicious first course or snack with drinks, spread with a little sweet butter. They can be added to salads or cut in slices or chunks and used as a salad by themselves. For 2 cups of radishes, use ½ cup vinaigrette or dress them with a few tablespoons of vinegar-and-chive-flavored sour cream.

Radishes are also good—and very decorative—cooked. For this dish, get bunches of fresh radishes with fresh leaves. You will cook the whole thing.

2 large bunches radishes with their leaves
3 tablespoons butter
salt

Wash and trim the radishes. Discard any leaves that are wilted. Cut the radishes into chunks—halves if they are small, thick slices or quarters if they are large. Chop the leaves coarse. Melt the butter in a large skillet and sauté the radishes for about 10 minutes over fairly high heat, tossing them around in the pan from time to time. After 10 minutes, add the leaves, mix them into the radishes and cook for a minute or 2 more, until the leaves are bright green and wilted and the radishes are tender but still crunchy. Season with salt (no pepper) and serve.

Simple Creamed Spinach

(SERVES 6)

3 pounds spinach
2 tablespoons butter
1 large, sweet (Bermuda or Spanish) onion, coarsely chopped
1 cup sour cream
salt and freshly ground pepper

Blanch the spinach in a large pot of boiling water, according to the directions on p. 100, and set it aside. Melt the butter in a large skillet, add the onion and sauté it gently, without browning, until it is transparent, 5–10 minutes. Meanwhile, coarsely chop the spinach. Add the spinach to the onion in the pan and continue to cook only until the spinach is hot. Stir in the sour cream and cook only until it is heated through, stirring from time to time. Don't let the sour cream boil. Season to taste with salt and freshly ground pepper and serve hot.

TOMATOES

Writing about tomatoes on a snowy day takes me back to the bliss of the August garden baking, growing, ripening under the sun with an intensity you can almost hear. The sight of a vegetable garden in the height of its opulence is palpable, pregnant. The best place to feel it is in the middle of a flourishing tomato patch. Mad dogs and Englishmen go out in the midday sun. So do crazy, passionate gardeners who want to know how those bursting red tomatoes come into being.

When you make this pilgrimage, try to remember to take a salt shaker along. To pick a dead-ripe tomato and eat it on the spot is to know how tomatoes taste at their best. Early in the season, there's no way to improve upon the tomato *au naturel*. Plain tomatoes accompany every meal in our house during tomato season. Our favorite summer breakfast is sliced tomatoes on hot, buttered toast; a favorite lunch, tomato sandwiches with a sprinkling of chopped basil or a slice of sweet red onion. After a while, we branch out a bit, including lots of tomatoes in a *Salade Niçoise*, p. 79 , stuffing raw ones with many good things, p.134 , all leading up to the grand, late-August climax of a glorious dish of Indiana Succotash, p. 109 .

When baskets of tomatoes cover every surface in the house (and every roadside stand) we finally begin to cook them. There is no end to the uses of tomatoes; we rejoice in the brief season when they become a staple of the kitchen and appear on the table in several different forms each day.

With the help of the freezer, we can extend the tomato season in several ways. The simplest is to wash the tomatoes, cut them into quarters or eighths and freeze them in plastic bags. When thawed they will have lost all their texture but not their flavor, and are extremely easy to peel. They are nearly as good as fresh tomatoes when used in soups and sauces—a bit more watery, perhaps, but the extra liquid can easily be boiled away. Homemade tomato soups and sauces, or simply a slightly concentrated puree of peeled tomatoes, keep their fresh flavor amazingly well and are much better than any tomato sold in a store out of season.

Never refrigerate tomatoes if you can avoid it. Their flavor and texture will never be the same.

To peel tomatoes. Immerse a tomato in boiling water for about half a minute, then remove it from the water. The skin will slip off easily as soon as the tomato is cool enough to handle. If you are peeling many tomatoes at once, try to resist the temptation to put them all in the water at the same time. Some of them will surely cook, making a mess and wasting a lot of their juice. Put them in the water a few at a time and spread them out to drain and cool.

Stuffed Raw Tomatoes

To prepare whole tomatoes for stuffing, cut a small slice from the top of the tomatoes and scoop out the seeds and pulp, using a grapefruit knife or spoon if necessary. Salt the tomato shells and invert them on a plate to drain for 15 minutes or so. Stuff them with any of the following:

Zucchini Caviar, p. 150
Shrimp Salad, p. 176
Eggplant Puree with Yogurt, p. 115
Rice Salad with Rosemary, p. 95
Lentils with Sorrel, p. 131
Eggplant and Peppers, p. 114
Fish Salads, pp. 76–79
Mussel Salad with Rice, p. 77
Stuffings for Raw Vegetables, pp. 123–124

Tomatoes with Swiss Chard Stuffing

(SERVES 6)

6 medium tomatoes, prepared for stuffing, above
4 slices bacon
1 medium onion, chopped
1 large clove garlic, chopped
2 pounds Swiss chard, blanched, p. 100 and chopped

½ cup unseasoned bread crumbs
salt and freshly ground pepper
lemon juice
4 tablespoons olive oil

Fry the bacon in a large skillet until it is crisp. Drain and crumble it and set it aside. Sauté the onion in the bacon fat just until it is transparent (about 5 minutes), add the garlic and chopped Swiss chard and mix them well with the fat and onions. Sprinkle in the crumbled bacon, the bread crumbs, salt, plenty of freshly ground pepper and a good squeeze of lemon juice and stir to combine well. If the mixture is too dry, add a little olive oil; if too bland, more salt, pepper and/or lemon juice.

Fill the prepared tomatoes with the stuffing. Put the oil and the tomatoes in a Dutch oven and heat it until you hear it begin to sizzle. Turn the heat to low, cover the pot and cook the tomatoes for about 15 minutes. Remove them from the pot and serve hot or cool. You can season the oil in the pan with a crushed clove of garlic and a tablespoon or so of chopped herbs and pour it over the tomatoes.

Variations.
Stuff raw tomatoes with any of the stuffings for Cooked Peppers, pp. 126-128, and cook them as directed above.

Sautéed Cherry Tomatoes

(SERVES 6)

3 tablespoons olive oil
4 cups cherry tomatoes, stemmed
2 tablespoons chopped chives
2 tablespoons chopped parsley
1 tablespoon chopped fresh basil
salt and freshly ground pepper

Warm the olive oil in a large pan and add the tomatoes. Stir to coat them with oil, cover the pan and cook the tomatoes over medium heat for 5 minutes. Sprinkle the tomatoes with the herbs, salt and pepper and carefully stir until the seasonings are well distributed, trying not to break the skin of the tomatoes. Continue to cook gently for a minute or 2, until the skins of a few tomatoes have burst. Put the tomatoes in a serving dish, pour the juices over them and serve immediately.

Tomato Bavarian Cream

(SERVES 6)

I found this little gem, in somewhat more complicated form, in Escoffier. It is amazing for its combination of lightness, richness and intense tomato flavor. It can be served as a first course, molded in individual soufflé dishes and garnished with a single leaf of watercress or parsley. It is a lovely accompaniment to cold, poached fish (but not salmon; it's the same color). I think it makes its most elegant appearance on a buffet table, molded in a ring mold, filled with cold beets and surrounded by the beet greens, lightly steamed, chilled and dressed with just a little oil and vinegar.

1 pound ripe tomatoes, preferably Italian plum tomatoes, peeled
1 envelope unflavored gelatin
salt
sugar
1 cup heavy cream, whipped

Puree the tomatoes in a blender or food processor or put them through a food mill. You will have about 2 cups of puree. Sprinkle the gelatin over ¼ cup of the puree and bring the rest of it to a boil in a small pot. Season the tomatoes with a little salt and sugar and simmer them for 2 or 3 minutes. Add the softened gelatin and stir very thoroughly to be sure it is well dissolved. Leave the tomatoes to cool to room temperature. Do not refrigerate them or the gelatin will set.

Mix the cooled tomatoes thoroughly with the whipped cream. Taste and correct the seasoning with salt and/or sugar. Pour the tomato cream into a 1-quart mold and chill until it is set, about 3 hours. Unmold the cream onto a platter (see directions for unmolding on p. 190) and garnish it with watercress, Swiss Chard Salad, p. 97, or cold beets and their greens.

Jessie Lynch's Fruit Relish

(6–8 PINTS)

I think this is one of the few relishes worth making. It can be made with less-than-perfect fruit as long as you add enough extra to make up for the parts you can't use. You need a big pot to make this relish; if you plan to cook it in 2 pots, divide the ingredients as you prepare them to be sure everything is evenly distributed. It's a wonderful hamburger and grilled meat relish, and delicious with scrambled eggs.

30 large ripe tomatoes, peeled
6 pears, peeled and cored (slightly unripe ones will do)
6 small onions, peeled
6 peaches, peeled and pitted
6 green peppers, seeded
3 cups sugar
2 tablespoons salt
1 pint vinegar
3 tablespoons mixed pickling spice, tied in cheesecloth

Coarsely chop all the fruit in a large wooden bowl if you have one, so none of the juices are lost. Put the fruit in a large, heavy bottomed pot and add the sugar, salt, vinegar and the bag of spices. Bring to a boil and continue to cook briskly, over medium heat, uncovered, for about 2 hours, stirring frequently with a wooden spoon. Be sure no fruit sticks to the bottom of the pot, and reduce the heat if necessary. Toward the end of 2 hours, the relish will begin to thicken, and it is essential to keep a close watch to be sure it doesn't burn. When it is greatly reduced in volume and about as thick as applesauce, the relish is done.

While the relish is cooking, sterilize some jars with tight-fitting lids. This is most easily done in a dishwasher, simply by letting the jars go through the regular wash-and-dry cycle and leaving the door closed. Time this so that the jars will still be hot when the relish has finished cooking. If you don't have a dishwasher, boil the jars and lids in a large pot of water for about half an hour, leave them in the hot water and remove them with tongs when you are ready to fill them.

Fill the jars to the brim with the hot relish. Screw the covers on loosely and set the jars aside to cool. When the relish is cool, tighten the jar lids.

Green Tomatoes

Green tomatoes are delicious. When you slice a large, well-formed green tomato it looks just like a ripe one, only the wrong color. But green tomatoes have a taste and texture all their own, utterly unlike ripe ones. They are usually picked only in very late summer or early fall when there's no chance they'll ripen, but when the crop is good enough, it is certainly worth picking some green ones, even at the height of the season. Fried green tomatoes are a real summer delicacy; you can save the other recipes for the tail end of the season.

Green tomatoes freeze very well. Wash them, cut them into quarters or eighths and put them in plastic bags. Freeze green cherry tomatoes too; they look particularly good in Green Tomato Chili, p. 139. Frozen green tomatoes are fine to use in all the recipes that follow, except for Fried Green Tomatoes.

Fried Green Tomatoes (or Eggplant or Zucchini)
(SERVES 4)

These tomatoes are a great summer treat. If you use 2 pans, you can fry enough for 4 in a relatively short time. If you want to cook more, you'll have to turn the oven on and keep the tomatoes warm until they're all cooked. The combination of a hot oven and a pan or 2 of boiling oil is more than I can stand in the summer; you may consider it worth the suffering to share this treat with lots of people.

Zucchini and eggplant are also excellent prepared this way. Cut them in French-fried-potato-sized pieces, shake them in flour and fry them until they are crisp and brown (you may need a little more oil). Drain on paper towels and serve.

4 or 5 large, firm green tomatoes
½ cup flour
salt and freshly ground pepper
oil for frying

Cut the tomatoes into ¼–inch slices. Put the flour, salt and pepper in a paper bag. Heat about an inch of oil in a large frying pan (or 2, if you like). Drop a few slices of tomato into the bag of flour, shake to coat them well, and put the tomatoes in the hot oil. Do not crowd the slices. As soon as they are brown on one side, turn them, using tongs, and brown the other side. You will have to adjust the heat so the tomatoes brown rapidly without burning. Put the fried slices on paper towels to drain. Eat the tomatoes while they are hot and crisp (everyone will want more).

Green Tomato Stew

(SERVES 6)

3 tablespoons olive oil
2 large onions, chopped
1 clove garlic, minced
1 small hot pepper, chopped or ½ teaspoon dried hot pepper flakes
8 large green tomatoes, cut in bite-sized pieces
1 teaspoon salt

Heat the oil in a large skillet, add the onions, garlic and hot pepper and cook over low heat, stirring frequently, until the onions are soft and golden brown. Add the tomatoes, stir them into the onion mixture, raise the heat to medium, partially cover the pan and cook the vegetables for 15 minutes, stirring from time to time. Remove the cover and stir the salt into the vegetables. Raise the heat and, stirring constantly, boil the liquid in the pan until it is reduced by about a half. Taste the tomatoes and add more salt if necessary. This stew can be made several hours in advance and left in its pan for reheating. Serve hot. Especially good with Pork Braised in Milk, p. 206.

Green Tomato Chili

(SERVES 6–8)

This is a fine dish for a crowd, and can be made more or less meaty, depending on your pocketbook and how large a supply of green tomatoes you want to use up. It freezes beautifully and, like all stews, improves with age, so make it a day or two in advance. Serve the chili with rice and beans. To be absolutely truthful, I most often cook this dish in cool weather, using green tomatoes which have been cut in quarters and frozen in plastic bags. They bring back the peace and fragrance of the summer garden as vividly as the red ones do.

> fat trimmed from beef or 2 or 3 tablespoons cooking oil
> 3 pounds beef chuck or round, trimmed and cut into 1-inch pieces
> 4 large onions, peeled and coarsely chopped
> 2 large cloves garlic, thinly sliced
> 12–15 large green tomatoes (3–4 pounds), cut into eighths or 3–4
>   pounds green cherry tomatoes
> 1 13½-ounce can beef broth
> 2–4 tablespoons chili powder
> salt

Render the beef fat in a heavy Dutch oven or heat the cooking oil. Dry the meat on paper towels and put it, about ⅓ at a time, into the hot fat to brown. Stir it to brown on all sides, remove it from the pan with a slotted spoon, and add more meat to the pan, removing it when it is brown. Put the onions and garlic into the pan and cook them over moderate heat until they are soft, 10–15 minutes. Scrape the browned bits from the bottom of the pan and mix them into the onions while they are cooking. Add the beef broth to the pot and stir in a good tablespoon of chili powder. Put in the meat and the green tomatoes, bring the liquid to a boil, turn down the heat, cover the pot and cook over low heat for about an hour, until the meat is tender. Taste the gravy and add more chili powder and salt to taste.

Serve with plain boiled rice and with black or pink beans which have been cooked according to package directions with an onion, a couple of cloves of garlic and a bay leaf. If you want to use canned beans, drain 2 cans in a colander and rinse with cool water. Sauté a chopped onion and 2 cloves of chopped garlic in 2 tablespoons oil for 5 minutes. Add the beans, a bay leaf, ¼ cup of water. Stir well and simmer over low heat for about ½ hour.

If you make the chili in advance and refrigerate or freeze it, add more chili powder to taste when you reheat it.

Green Tomato Mincemeat

(ABOUT 6 QUARTS)

It is wonderful to know, while you are picking the tomatoes for this mincemeat, that they will be part of the Christmas feast. Mincemeat made with green tomatoes is both tarter and lighter than the usual kind. This recipe makes enough mincemeat for 8 or 9 good-sized pies or lots and lots of tarts. You must have a huge, heavy bottomed pot to cook it in. Try to borrow it if you don't have one, or consider making a bit less, but do *not* try to make it in a flimsy pot: it burns easily and is immediately ruined by a scorched taste. Even a small jar of homemade mincemeat makes a nifty Christmas present.

2 pounds beef, ground
1 pound suet, ground
25–30 large green tomatoes, chopped
*2 pounds dried currants or 2 boxes (sometimes the boxes weigh a
    little less)*
2 pounds raisins
1 cup diced citron or mixed candied fruits
3 cups brown sugar
1 cup molasses
4 cups apple cider
grated rind and juice of 2 lemons
*1½ teaspoons each of ground nutmeg, cinnamon, cloves, mace, salt,
    mixed together*
1 pint brandy (a cheap brand will do)

Put all the ingredients except the spice mixture and the brandy into a heavy bottomed pot that will hold at least 12 quarts. Mix everything together thoroughly with your hands. Bring it all to a boil, stirring frequently, turn down the heat and simmer, uncovered, for about 2 hours. Continue to stir very frequently. Stir in the spice mixture and continue to cook and stir, making sure that the mincemeat does not stick to the bottom of the pot when it thickens. When the mincemeat is thick, turn off the heat and stir in the brandy. Put the mincemeat in sterilized jars. (Directions for sterilizing jars can be found at the end of the recipe for Fruit Relish, p. 137 .) Try to make the mincemeat as early as possible—its flavor develops while it is in the jar, and it will keep for many months in a cool, dry place.

Summer Squash Puree

(SERVES 6)

The best way to cook really young, really fresh summer squash, yellow, white or green or all three together, is to steam it in butter, p. 101. Stuffing, sautéing with other vegetables or frying are fine for the large number of bigger, less delicate squash that are so much easier to find. This puree is a particularly delicious combination, and a good way to use large, yellow squash.

3 medium summer squash, washed
1 pound Swiss chard
4 tablespoons butter
salt and freshly ground pepper

Plunge the whole, unpeeled squash into a large pot of rapidly boiling water, cover the pot and boil the squash for 20 minutes. Remove it from the pot and add the Swiss chard leaves to the boiling water. After 5 minutes, drain the chard into a colander and rinse it with cold water to stop the cooking. Press out as much water as possible. Trim the ends off the squash and chop the 2 vegetables quite fine, to make a coarse puree, using a food processor if you have one. Put the puree in a sieve and let it drain (save the juice for soup). This can be done hours in advance. Heat the puree gently with the butter and season to taste with salt and freshly ground pepper. Serve hot.

Sautéed Summer Squash

(SERVES 6)

3 tablespoons butter
3 medium summer squash, thinly sliced
1 large ripe tomato, peeled, seeded and coarsely chopped
1 tablespoon chopped tarragon
salt and freshly ground pepper

Melt the butter in a large frying pan and sauté the squash, turning it frequently for about 10 minutes. Add the tomato and the tarragon and continue to cook the squash, uncovered, until it is just becoming translucent, about 5 minutes more. The tomato should make just a little juice in the bottom of the pan. If it is at all watery, raise the heat under the pan and boil it rapidly to reduce the liquid. Season the squash with salt and freshly ground pepper and serve immediately.

STUFFED SUMMER SQUASH
(YELLOW, PATTYPAN OR ZUCCHINI)

(SERVES 6)

While I do not subscribe to the garbage-pail school of stuffing vegetables, I have found over the years that almost anything can be made into a good stuffing for summer squash. The secret is not to use too many different flavors in any one stuffing. If you have a few odds and ends that would make good stuffings, it is almost as easy and far better to make little bits of several different stuffings and to serve a variety of stuffed squashes. A very attractive meal can be made of squash stuffed 3 different ways—with a meat, a vegetable and a grain stuffing. The basic preparation of the squash is the same for all varieties. Simple blanching of the whole squash preserves its delicate flavor and provides a firm shell for the seasoned filling. This is a very good way to prepare oversized squash (I have made dinner for 12 from a zucchini that got out of hand). Of course, you will need a very large pot to blanch it; as an alternative, set it on a rack in a roasting pan and steam it, covered, for 20–25 minutes. If the squash are young, 10 minutes will be enough time to cook them. Larger squash (a pound or more, 8–10 inches) will need a good 15 minutes in the water. They will continue to cook a little after you remove them from the pot. When the squash is cool enough to handle easily, cut it in half lengthwise for zucchini and summer squash, horizontally for pattypan. Remove the seeds and flesh of the squash, leaving a shell about ½-inch thick. Sprinkle the halves with salt and invert them on a plate to drain. Discard the seeds only if they are woody. Chop the flesh of the squash and add it to the stuffing.

The recipes that follow should serve as models only—one is stuffed with vegetables, one with meat or chicken and one with rice.

Summer Squash Stuffed with Green Bean Puree

(SERVES 6)

3 medium summer squash, pattypan or yellow
salt
1 pound green beans
½ cup cream
½ cup fresh Tomato Sauce, p. 248

Drop the squash into a large pot of boiling water. Cook at a full boil for 15–20 minutes, then remove them from the pot with a slotted spoon and set them aside to cool. Add the green beans to the boiling water, bring the water back to the boil and cook the beans for 5 minutes—no more. Drain them.

Cut the squash in half crosswise (pattypan) or lengthwise (yellow). Scoop out the flesh, leaving a ½-inch shell. Sprinkle the shells with salt and turn them upside down in a colander to drain.

Chop the beans and the flesh of the squash in a food processor or puree them in a blender, using a little cream if liquid is needed. Season the puree well with salt and add more cream if it is very thick.

Pat the squash shells dry with paper towels and put them on a platter. Spread a thin layer of tomato sauce in the shells and fill them with the bean puree. Serve at room temperature as a first course or with grilled meat or fish.

Pattypan Squash Stuffed with Meat and Green Tomatoes
(SERVES 6)

3 pattypan squash, each about 6 inches in diameter
3 tablespoons olive oil
6 scallions including green tops, thinly sliced
2 large cloves garlic, minced
1 hot red pepper, finely chopped (1–2 tablespoons)
1 pound boneless pork or chicken, minced or 2 cups leftover meat,
*   minced*
2 medium green tomatoes, chopped or 1 cup Tomato Sauce, p. 248
1 teaspoon chopped marjoram or oregano
chopped flesh of the squash
salt and freshly ground pepper

Plunge the whole, unpeeled squash into a large pot of rapidly boiling water. Cover the pot and let the squash cook for 15–20 minutes. Drain the squash and let it cool.

While the squash is cooling, heat the oil in a large skillet, add the scallions, garlic and hot pepper and sauté gently for about 5 minutes. Add the minced meat, season it with salt and cook it, 5 minutes for chicken or 10 minutes for pork. Stir in the chopped tomatoes or the tomato sauce and the marjoram and let the stuffing simmer gently while you prepare the squash.

Cut the squash in half horizontally, remove the seeds and scoop out the flesh, leaving a scallop-edged shell about ½-inch thick. Chop the flesh of the squash and add it to the stuffing in the pan. Taste the stuffing and season it with salt, pepper and more herbs if necessary.

Remember that the stuffing will have a blander taste when it is cold, so be generous with the seasoning. Pat the squash shells dry with paper towels and put them on a platter. Spoon the stuffing into the shells. Serve the stuffed squash at room temperature. If you make it in advance and refrigerate it, remove it from the refrigerator about an hour before serving.

Zucchini Stuffed with Rice

(SERVES 6)

3 medium zucchini
1 cup rice
Cooked Basil-Tomato Sauce, p. 249, made with olive oil instead of
    butter
3 tablespoons freshly grated Parmesan cheese
salt and freshly ground pepper
3 tablespoons chopped parsley

Plunge the whole, unpeeled zucchini into a large pot of rapidly boiling water. Cover the pot and let the squash boil for 15–20 minutes. Drain the squash and let it cool.

While the squash is cooking and cooling, cook the rice according to your usual method (or package directions) and make the very simple sauce. When the rice is done, drain it well. Mix it with the sauce and the grated cheese while it is still hot, then let it cool.

Cut the squash in half lengthwise and scoop out the flesh and seeds, leaving a shell about ½-inch thick. Sprinkle the shells with salt and invert them on a platter to drain for 10 or 15 minutes. Chop the zucchini flesh and add it to the stuffing. Taste the stuffing and season it with salt, pepper and more grated cheese if necessary.

Put the squash shells on a platter and pat them dry with paper towels. Sprinkle half the chopped parsley into the cavities, then fill them with the rice stuffing. Sprinkle the remaining parsley on top and serve the squash at room temperature. If it has been refrigerated, remove it from the refrigerator at least an hour before serving.

Stuffed Squash Blossoms

(SERVES 6 AS FIRST COURSE)

24 wide-open squash blossoms
3 cups Rice Salad with Rosemary, p. 95
about 2 tablespoons olive oil
2 or 3 sprigs rosemary
2 cloves garlic, cut in half

Choose large squash blossoms which are wide open. *Do not wash them.* (Water will make them limp and impossible to stuff.) Shake each one or brush it lightly with your fingers to remove any odd bits of garden debris. Put a good tablespoon of rice salad into the open blossom, then fold the petals one by one (there are 5) over the stuffing. The oil on your fingers will make the petals stick together to form a lightly sealed package. Place it gently on a plate and proceed until all the blossoms have been stuffed. Put the oil in a large skillet, add the garlic and sprigs of rosemary and heat it over *very* low heat until the oil is well-seasoned, 5–10 minutes. Remove the garlic and discard it. Very gently place the stuffed blossoms side by side in the warm oil. Turn the heat to medium low and cook them for 2 or 3 minutes, then turn them very gently, using tongs or 2 spoons, and cook them for 2 or 3 minutes on the other side.

You will probably have to cook the blossoms in several batches. Arrange them symmetrically on a platter and garnish with a fresh blossom or 2 or a tiny squash taken from the plant when you pick the blossoms. Serve at room temperature.

ZUCCHINI

Zucchini is the ideal crop for the beginning gardener. The seeds are big; when you plant six of them in a "hill" you will remember where they are. (Not like the seeds of, say, carrots or leeks, which are like large grains of dust and are lost to the eye the minute they drop to the earth.) Zucchini seeds almost always sprout. And, once they have sprouted, you can almost see them grow—and grow—and grow.

If you are sensible, you will leave as much space between the hills as the seed package suggests, although even experienced gardeners, forgetting from one year to the next how enormous those plants will get, often end up with fence-to-fence zucchini. Very soon after the plants get big, they burst into prolific golden bloom. At the stem end of the female flower, a tiny zucchini can be seen, no bigger than a baby's thumb. Within a few days it will be 6 inches long and ready to pick. So will many others. Under a leaf there's an 8-inch one you'd almost overlooked; under another leaf is a zucchini that is 10 inches long. One day soon afterward, when the proud gardener already has a dozen or more zucchini ready to be cooked, an eighteen-inch giant is found lying on the ground, looking more like a watermelon than a squash.

It's almost impossible to have enough zucchini without having too much. Fortunately, it is almost as versatile as it is prolific. You can eat it raw, steamed, sautéed, fried, broiled and baked. It can be put into soups, stews, salads, soufflés, custards, cakes and pancakes. It can be stuffed, or used as a stuffing. The flowers, and even the tender leaves, are delicious. It can be pickled; it can be cooked and frozen for a time in winter when it will be most welcome (see the recipe for Zucchini Soup Base, p. 63, the best way to use superabundance of zucchini).

Each year, after bestowing zucchini on everyone who will accept it (we once carried some 1,000 miles to give to relatives), the cook's ingenuity is tested, and new recipes emerge. Here are a few favorites.

Zucchini Caviar

(ABOUT 1 QUART)

3 medium zucchini (about 2 pounds)
2 scallions including green tops, finely chopped
1 small green pepper, seeded and finely chopped
1 ripe tomato, peeled, seeded and finely chopped
1 tablespoon chopped parsley
Vinaigrette Dressing, p. 251

Plunge the whole, unpeeled zucchini into rapidly boiling water, cover the pot and cook the squash for 10 minutes. Drain the zucchini and let it cool. Chop the zucchini fine and put it into a sieve to drain. Press the juice out of the squash and combine it thoroughly with the other vegetables and the dressing.

Zucchini Caviar is best made a day in advance and will keep well in the refrigerator for several days. It is good as an appetizer or snack, spread on brown bread, and makes a delicious stuffing for raw tomatoes.

Zucchini Flan

(SERVES 6 AS FIRST COURSE)

2 tablespoons butter
4 scallions including green tops, thinly sliced
6 very small zucchini (4 or 5 inches long), each cut lengthwise into 4
    wedges.
2 tablespoons chopped parsley
salt and freshly ground pepper
3 eggs
1 cup heavy cream   } beaten together with a fork
a pinch of nutmeg
½ cup grated Swiss cheese

Melt the butter in a skillet, add the scallions and sauté them over low heat until they are slightly wilted. Add the zucchini and parsley and cook, stirring from time to time, and seasoning it with salt and pepper. Use a little extra salt if you plan to serve the flan at room temperature.

Arrange the zucchini wedges, spoke-fashion, in a well-buttered 9- or 10-inch glass pie plate. Scrape the scallions and parsley into the egg-cream mixture and stir it. Pour the mixture over the zucchini, being careful not to spoil the pattern. Cover the plate loosely with waxed paper and steam it on a rack for about 20 minutes, following the directions for steaming custards on p. 31. Serve hot or at room temperature.

Zucchini with Hot and Sweet Peppers
(SERVES 6)

⅓ cup olive oil
3 medium zucchini (about 2 pounds), cut in ½-inch cubes
2 large cloves garlic, minced
3 ripe tomatoes, coarsely chopped
salt and freshly ground pepper
2 sweet red or green peppers, cut in bite-sized chunks
2 hot red peppers, finely chopped (3–4 tablespoons)
3 tablespoons chopped parsley

Wash and cut up all the vegetables before starting to cook this dish. Heat the oil in a deep 12-inch skillet or a Dutch oven. Add the zucchini and cook it over medium high heat, tossing it constantly, for about 5 minutes. *Do not overcook it.* Push the zucchini to the side of the pan, add the garlic and cook it for a minute or 2. Add the tomatoes and some salt and pepper and mix them well with the garlic and pan juices, then with the zucchini. Continue to cook and stir, over high heat, for another 5 minutes. Turn off the heat and stir in the sweet pepper, the hot pepper and the parsley. The heat of the zucchini will cook them very slightly. Taste and correct the seasoning, adding more chopped hot pepper if you like. Serve at room temperature.

Zucchini Pancakes

(18–20 PANCAKES)

Two hungry and appreciative people could easily eat this whole batch of pancakes. Unless you want to stand at the stove for a long time, save these for small lunches or dinners. The grated and drained zucchini and onion mixture can be frozen in recipe-sized packages. It's a nice thing to find in your freezer. Thaw the vegetables and drain them well before making the pancakes.

> 3 medium zucchini (or 1 great big one without the seeds)
> 1 small onion, peeled
> 1 teaspoon salt
> 3 eggs
> 3 tablespoons flour
> 2 tablespoons freshly grated Parmesan cheese, optional
> oil for frying
> fresh Tomato Sauce, p. 248, optional

Grate the zucchini and the onion together, mix in a teaspoon of salt and put the vegetables in a colander to drain for about 10 minutes. Squeeze out the juice with your hands (and save it to make soup). You should have about 3 cups of grated zucchini.

Beat the eggs well, then beat in the flour and the cheese if you are using it. Add the zucchini and combine well. Taste and add more salt if necessary.

Heat about ½-inch of oil in a large frying pan and drop in the batter by the tablespoonful. Fry the pancakes over medium heat, until they are well browned on both sides. Drain them on paper towels and serve plain or with fresh tomato sauce.

You can make this batter hours in advance and keep it in the refrigerator.

Ratatouille

(SERVES 6–8)

1 medium zucchini (about 1 pound), thinly sliced
1 medium eggplant (about 1 pound), cut in quarters lengthwise and
  sliced
salt
4 tablespoons olive oil
1 large, sweet (Bermuda or Spanish) onion, sliced
3 large, ripe tomatoes or 10–12 plum tomatoes, peeled and coarsely
  chopped
3 cloves garlic, thinly sliced
3 medium green peppers, seeded and cut into small pieces

Sprinkle the zucchini and eggplant with salt and put them in a colander to drain while you prepare the other vegetables. Heat 2 tablespoons of the oil in a large skillet and cook the onion in it until it is transparent, 5–10 minutes. Add the garlic, cook it for a minute, then add the tomatoes and bring them to a boil. Season with salt and pepper. Pour the tomato mixture into a bowl. Pat the zucchini and eggplant slices dry with paper towels. Heat the remaining 2 tablespoons of olive oil in the pan and add the eggplant. Turn it in the warm oil and cook it gently for 5 minutes or so, turning it frequently with a spatula. Spoon 2 or 3 tablespoons of the tomato mixture over the eggplant and spread the zucchini in a layer on top of it. Add 2 or 3 more tablespoons of tomatoes, then the peppers, in a layer. Pour the rest of the tomatoes over all. Cover the pan, and when the tomatoes are bubbling, lower the heat and cook the vegetables over low heat for about 20 minutes. Uncover the pan; taste the juices and add more salt and pepper if necessary. Turn the vegetables over with a spatula and continue to cook them over medium heat, uncovered, until they are soft. Raise the heat if necessary to reduce the juices in the pan to a few spoonfuls.

Ratatouille tastes best a day or so after it is made, when the flavors have blended. Bring it to room temperature before serving.

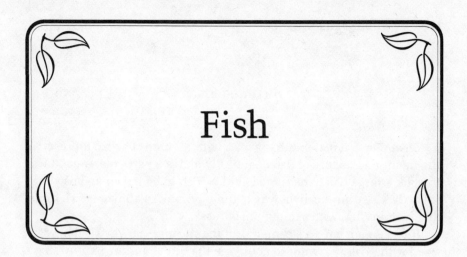

Fish

FISH

Fish is an ideal summer food—light, varied, quick to cook, good hot or cold. There is no reason ever to use the oven to cook fish in summer; steaming, poaching and sautéing are all ideal methods of cooking. Baking is a fine way to cook fish, too, but it is the slowest method and it does heat up the kitchen. Save baked-fish dishes for the cooler months and if you want to broil fish, do it over charcoal.

Most of the fish recipes given here can be used for any fish that is fresh and easily available. Deal with a good fish store and take their advice on the best fish to buy on a given day. Remember that fish must be absolutely fresh, that overcooked fish is unpalatable, and that cooked fish falls apart easily and must be handled with care. Buy carefully, cook carefully, season with a light hand and you can happily eat fish all summer long.

Sauces to serve with hot or cold steamed or poached fish can be found in the index.

Steamed Fish

Steaming is a method that works with all kinds of fish. It preserves the flavor and texture of fish beautifully and is a particularly good way to cook a large fish to be served cold or fish to be flaked and used in a salad. It is also an excellent way to quickly cook small whole fish for individual servings with a minimum of fuss.

If you do not have a steamer, or if the steamer you have is the wrong size for the fish you want to cook, see the directions for improvising a steamer on p. 103. General directions for steaming fish precede the recipes and a list of appropriate sauces can be found in the index.

To steam fish in a colander. A colander is an ideal steaming container for fish fillets, rolled up and held together with a toothpick, or for a thick, center cut of a large fish such as cod, bass or salmon.

Put 2 cups of dry white wine in your steaming pot and add water to a depth of 1–1½ inches. Add a bay leaf and a sprig or 2 of thyme or dill. Bring the liquid to a boil and lower the colander into the pot. Cover the pot and steam, over medium high heat: 6–8 minutes for rolled fillets, about 20 minutes, or longer, for a large piece. Test by prodding the fish to the bone with a fork or a sharp knife; push the flesh aside and be sure it is opaque throughout.

Strain the cooking liquid and save it to use in a fish soup or reduce it and use it to make Cream Sauce for Fish, p. 160.

To steam fish on a rack. Put a rack in the steamer and add 1½–2 inches of water. Bring the water to a boil. Put the fish on a platter, put it on the rack and cover the steamer. Steam the fish over medium-high heat until it is done: 8–10 minutes for fillets, about 10 minutes for inch-thick steaks and about 15 minutes for a whole, 1½-pound fish. Stick a fork cautiously into the fish at its thickest part to be sure that it is opaque throughout. If you are steaming a whole fish, put the fork all the way to the bone to be sure the fish is no longer translucent.

When the fish is done, pour off the juice that has accumulated in the platter and save it to use for a soup or sauce.

Large Whole Cold Steamed Fish

(SERVES 6–8)

a 5–6 pound fresh fish (bass, sea trout, bluefish or whatever is fresh
*   and good)*
2 cups dry white wine
a bay leaf
2 or 3 sprigs of thyme or dill
boiling water
cheesecloth

Have the fish cleaned; have the head removed or left on, as you wish. Read the directions for improvising a steamer, p. 103 and get ready a rack, a pan and a platter large enough to hold the fish.

Put the wine and seasonings in the pan. Put in the rack, raised at least 2 inches from the bottom of the pan, and add boiling water to a depth of 1–1½ inches; the rack should not touch the water.

Wrap the fish in cheesecloth and put it on the platter. Bring the liquid in the pan to a boil and put the platter of fish on the rack. Cover the pan and steam the fish over medium heat for 20–25 minutes.

Pull aside the cheesecloth and stick a fork into the fish, down to the bone. Pull the flesh aside to see if it is opaque throughout. If it is not, continue steaming the fish for 10 minutes or more, until the fish is done. When done, remove it from the pan and let it cool. Add the juices on the platter to the liquid in the pan and save it to use in a fish soup.

When the fish is cool, the skin will peel off easily when you remove the cheesecloth. Do this carefully, rolling the fish over on its platter to skin it on both sides. Serve the fish cold. It is especially good with Egg-Lemon Sauce, p. 233.

Small Whole Steamed Fish or Fish Steaks

(SERVES 4)

Buy the best whole, small fish or fish steaks in the market. All kinds of fish are good when prepared this way.

4 small, whole fish (1–1 ½ pounds each) or 4 fish steaks about 1 inch
   thick
4 scallions, finely sliced
4 tablespoons soy sauce
2 tablespoons hot oil or 2 tablespoons vegetable oil and a pinch of
   hot pepper flakes
2 large cloves garlic, chopped

Have the fish cleaned and their heads removed or left on, as you
wish. Cut 2 or 3 diagonal slashes in the skin of each fish on both sides.
Put the four fish in one layer on the platter that will be used for steaming. Sprinkle the fish with the scallions, soy sauce, oil and garlic. Turn
to coat them well on both sides and let them marinate for an hour or so.
   Following the directions for steaming fish on a rack, p. 156 , steam
the fish for about 15 minutes or until they are done. Serve immediately.

Variations.
Any number of seasoning combinations are good. Try:
Olive oil, anchovies, garlic and basil or
Herb butter and grated lemon rind or
¼ cup white wine, sliced cucumbers and chopped dill

or

Steam the fish plain and serve it with Sour Cream Hollandaise, p.
   238, Cooked Basil-Tomato Sauce, p. 249, or Tomato Sauce with
   Cream and Tarragon, p. 249.

Poached Fish, Hot or Cold

(SERVES 8–10)

There are those who say that the best way to poach a fish is in plain
water. I simply cannot bring myself to do this, and therefore I poach fish
only when I have a good fish stock on hand, made from heads and
trimmings from fish bought for other purposes or perhaps from a gift of
a very bony catch given to me by an enthusiastic fisherman. In any case,
if you are planning to poach fish, start out with enough Fish Stock, p.
69. For a large piece of bass or salmon (about 5 pounds) you will need

10–12 cups of stock. For poached fillets, 3 cups will be enough for both the fish and its sauce.

Because this is such a splendid dish for a buffet, and because poached fish can be used in so many ways—in salads, pâtés, or cold with sauces—I have recommended poaching a large piece of fish. Cook a smaller piece by exactly the same method, using a little less stock.

10–12 cups Fish Stock, p. 69
A 5-pound center cut of fish (bass, salmon, cod)
cheesecloth

Bring the stock to a boil. Wrap the fish in cheesecloth, put it in a heavy pot and gently pour the fish stock over it. If the stock doesn't cover the fish, move the fish to a smaller pot. Bring the liquid to a boil, cover the pot and simmer the fish, covered, for 5 minutes. Turn off the heat and leave the fish in the hot liquid.

To serve hot. After 20 minutes, test the fish by sticking a fork into it all the way to the bone. Pull the flesh aside. If it is opaque throughout, the fish is done. If it is not done, bring the liquid back to a boil, turn it off and let the fish sit for an additional 10 minutes.

In the meantime, make a sauce. The fish will be equally good with melted butter mixed with lemon juice and a generous sprinkling of chopped dill or with a Cream Sauce for Fish, p. 160, made with some of the stock the fish was cooked in.

To serve cold. Let the fish cool in the liquid. When you remove the cheesecloth, the skin will peel off with it. Handle the fish carefully so it doesn't break. Put the fish on a platter and garnish it with raw vegetables. A list of sauces to serve with cold fish can be found in the index. Cucumber Sauce, p. 232, is a classic accompaniment to poached salmon.

Poached Fish Fillets with Cream Sauce

(SERVES 6)

3 cups Fish Stock, p. 69
butter
3 pounds fish fillets
salt and freshly ground pepper
Cream Sauce for Fish, p. 160

Put the fish stock in a saucepan, bring it to a boil and reduce it to 2 cups. Butter a large frying pan. Season the fillets with salt and freshly ground pepper and lay them in the pan, as nearly as possible in one layer.

Using 1 cup of the stock, make Cream Sauce for Fish or one of its variations. When the sauce is done, remove it from the heat and cook the fish.

Pour the second cup of the stock over the fillets and put them over medium heat. As soon as the liquid begins to simmer, lower the heat, cover the pan and let the fish cook *as slowly as possible* until the fillets are opaque throughout. This should take 7 or 8 minutes. Reheat the sauce over low heat, stirring constantly so that the egg yolk in the cream sauce will not scramble. Remove the fish carefully to a platter and pour the sauce over it. Garnish the platter with some sprigs of parsley or dill and serve immediately.

Cream Sauce for Fish

(ABOUT 1½ CUPS)

2 tablespoons butter
2 tablespoons flour
1 cup hot, concentrated Fish Stock made with wine, p. 69
½ cup heavy cream
1 egg yolk
lemon juice
salt and freshly ground pepper

Melt the butter in a saucepan. Add the flour and cook for 1 or 2 minutes over low heat *without browning,* stirring constantly with a wire whisk. Add the hot fish stock and stir rapidly over moderate heat until the sauce is thick and smooth. Let the sauce simmer over very low heat for 10 minutes or so, stirring from time to time. Stir a few spoonfuls of the hot sauce into the cream-egg yolk mixture, then pour the cream mixture into the sauce and stir constantly over low heat for another 2 or 3 minutes. Do not allow the sauce to boil after adding the egg yolk. Season carefully with lemon juice, salt and pepper.

Variations.

Sorrel Sauce. *Sauté ¼ pound chopped sorrel (about 2 cups) in 1
    tablespoon butter until the sorrel is wilted. Add it to the sauce
    before adding the cream and egg yolk and simmer for 5 minutes
    before finishing the sauce as directed above. You may not wish
    to add lemon juice; the sorrel has a rather tart flavor.*

Mussel Sauce. *Substitute a cup of the juice from* Moules Marinière,
    *p. 172 for the fish stock and garnish the fish with some steamed
    mussels.*

Shrimp Sauce. *Substitute 1 cup shrimp stock (saved from* Shrimp
    Boiled in Beer, *p. 175, or* Shrimp in Dill, *p. 175) for the fish
    stock; simmer ¼ pound of shelled shrimp in the sauce until they
    are pink, then pour the sauce over the fish.*

Lemon and Herb Sauce. *Add 2 or 3 tablespoons of chopped herbs
    and an extra tablespoon or 2 of lemon juice to the sauce.
    Simmer 5 minutes.*

Poached Salmon Steaks with Beurre Blanc

(SERVES 6)

Many fish-lovers agree that light, delicate and creamy *beurre
blanc* is the best sauce for fish. It is disconcertingly tricky to make, but
for those who are willing to practice a bit, it is worth learning. There is
only one way to make the sauce fail—overheating it. This is a sauce
made over warmth, not heat. Follow the directions carefully and
proceed with confidence. If the sauce should overheat, do a quick menu
change and use the melted, flavored butter to make a Béarnaise Sauce,
p. 238.

SAUCE
2 or 3 shallots, minced (a good tablespoon)
3 tablespoons wine vinegar
3 tablespoons dry white wine or vermouth
1 teaspoon salt
1 cup (2 sticks) unsalted butter

F ISH
3 cups Fish Stock, p. 69
6 salmon steaks
salt and freshly ground pepper

Put the shallots, vinegar and wine in the top of a double boiler and boil them over direct heat until they are reduced to about 1 tablespoon. This can be done several hours in advance. Cut the butter into 1-inch pieces and let it come to room temperature. Keep some water warm in the bottom of the double boiler.

Put the fish stock in a deep frying pan and bring it to a boil. Lower the heat and put the fish steaks into the barely simmering stock. Cover the pan and let the fish cook *as slowly as possible* until it is opaque throughout, 10–12 minutes. Arrange the fish on a platter, cover it loosely with foil and set the platter over a pan of barely simmering water to keep the fish warm if the sauce is not ready. (Save the stock to use again, to cook fish or in a soup or sauce.) While the fish is cooking, complete the preparation of the sauce.

Put the reduced shallot mixture over the warm water to heat it slightly. Add 2 pieces of butter and whisk them in. As soon as the butter is creamy, beat in some more. Be prepared to take the pot in and out of the warm water the whole time you are making the sauce. Beat in the butter, piece by piece, removing the pot from the heat when the butter seems to be getting too soft, putting it back when it shows signs of solidifying. Ideally, the sauce should have the texture of thick heavy cream, but if it's a choice of too thick or too thin, *under* rather than *over* heat it. Put the sauce in a bowl.

Garnish the platter of fish with some parsley or watercress and spoon some *beurre blanc* on each piece as you serve it.

Fish Loaf
(SERVES 6 FOR LUNCH, 12 AS FIRST COURSE)

This is a splendid lunch dish. It should be made a day in advance. Arrange to be out of the kitchen while the oven is on.

6 large onions, chopped
3 tablespoons butter
1 tablespoon vegetable oil

2 pounds fish fillets, preferably a mixture of several kinds
3 eggs
3 tablespoons unseasoned bread crumbs
juice of ½ lemon
2 teaspoons salt
freshly ground pepper

Garnish
lemons, capers and watercress or parsley

Preheat the oven to 350°.

Sauté the onions in the butter and oil until they are golden brown. While they are cooking, cut the fish into very small pieces, chop it by hand or in a food processor, or grind it. Make it as coarse or as fine as you like—it's entirely a matter of taste. Beat the eggs in a large bowl and add the fish, the cooked onions, the bread crumbs, lemon juice, salt and lots of pepper.

Put the mixture in an oiled 9 x 5-inch loaf pan or a 2-quart baking dish and bake it for 1 hour. Chill it for 3–4 hours.

Turn the loaf out onto a platter and decorate it with capers, lemon slices and watercress or parsley. Pass around plenty of extra capers and lemon wedges when you serve.

Fish Mousse
(SERVES 8 AS FIRST COURSE, 6 AS MAIN COURSE)

This is as light and elegant a fish mousse as I have ever tasted. It can also be made with shrimp or scallops or a combination of fish and seafood. It is the easiest dish in the world to make if you have a food processor.

Resist the temptation to add anything to the fish mixture. Experiment with the sauces; the fish is perfect the way it is. I can never decide whether it is better hot or cold.

1 pound boneless fish of any kind or scallops or shelled shrimp
3 eggs
1 cup heavy cream
salt and freshly ground pepper
butter

Cut the fish into 2-inch pieces and process it with the metal blade of a food processor until it is smoothly chopped. With the processor still running, add the eggs through the tube. Stop the processor and scrape down the mixture from the sides. Add about a teaspoon of salt and 5 or 6 grinds of pepper. Turn the processor on again and add the cream. Process until everything is well blended.

If you don't have a processor, grind the fish twice or get the fish-monger to do it for you. Beat in the eggs and cream very well by hand.

Generously butter a fish mold or a 1-quart soufflé dish. Scrape the fish mixture into the mold. Put a rack in a large pot with a tight-fitting lid or improvise a steamer, following the suggestions on p. 103 . Put an inch of water in the bottom of the pot and bring it to a boil. Cover the mold with waxed paper and put it on the rack. Cover the pot and steam the mousse over medium heat for 15–20 minutes, or until a knife inserted in the center comes out clean.

Turn the mousse out on a serving dish and garnish it with something pretty and green—watercress or fresh herbs. Serve the mousse hot with Cooked Basil-Tomato Sauce, p. 249 or cold with Herb or Green Mayonnaise, p. 243, or any of the sauces for fish found in the index.

Fish and Spinach Pie
(SERVES 8 AS FIRST COURSE AND 6 AS MAIN COURSE)

2 pounds spinach, thoroughly washed
1½ pounds fish fillets, very thin or thinly cut (any kind is good)
1 lemon, cut in half
salt and freshly ground pepper
½ pound cooked shrimp, chopped }
2 tablespoons chopped fresh dill }   *mixed together*
3 tablespoons butter, cut in small pieces

Bring several quarts of water to a boil in a large pot. Put the spinach into the boiling water, bring back to a boil and immediately drain the spinach into a colander. Rinse it with cold water to stop the cooking and spread it on paper towels to drain. Butter a 9 or 10-inch glass pie plate or shallow casserole. Line the plate with half the spinach leaves, overlapping the leaves and letting them hang over the edge of the plate a bit. Sprinkle the spinach with salt, freshly ground pepper and a generous squeeze of lemon juice. Cover the spinach with a layer of half the fish. Season the fish with more salt, pepper and lemon juice, spread the shrimp-dill mixture on top, dot it with 2 tablespoons of the butter and cover it with the rest of the fish. Season it once again with salt, pepper and lemon juice and cover the fish with the rest of the spinach to form the top crust of the "pie." Dot the spinach with the rest of the butter.

You can prepare this dish to this point several hours in advance, cover and refrigerate it. Remove the pie from the refrigerator half an hour before you intend to serve it. Put a rack in a large pot with a tight fitting, domed lid or improvise a steamer, following the suggestions on p. 103 . Put about an inch of boiling water in the pan, put the plate of fish on the rack, put a piece of waxed paper loosely over the fish, cover the pot and steam the pie over medium heat for about 20 minutes. Poke carefully into the center with a fork to be sure that the fish is white and opaque throughout. Decorate the pie with slices of lemon and/or a few whole cooked shrimp.

Serve the pie in wedges with Hollandaise Sauce, p. 237.

Sorrel and Fish Rolls

(SERVES 6)

This dish is a bit of a nuisance to make but is well worth it. If you can't get sorrel, you can make it with spinach, chard or lettuce leaves. But try to get sorrel.

24 or more large sorrel leaves
6 fish fillets, cut in half crosswise
1 can (2 ounces) flat anchovy fillets, drained
4 tablespoons unsalted butter,
    at room temperature
1 medium clove garlic, minced   } thoroughly mashed together
4 tablespoons chopped parsley
plenty of freshly ground pepper
4 tablespoons butter
2 egg yolks
juice of ½ lemon   } beaten together with a fork

Blanch the sorrel leaves by dipping them quickly, one at a time, into boiling water and immediately laying them flat on paper towels to drain. If you leave the sorrel in the water for more than a few seconds it will become very difficult to handle. It's a good idea to blanch more leaves than you need, in case some of them tear. After the leaves have drained, place the leaves one on top of another to make 12 two-layered leaves.

Put about a tablespoon of the anchovy mixture on each piece of fish, fold the fish in half and place it at the widest end of the leaf. Roll the fish up in the leaves and put it, seam-side down, on a platter. Repeat until all the fish and sorrel are rolled up. You may cover and refrigerate the fish for several hours at this point.

Half an hour before serving, remove the fish from the refrigerator. Melt the butter in a skillet large enough to hold all the fish rolls. Put the rolls in the butter, cover the pan and cook over medium-low heat for 15–20 minutes. Remove the fish carefully to a platter, using a slotted spoon. Mix a few spoonfuls of the pan juices into the egg-lemon mixture, then pour it into the pan. Whisk constantly over low heat until the sauce thickens slightly—less than 5 minutes. Don't let it boil, or the eggs will scramble. Taste the sauce, correct the seasoning, pour it over the fish and serve.

Fish Steaks with Mixed Vegetables

(SERVES 6)

6 tablespoons butter
1 large bulb fennel with leaves, thinly sliced (about 3 cups)
6–8 scallions, thinly sliced (about ½ cup)
2 large potatoes, peeled and diced (about 2 cups)
4 small carrots, scraped and cut into matchsticks
3 tablespoons chopped parsley
1 teaspoon fresh thyme leaves
juice of ½ lemon
salt and freshly ground pepper
6 fish steaks (any firm-fleshed fish such as bass, cod, tile, halibut)
2 egg yolks

Melt the butter in a large skillet with a close-fitting lid. Add all the vegetables and the herbs and mix them well with the butter. Sauté them for about 10 minutes, stirring frequently. Season with lemon juice, salt and pepper. Remove half the vegetables from the pan. Season the fish with salt and pepper and place it on top of the layer of vegetables. Spread the rest of the vegetables on top of the fish. Cover the pan (a cover can always be improvised with foil if you don't have one that fits), turn the heat to high and when the juices begin to boil, turn the heat to medium. Cook the fish and vegetables for about 20 minutes, or until the fish is opaque throughout. Turn off the heat, tilt the pan and spoon the juices into a small pot. Combine the juices with the egg yolks, heat gently until the sauce just thickens, pour it over the fish and vegetables and serve.

Sweet and Sour Salmon
(SERVES 12 AS A FIRST COURSE)

This is a lovely dish for a buffet table, especially if it is made in a fish mold. It looks like an odd combination of ingredients; our associations with sweet and sour fish are largely Chinese. But it is typically Jewish to combine sweet, sour, ginger and fruit flavors with fish or meat. My mother has made this dish, both with a clear aspic and with a gingersnap-thickened sauce, for as long as I remember, and I think it deserves a place with any salmon dish I know. It's also good made with other kinds of fish.

COURT BOUILLON
2–3 pounds fish heads and trimmings
3 large onions, sliced
1 tablespoon mixed pickling spice
juice of 2 lemons
rind of 1 lemon
2–3 tablespoons wine vinegar   *boiled together for about*
⅓ cup brown sugar   *½ hour and strained*
3–4 bay leaves
6 peppercorns
1 teaspoon salt
3 cups water

3-pound piece of salmon or 3 pounds salmon steaks
½ cup golden raisins

For Clear Sauce
1 envelope gelatin, softened in ¼ cup water

For Thick Sauce
12–14 gingersnaps, crumbled
ground ginger, optional

Put the strained *Court Bouillon* in a pot and bring it to a boil. Lower the heat, add the fish, cover the pot and barely simmer the fish until it is cooked through, about 15–20 minutes for one large piece, about 10 minutes if you are cooking steaks. Poke a fork into the thickest part of the fish to be sure it is opaque throughout. Take the fish out of the broth, remove the skin and bones and flake it into small pieces. Gently mix the raisins with the fish and set it aside.

If you are making a clear sauce. Dissolve the softened gelatin in the hot fish broth, taste it and adjust the seasoning with salt, pepper, lemon juice and/or brown sugar. Put the fish in a 1½-quart mold. Pour in the broth, cover the mold and refrigerate it for at least 4 hours. To unmold, run a knife around the edge of the mold and dip it very briefly into hot water. Invert a serving dish over the mold and, grasping dish and mold firmly, turn them over. A tap on the mold should free the fish. Garnish the platter with lemon slices and parsley.

For a thick sauce. Add a little broth to the crumbled gingersnaps, whisk until smooth and combine the mixture with the rest of the broth. Taste and adjust the seasoning with salt, pepper, lemon juice and/or brown sugar and a pinch of ground ginger, if you like. Combine the fish with the sauce, put it in a serving dish and chill for several hours before serving.

Whichever sauce you choose, this dish can be made a day in advance.

Gravlax

(SERVES 12–15)

A Scandinavian specialty, this salmon is "cooked" by its own briny juices. It is a great delicacy, worthy of a very special occasion.

3–3½ pounds center cut of salmon
1–2 large bunches fresh dill
¼ cup salt, preferably kosher salt
2 tablespoons sugar
2 tablespoons peppercorns, coarsely crushed

} mixed together

Have the salmon cut in half lengthwise, the bones removed and the skin left on. If you are using hothouse dill, which is not very pungent, chop it coarsely to release the flavor. Put several sprigs or a good sprinkling of dill in a glass, pottery or enameled dish just large enough to hold the fish. Place one piece of fish skin-side down on top of the dill. Spread half of the salt mixture on the fish, cover it with the rest of the dill, sprinkle on the rest of the salt mixture and lay the second piece of fish on top, skin-side up. Cover the dish well with several layers of aluminum foil and weight it with a brick or several cans of food set in a loaf pan. Refrigerate for 2–3 *days*. Turn the fish every 12 hours or so to allow both of the skin-covered sides to steep in the juices which accumulate in the dish. Spoon a bit of the juice between the pieces of fish when you turn it.

Remove the fish from the dish and drain it on paper towels. Gently scrape all the dill and pepper from the cut surfaces of the fish. Put the fish skin-side down on a cutting board and, holding a very sharp knife almost parallel with the fish, cut it into thin slices. Serve the fish with buttered brown bread and with the following mustard sauce.

Mustard Sauce

The traditional mustard sauce for *Gravlax* is quite sweet—too sweet for my taste. I suggest you start with just a little bit of sugar and add more to taste.

6 tablespoons good prepared mustard
1 scant tablespoon powdered mustard
1–2 tablespoons sugar
3 tablespoons wine vinegar
½ cup vegetable oil
2–3 tablespoons finely chopped dill

Mix the mustards, sugar and vinegar together with a fork. Gradually beat in the oil until the sauce is smooth and well combined. Taste and adjust the seasoning. Stir in the chopped dill.

Seviche

(SERVES 6–8)

Seviche is fish cooked by lemon juice, not by heat. It has a lovely, firm texture and does not taste the least bit raw. Garnish the fish with lots of raw vegetables and serve it with bread and sweet butter.

2 pounds fish fillets (sole or flounder) or scallops or some of each
juice of 4–5 lemons or 1 container frozen (not bottled) lemon juice

SAUCE
2 tablespoons wine vinegar
⅓ cup orange juice
⅓ cup olive oil
1 hot pepper or more, minced
    or a large dash Tabasco sauce   } *beaten together with a fork*
3 scallions including green tops,
    thinly sliced
1 clove garlic, minced
salt and freshly ground pepper

Cut the fish into small serving pieces, put it in a shallow dish and pour the lemon juice over it. Cover the dish and let the fish marinate in the refrigerator for at least 6 hours, preferably overnight. Turn it once. The lemon juice will "cook" the fish, turning it white. Cut into the thickest part of one of the pieces to be sure it is white throughout.

Drain the fish and pat it dry with paper towels. Discard the marinade. Put the fish in a serving dish, pour the sauce over it and refrigerate for at least an hour. Serve cold, garnished with raw vegetables. *Seviche* will keep in the refrigerator for several days.

Steamed Clams

When you serve steamed clams, you can put a large bowl on the table to receive the empty shells. We always make a tablecloth of newspaper and put the shells right on the table. This is a messy but incomparably delicious meal.

It's always hard to think of anything to serve with steamed clams. If you can't bear the thought of serving only as many clams as everyone can eat, you could make it a meal entirely without cutlery and serve a bowl of raw vegetables with Arugula Dip, p. 12, first and finish up with a bowl of fresh fruit or a watermelon.

Soft-shell or steamer clams are the best kind to use for this dish, but any kind of small clams are delicious.

6 quarts steamer clams or small hard-shelled clams
½ pound (2 sticks) butter, melted ⎫
juice of a large lemon (4 tablespoons) ⎬ mixed together

Wash the clams in several changes of water and scrub them thoroughly with a stiff brush. Put about an inch of water in a large soup pot and add the clams. Put the pot on high heat, cover it tightly and steam the clams just until they all open, about 10 minutes. It may be necessary to stir them around in the pot several times so that the clams on the bottom do not become overcooked while those on top are still closed. Do not overcook the clams or they will become very tough. As soon as they open, put the clams in a large bowl and strain the broth through cheesecloth into individual cups. Serve individual cups of lemon butter.

Take a steamer clam from its shell with your fingers, holding it by its long neck; dip it into the hot broth to wash off any sand that may still be clinging to it, and dip it in the lemon butter before eating. Drink the broth, but be careful not to disturb the layer of sand that has undoubtedly collected in the bottom of the cup no matter how carefully you washed the clams.

MUSSELS

To clean mussels. It takes time to clean mussels. Do it at your convenience and put the cleaned mussels in the refrigerator until cooking time. Scrub the mussels thoroughly with a stiff brush under running water. Scrape the barnacles off the shells and debeard the mussels, using a sharp knife. Discard any which feel noticeably heavier than the others. If any of the mussels are gaping open, give them a sharp rap and set them aside. If they are not tightly closed after a few minutes, discard them too. You can expect to throw away several mussels out of each quart you buy.

Moules Marinière

(SERVES 6 AS A MAIN COURSE)

It is hard to believe that any dish as good as *Moules Marinière* could also provide the basis for so many other delicious dishes. If you are lucky enough to be near a beach where you can gather mussels, it will also be almost free, but even if you have to buy the mussels, it is still an inexpensive dish with a very luxurious flavor.

3 quarts (6 pounds) mussels, cleaned according to the directions
3 tablespoons butter
6 scallions or 4 shallots or 1 medium onion, chopped
2 large cloves garlic, chopped
4 tablespoons chopped parsley
2 cups dry white wine

Melt the butter in a pot large enough to hold all the mussels when they are open. Gently sauté the scallions and garlic without browning for 3 or 4 minutes. Stir in the parsley, pour in the wine and bring to a boil. Put all the mussels in the pot and cover it tightly. After 2 minutes or so, stir the mussels around in the pot so that those on top will have a chance to steam. Do this several times if necessary. As soon as all the mussels are open (5–8 minutes), remove the pot from the heat. Do not overcook; mussels start to toughen as soon as they open. Discard any few mussels which have not opened by this time; they are likely to be nothing but shells full of sand or mud.

Serve the mussels in a bowl with a ladleful of their juices poured over them. Be sure everybody has a spoon and plenty of French bread so that not a drop of the delicious juices will be wasted. Put a large bowl on the table to receive the empty shells.

Mouclade

(SERVES 6 AS A FIRST COURSE)

Mouclade is a rich version *Moules Marinière*, ideally served as a first course. Prepare a half-recipe of *Moules Marinière* but substitute 1 tablespoon chopped fennel leaves or ¼ teaspoon anise seeds for the garlic.

> ½ recipe Moules Marinière, p. 172, with substitutes as directed
>   above
> 3 egg yolks
> ½ cup heavy cream
> ½ teaspoon cornstarch dissolved in 2 tablespoons water, optional

Remove the top shells and arrange the mussels on a platter. Strain the juice through several layers of cheesecloth and put it to heat in a small saucepan. Beat the egg yolks and cream together in a bowl, then beat in about ½ cup of the hot mussel juice. Add this mixture to the liquid in the pot and stir, over low heat, for 4 or 5 minutes. Do not allow the sauce to boil or the eggs will scramble. If the yolks have not thickened the sauce after 5 minutes of slow but steady cooking, stir in the cornstarch. The sauce will thicken lightly. Pour it over the mussels and serve.

Mussels on the Half-Shell with Horseradish Sauce
(SERVES 6–8 AS A FIRST COURSE)

½ recipe Moules Marinière, p. 172
1 recipe Horseradish Sauce, p. 240

Remove the mussels from the juice in the pot. Strain the juice through cheesecloth and save it, in the refrigerator or the freezer, to use in Egg-Lemon Sauce for Fish, p. 233, Cream of Mussel Soup, p. 71, or instead of fish stock in any of the fish soup recipes in this book.

Remove the top shell from each mussel and arrange the mussels on a platter. Cover and refrigerate until serving time. Put a dab of Horseradish Sauce on each mussel before serving.

Mussels Vinaigrette or Mayonnaise

This is a simple way to fix mussels which have been steamed so that their juices can be used to make Cream of Mussel Soup, p. 71, or a Mussel Sauce for fish, p. 161. Both of these are excellent fillings for raw tomatoes.

One recipe Vinaigrette Dressing, p. 251, is approximately the right amount to dress 1 cup of mussels out of their shells. A little extra garlic, a very finely chopped red or green pepper and/or a teaspoon or so of finely chopped hot pepper are excellent additions. Mix the mussels with the dressing at least an hour before serving.

Half a cup of Herb or Green Mayonnaise, p. 243, is enough for a cup of mussels out of their shells. Be sure the mayonnaise is well seasoned with salt and freshly ground pepper and add a little lemon juice if you wish. Add the mayonnaise little by little to the mussels until they are properly coated with, but not drowned in, the sauce.

SHRIMP

Shrimp have become so expensive that one can scarcely make a meal of them. Fortunately, they make an excellent first course and a beautiful garnish for fish dishes or soups. An easy way to serve shrimp at an informal summer party is in their shells.

Shrimp Boiled in Beer

(SERVES 4)

1 can beer
1 teaspoon celery seed
2 cloves garlic, chopped
1 pound shrimp in their shells, rinsed

Put the beer in a 2-quart saucepan, add the celery seed and garlic and bring it to a boil. Put in the shrimp, cover the pot and bring the beer back to the boil. Remove the pot from the heat and let the shrimp cool, covered. Shake the pot from time to time so that all the shrimp have a chance to steep in the seasoned beer. Drain the shrimp into a colander and serve warm or cold.

Strain the liquid and use it to make a sauce for fish, p. 161 .

Shrimp in Dill

(SERVES 4)

1 quart water
1 tablespoon salt
1 tablespoon dill seed
1 large bunch fresh dill, washed
1 pound shrimp in their shells, rinsed

Put the water, salt, dill seed and half the fresh dill in a 2-quart saucepan and bring it to a boil. Turn down the heat and let the stock simmer for 10–15 minutes. Line a 1½-quart bowl or plastic container with the remaining dill.

Bring the stock back to the boil and add the shrimp. Bring the stock back to the boil again, then turn off the heat. Stir the shrimp around in the broth to be sure they are all pink, remove them with a slotted spoon and put them into the bowl lined with dill. Strain the broth over the shrimp and let it cool. Refrigerate overnight, drain and serve with a lemony homemade mayonnaise.

Shrimp Salad

(SERVES 6)

For an elegant first course, make this salad with Shrimp in Dill, p. 175.

½ pound Shrimp in Dill, shelled and cut in half
½ cup homemade mayonnaise
1 small can water chestnuts, drained and sliced
salt and freshly ground pepper
lemon juice
6 small, ripe tomatoes

Mix all the ingredients together. Fill the tomatoes with the salad.(For directions on preparing tomatoes for stuffing, see p. 134.) Serve the stuffed tomatoes on a bed of Swiss Chard Salad, p. 97.

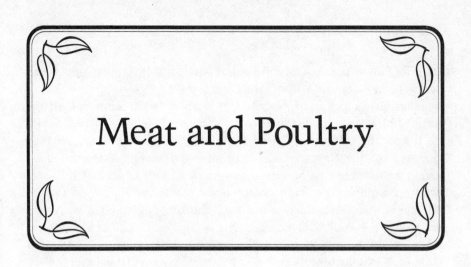

Meat and Poultry

COLD BEEF, LAMB, PORK, VEAL OR CHICKEN ROASTED ON TOP OF THE STOVE

(SERVES 6–8)

Meats can be beautifully roasted on top of the stove in a Dutch oven or a heavy casserole. This is the best method to use in summer to get plain, cold, sliced meat—a simple and indispensible food, especially if you entertain a lot and want to avoid last-minute cooking. Meat cooked this way is juicy and can be flavored with herbs and aromatic vegetables. There's no reason for meats roasted on top of the stove to be overcooked—rare or medium-rare roast beef and lamb and juicy, just done pork, veal and chicken are easy to produce by this method. A small turkey is good too—just double the vegetables and be prepared to let it simmer for at least 3 hours. Just as in oven roasting, you can use a meat thermometer to ensure that the meat will not be cooked more than you want it to be. With one of these meats on a buffet table, everything else can (and should) be vegetables.

Cold, sliced meats should be served with 1 or 2 sauces or relishes. Choose among the various mustards or mayonnaises, Fruit Relish, p.

177

137, Hot Sauce, p. 240, Onion-Vinegar Sauce, p. 246, Green Peppercorn Sauce, p. 234, or Pesto without the cheese, p. 44.

The basic mixture of aromatic vegetables is the same for all the meats, but you can and should vary the herbs. Parsley is included with all the meats. Choose one herb to dominate, add others only if they complement the flavor. Basil, rosemary and tarragon are not good together. Rosemary is the classic herb to use with lamb, but it is also good with pork. You may combine it with a sprig or 2 of thyme. Tarragon, the classic herb to use with chicken, is also good with veal and combines well with chervil. Dill is good with chicken, veal and lamb. Basil is good with any of the meats and can be combined with a sprig or 2 of marjoram, oregano or thyme. My favorite seasoning for beef cooked this way is plenty of fresh thyme and lots of parsley. The strength of various herbs differs enormously; you cannot use the same quantity of each. Add herbs cautiously; taste the vegetables in the middle of the cooking and add more herbs if the flavor is not pronounced enough.

The meat will produce delicious juices. If it is to be eaten hot, the juices and cooked vegetables make a perfect garnish. If it is to be eaten cold, however, especially if the meat is at all fat, it may be difficult to remove the fat from the vegetables. If you add a little hot stock or water to the juice and vegetables in the pan after the meat has cooked, it will be easier to remove the congealed fat when it is cold. The cold vegetables also make a good garnish, or can be used in a soup.

Meat and Chicken. All weights (except chicken) are for meats *after boning.* Have as much fat removed as possible.
Beef: 3–4 pounds sirloin or round roast, rolled and tied if necessary
Lamb: 3–4 pounds boned leg or shoulder, rolled and tied
Pork: 3–4 pounds boned loin, shoulder or fresh ham, rolled and tied
Veal: 3–4 pounds boned leg or shoulder, rolled and tied
Chicken: a 4–5-pound roasting chicken

VEGETABLE AND HERB MIXTURE

  4 tablespoons butter
  1 large onion, finely chopped
  3 large cloves garlic, finely chopped
  2 stalks celery with lots of leaves, finely chopped
  2 medium carrots, scraped and finely chopped

1 medium turnip, peeled and finely chopped, optional
½ cup chopped parsley
salt and freshly ground pepper
1–2 tablespoons finely chopped basil or dill or chervil
2–3 teaspoons finely chopped thyme, rosemary or tarragon or
marjoram

Melt the butter in a large skillet. Add all the chopped vegetables and herbs and sauté them gently, stirring frequently, until they are wilted and the onions are transparent, 10–15 minutes. Season with salt and lots of freshly ground pepper. Remove the pan from the heat. The vegetables may be prepared up to a day in advance; this reduces preparation time for the meat considerably. The vegetable mixture can be frozen and it is very handy to have it readymade. Especially if you have a food processor, it's a good idea to chop up some extra vegetables to give them their preliminary cooking and freeze them.

To Cook the Meat
2 tablespoons olive oil
a bay leaf

Heat the oil in a heavy bottomed casserole or Dutch oven just big enough to hold the meat. Brown the meat very thoroughly, searing each surface well, over high heat. Be careful not to pierce the meat with a fork; use tongs or 2 spoons to turn it and to remove it from the pan when it is well browned. Season the meat with salt and freshly ground pepper. Pour the oil out of the pan and wipe the pan with paper towels. Put the meat back in the pot and pour the vegetable mixture over and around it. Add the bay leaf. Turn the heat high until you hear things begin to sizzle, then turn it low, cover the pan and cook the meat until it is done the way you like it. Medium-rare beef will take an hour or so (140° on meat thermometer), medium-rare to medium lamb 15 minutes longer (150° on thermometer). Veal and pork may take up to 2 hours (175-180°). Turn the meat once, in the middle of cooking, and spoon some vegetables over the top.

When the meat is done, put it on a platter and let it cool before slicing. If you are cooking it a day in advance, wrap it well and refrigerate it in 1 piece. Slice the meat shortly before serving.

To cook the chicken. Chicken should be browned gently in 1 tablespoon each butter and olive oil. It will take at least 15 minutes.

Turn it carefully to brown all the surfaces, using 2 spoons so you don't pierce the skin. Remove the browned chicken from the pan and season it with salt and freshly ground pepper. Throw away the oil and butter in the pan only if they have burned. Spread some of the vegetables on the bottom of the pan and lay the chicken, breast-side up on top of them. Put the rest of the vegetables on and around the chicken and add the bay leaf. Turn up the heat until you hear a sizzling sound, then turn it down, cover the pot and cook the chicken over low heat until it is done, 1½–2 hours. After 1 hour, turn it on its side for 20 minutes, then on the other side for 20 minutes or so. The chicken is done when the leg can be moved easily in its socket and when the juices run clear yellow, not pink, when the thigh is pierced with a fork. Remove the chicken to a platter and let it cool. Refrigerate it whole if you are not using it immediately, and slice it just before serving. Cold roast chicken is a classic picnic dish. Two unusual sauces for cold chicken are Tuna Mayonnaise, p. 244 and Anchovy Sauce, p. 231.

VEGETABLE MEATBALLS (OR MEAT LOAF)

(MEATBALLS MADE WITH 1 POUND OF MEAT WILL SERVE 4)

Vegetable meatballs are good all year round, but especially in summer, because there are always extra bits of cooked vegetables available and because they are especially good cold. I have made meatballs with many different cooked vegetables and I suggest you experiment, using about a cup of chopped, cooked vegetable to every pound of meat. You can multiply this 2, 3 or even 4 times for a big crowd. All the mixtures can, of course, be used equally well to make meat loaves, but it does involve turning on the oven. To make a meat loaf from any of these meat-vegetable mixtures, preheat the oven to 350°, put the meat mixture on a baking pan, shape it into a loaf and cover and surround it with pieces of tomato. Bake it for about an hour, uncovered, and serve it hot or cold.

Meatballs can be deep fried and served with lemon juice and chopped parsley, or browned in a little olive oil and cooked in a very simple sauce, consisting of some cut-up tomatoes and a sprinkling of herbs. Here are a few of the most successful combinations. Quantities given are for 1 pound of ground meat.

Tomato Meatballs

1 cup Tomato Sauce, p. 248
1 medium clove garlic, minced
1 egg   } mixed together
1 teaspoon salt
plenty of freshly ground pepper
1 pound lean ground beef or veal or pork or a mixture
½ cup unseasoned bread crumbs

FOR FRIED MEATBALLS
flour
oil for frying

FOR MEATBALLS IN A SAUCE
olive oil for browning
2 or 3 large tomatoes, cut up
2 or 3 tablespoons chopped herbs

Combine the tomato-egg mixture with the meat in a large mixing bowl. Mix and knead it together, using your hands, and gradually add bread crumbs until you have a mass firm enough to shape into meatballs. Add only as much bread crumbs as you need. Different vegetable mixtures will require different amounts of bread crumbs. Shape the mixture into small meatballs for frying, larger ones for sautéing.

To fry the meatballs. Roll them in flour. Heat about an inch of oil in a large skillet. When it is hot, put in the meatballs, adding only as many as will fit in the pan without touching each other. Brown them very well on all sides, turning them frequently, over medium high heat. Drain the meatballs on paper towels, pile them on a plate and serve hot or cold with plenty of lemon wedges and chopped parsley, or with a bowl of yogurt beaten with some crushed garlic and salt.

To sauté or stew the meatballs. Put about 2 tablespoons of olive oil in a large skillet. Brown the meatballs, a few at a time, over medium heat. When they are all browned, remove them from the pan, add the cut-up tomatoes to the oil in the pan, scrape up all the browned bits and stir them into the tomatoes. Add some chopped herbs, return the meatballs to the pan, baste them with the tomatoes, cover the pan and cook over low heat for about 30 minutes, turning them once in the sauce. Remove the meatballs and boil the sauce for 2 or 3 minutes to reduce it slightly. Pour the sauce over the meatballs and serve them hot or at room temperature. They are especially good in hero sandwiches.

Eggplant and Pepper Meatballs

1 cup Eggplant and Peppers, p. 114
1 egg
1 medium clove garlic
1 pound lean ground beef or veal or pork or a mixture
½ cup unseasoned bread crumbs
salt and freshly ground pepper

Puree the vegetables with the egg and the garlic in a blender or food processor. Mix them with the meat and enough bread crumbs to enable you to form the meat into meatballs. Season the mixture with salt and pepper and follow the procedure for Tomato Meatballs, p. 181.

Zucchini Meatballs

1 cup cooked zucchini, finely chopped
1 small onion, chopped and sautéed in 2 tablespoons olive oil
2 large leaves basil, finely chopped
1 tablespoon freshly grated Parmesan cheese, optional
1 teaspoon salt
lots of freshly ground pepper
1 egg
1 pound lean, ground beef or veal or pork or a mixture
½ cup unseasoned bread crumbs

Mix the zucchini and onion and all the seasonings with the egg and the meat. Add bread crumbs and form the mixture into meatballs. Follow the directions for Tomato Meatballs, p. 181. These are especially good fried.

Swiss Chard Meatballs

Substitute 1 cup of blanched, chopped Swiss chard for the tomato sauce in the Tomato Meatballs, p. 181. This mixture will probably require a smaller amount of bread crumbs.

Ratatouille Meatballs

By now you should be getting the idea. Substitute 1 cup of pureed Ratatouille, p. 153, for the tomato sauce.

BEEF

Jellied Beef with Summer Vegetables

(SERVES 6–8)

This is a very special dish for a very special dinner party or buffet. It is as beautiful as it is delicious. The classic French *boeuf en gelée* is a rather tame affair compared with this handsome extravaganza of meat, spicy aspic and as great a variety of summer vegetables as you want to include. The dish depends upon an intensely flavored, firm meat jelly which is produced by simmering bones in a highly seasoned broth. It does take time to prepare, but most of that time you don't have to pay any attention to what's simmering on the stove.

Although the list of ingredients looks formidable, it is not a difficult dish, and if you make it in several stages, it doesn't even seem very time consuming. As long as you remember to refrigerate everything in between, the preparation can be interrupted and/or resumed at any point and can stretch over 2 or 3 days. But don't assemble the dish until a couple of hours before serving.

On aspic. This and any of the other aspics in this book—the cold chicken soup and the sauces for cold veal, pork and duck—could be clarified. I do not recommend this. In the clarifying process the aspic loses a good deal of its flavor. One of the pleasures of home cooking is that you can serve and enjoy a slightly cloudy but very flavorful aspic. Straining the hot broth through several layers of cheesecloth, as directed in these recipes, removes large particles and makes an aspic clear enough to be attractive. If this does not convince you, directions for clarifying aspic can be found in any good standard cookbook.

BROTH
2 tablespoons butter
½ pound salt pork, diced or bacon cut into small pieces, blanched in boiling water for 5 minutes and drained

2 large onions, sliced
2 large cloves garlic, sliced
2 large carrots, sliced
2 or 3 stalks celery with leaves, cut in chunks
4 or 5 sprigs parsley
2 or 3 large ripe tomatoes, cut in chunks
2 13½-ounce cans beef broth
4 cups dry white wine
2 tablespoons mixed pickling spices, tied in cheesecloth
1 large bay leaf
1 tablespoon salt
6 peppercorns, bruised
about 3 pounds veal bones or beef and veal bones combined
2 large pig's feet, split (2–3 pounds)

MEAT
2 tablespoons olive oil
4–5 pound piece boneless rump or sirloin or round of beef
¼ cup brandy, optional

ASSORTED VEGETABLES
Use as many different kinds and as much as you like of any of the
following:

shelled peas
snow peas
green beans, cut in ½-inch pieces
zucchini or yellow squash, sliced or cut into small wedges
carrots, sliced or cut in matchsticks
small turnips or kohlrabi, peeled and sliced or cut in quarters
celery, sliced
fennel, sliced
red radishes, thickly sliced
tiny new potatoes
*tiny beets, peeled and left whole (cook these last so they don't turn
    all the others red)*

For the broth. Melt the butter in a large, heavy soup pot or Dutch
oven (4–5 quarts). Add the salt pork or bacon and cook for 5–10

minutes, until it is lightly browned. Add the onions, garlic, carrots, celery, parsley, tomatoes and sauté them for 10 or 15 minutes. Add the broth, wine, spices, bay leaf, salt and peppercorns, bring it to a boil and add the bones and pig's feet. Bring the liquid back to the boil, skim off the foam, turn down the heat, cover the pot and cook over medium-low heat for at least 4–5 hours, even more if it is convenient.

For the meat. Heat 2 tablespoons of olive oil in a large skillet and sear the meat, browning it on all sides. If you are using the brandy, heat it, pour it over the meat and ignite it with a match. Let it burn itself away.

If the pot is large enough, add the meat to the pot of bones and vegetables. If you do not have a large enough pot, strain the broth and return it to the pot. Taste the broth and add salt if necessary. Bring the broth to a boil and add the meat, making sure that the liquid comes at least halfway up the sides of the meat. Lower the heat, cover the pot and simmer slowly for 2–3 hours or until the meat is very tender and the juice runs clear, not rosy, when it is pierced with a fork. When the meat is done, remove it from the pot, wrap it well in foil and refrigerate it. Strain the broth through a double layer of cheesecloth, taste it and make sure it is seasoned well. Remember that it will not taste as highly seasoned when it is cold. Set aside 2 cups of broth for cooking the vegetables and put the rest into the refrigerator to cool and jell.

For the vegetables. Prepare the vegetables you have chosen by washing, peeling, slicing or dicing them. Bring the reserved broth to a boil in a saucepan. Cook the vegetables in the order given—milder ones first, then the vegetables which will give the broth a strong flavor. Add one batch of vegetables, cover and cook rapidly until they are *just barely cooked.* Remove them from the broth with a slotted spoon and set aside. Add another vegetable to the boiling broth and cook it. Continue until all the vegetables are cooked, adding a little water to the broth if it becomes too concentrated. Chill each vegetable in a separate container (or separate pile on a plate).

To assemble. Remove the layer of congealed fat from the top of the aspic. Scrape off any little bits of fat or wipe them off with a paper towel dipped in hot water. Scoop about 2 cups of the aspic into a bowl and whisk it for a second or 2. Cut the meat into thin slices and arrange them down the middle of a large platter, spreading a little of the aspic on each slice as you put it on the platter. Arrange piles of different vegetables in an attractive pattern surrounding the meat, and spoon a layer of very slightly whisked aspic over all. Put any remaining aspic in a small bowl to be served as a sauce.

Cold Roast Beef

Cold roast beef is a wonderful dish to serve in summer if you want to spend your cooking time on vegetables or if you want something really super for elegant picnic sandwiches. Stuffed vegetables, a potato and vegetable salad, Peperonata or any of the steamed vegetable custards would round out a beautiful and luxurious spread. If you can arrange to be out of the kitchen for about an hour, you can roast a large piece of beef by the very-high-temperature method without undue discomfort.

Figure on ¼ to ⅓ pound of beef, after boning, per person, if it is the only meat to be served. It will be delicious and go a lot further if very thinly sliced.

Use meat of good quality, boned and tied. The best cuts are a boned rib roast, a boned shell or eye round. Take the meat out of the refrigerator and let it come to room temperature (this should take about 10 minutes per pound).

Preheat the oven to 500°. Put the meat in a roasting pan, preferably on a rack, and roast it in the middle of the oven for 5 minutes per pound. Turn off the oven but do not open the door. Leave the roast in the oven for 1 ½ hours. It will be medium rare and very juicy. For really rare meat, reduce the roasting time to 4 minutes per pound. Let the meat cool, wrap it well and refrigerate it until about an hour before serving time. You can roast the meat a day or 2 in advance of serving it, but slice it just before serving with one or several of the sauces for cold meat as suggested on pp. 177-178.

Marinated Minute Steaks

(SERVES 6)

*1½–2 pounds minute steaks, preferably skirt steaks, well trimmed
and cut into serving pieces
Hot Oil Marinade, p. 218
rendered beef fat (trimmed from meat) or 2 tablespoons cooking oil*

Put the meat in one layer in a dish and pour the marinade over it. Turn it several times to be sure it is well coated and let it marinate for at least 2 hours. Remove the meat from the marinade and dry it with paper towels. Reserve the marinade.

Render the fat trimmed from the meat or heat the cooking oil in a large skillet. Cook the meat rapidly, browning it well and turning it only once, using tongs to keep from piercing the meat. It should take no more than 5 minutes for medium-rare steak. Put the steaks on a platter and pour the marinade into the pan. Swirl it around, scraping any browned bits into it, and pour it over the meat. Serve immediately.

Steak alla Pizzaiola

(SERVES 6)

Made with fresh tomatoes and fresh basil, this familiar Italian-restaurant dish has an entirely different taste. It is a quick, easy and very good way to garnish pan-broiled steak, chops and fish.

> *2 tablespoons olive oil*
> *2–3 cloves garlic, finely chopped (use more or less depending on how much you like garlic)*
> *2 pounds ripe tomatoes, peeled and coarsely chopped*
> *4–6 large leaves fresh basil, finely chopped or ½ teaspoon dried oregano*
> *salt and freshly ground pepper*
> *fat trimmed from the beef or 2 tablespoons olive oil*
> *6 individual boneless steaks or 2–3 pounds boneless sirloin or porterhouse steak cut into serving pieces*

Heat the olive oil in a small saucepan; add the garlic, and cook it for a minute or 2 without browning. Add the tomatoes and the basil or oregano and cook briskly, stirring from time to time. Cook the tomatoes only long enough for their liquid to evaporate. This will take 5 minutes, more or less, depending on the size of the pot. The flavor of the sauce depends on not overcooking the tomatoes. Season the sauce to taste with salt and freshly ground pepper and set it aside. The sauce can be made several hours in advance.

Trim the fat from the meat and render it in a large, heavy skillet. If the meat is very lean, heat 2 tablespoons of olive oil instead. Sear the steak well on one side over high heat, turn the meat and let it brown for a minute or 2 on the second side. Spread the tomato sauce on and around the steak, cover the pan and continue to cook over medium heat for 4–6 minutes for medium-rare steak. Put the meat on a platter, scrape the brown bits from the pan into the rest of the sauce and pour it over the meat. Serve hot *or cold.*

CHICKEN

Chicken Mousse

(SERVES 8–10)

This mousse is perfect for an elegant cold lunch, as a first course for an otherwise meatless dinner or, best of all, unmolded and beautifully decorated on a summer buffet table. It needs no sauce. It is especially good served with cold, crisp steamed snow peas and, if you're lucky enough to have them, steamed Day Lily Buds, p. 111.

4 cups stock from Smoked Ham or Tongue, p. 209

or

3 slices bacon, chopped
1 medium onion, chopped
1 carrot, cut up
1 cup dry white wine } *made into stock as directed below*
2 13½-ounce cans chicken broth
1 bay leaf
about 4 pounds chicken parts
2 teaspoons finely chopped tarragon
2 packages unflavored gelatin
½ cup finely chopped parsley
1 cup heavy cream, whipped

If you are using ham stock. Bring it to a boil in a large pot and cook the chicken in it.

To make the chicken stock. Melt the bacon over low heat in a large pot, add the onion and carrot and cook them together, without browning, for about 5 minutes. Add the wine, chicken broth and bay leaf and bring it to a boil. Simmer the stock for 15 minutes.

Add the chicken to the boiling stock, turn the heat to medium, cover the pot and cook the chicken until it is very tender, about 30 minutes.

Remove the chicken and let the stock continue to simmer, uncovered, while you take the chicken meat from the bones and chop it, either in a food processor or by hand. Use a blender only if you can chop the chicken without pureeing it.

Strain the stock. You should have approximately 3 cups. If you have a lot more, put it back in the pot and boil to reduce it. If you have a lot less, add water to make 3 cups. Stir the tarragon into the hot stock. Sprinkle the gelatin over ½ cup of water and when it has softened, stir it into the hot stock until it is dissolved. (The gelatin will not dissolve properly unless the stock is hot. If it has cooled, add a little stock to the softened gelatin and heat it until it's completely dissolved.) Taste the stock and add salt and freshly ground pepper to taste. Remember to season it highly; after it is cold and has been mixed with the chicken and cream, the flavor will be much less intense.

Cool the stock in the refrigerator but don't let it get so cold that it jells. When the stock is cold, remove all the fat from the surface. If you are planning to make a decorated mold, set aside ½ cup of the stock. Stir the chopped chicken and parsley into the stock. Whip the cream and fold it in. Pour the mousse into any 2-quart mold, a loaf pan if you want to serve it in slices, or a ring mold.

To decorate a ring mold. Pour the reserved stock into the mold and refrigerate it for a few minutes, until the aspic sets. Make an attractive pattern with slices of vegetables and/or with tarragon or parsley leaves. Spoon the chicken mixture carefully into the mold, being careful not to disturb the pattern. Refrigerate at least 4 hours; you can make this mousse 24 hours in advance.

To unmold the mousse. Run a knife around the outer and inner rings of the mold. Set the mold into hot water *for a few seconds only.* Invert a platter over the mold. Then, grasping both mold and platter firmly, turn them both upside-down. The mousse should slide onto the platter. If it does not, wring out a dish towel in hot water, hold it on the mold for a second or 2, and rap the mold in several places to loosen the mousse. Do not let the bottom of the mold get too hot or the thin layer of aspic will melt and the decoration will be ruined.

Fill the center of the mold and decorate the platter with green vegetables. Refrigerate until serving time.

Chicken Breasts in Dill Sauce

(SERVES 6)

You can easily extend this dish into a whole meal by adding lots of cooked and/or raw vegetables to the platter. Steamed broccoli, green beans, cold cooked beets, raw green peppers and tomatoes are all especially good with the dill sauce. If you are serving lots of vegetables and want to make some extra sauce, change all the 3s the sauce recipe to 4s and add another small clove of garlic and as much extra lemon, sugar and salt as you think the sauce needs.

3 cups chicken stock, preferably homemade, p. 72
3–4 sprigs dill
6 whole chicken breasts, boned, skinned and cut in half

Dill Sauce
3 tablespoons butter
1 clove garlic, minced
3 tablespoons flour
3 cups chicken stock (saved from cooking the chicken)
2 teaspoons vinegar
2 teaspoons sugar
juice of ½ a small lemon, or more
½ teaspoon salt
freshly ground pepper
3 tablespoons fresh dill, chopped

Heat the stock with the sprigs of dill in a large skillet until it is just simmering. Add the chicken breasts and poach them, covered, in the barely simmering stock for about 10 minutes or until they are just cooked through. Cook them in 2 batches if necessary. Arrange the chicken on a serving platter. Strain the stock, measure it and add enough additional stock or water to make 3 cups.

Melt the butter in a saucepan over low heat, add the garlic and cook it for 2 or 3 minutes without browning. Stir in the flour with a wire whisk and continue to cook, without browning, for 2 or 3 more minutes. Whisk in the stock, stirring constantly, and cook the sauce over medium heat until it thickens. Add all the seasonings and cook the sauce over low heat, stirring frequently, for about 15 minutes. Taste the sauce and adjust the seasonings. The sauce will be quite thin but it will thicken as it cools.

Spoon half the sauce over the chicken breasts and put the rest in a bowl. Serve at room temperature.

You can prepare this dish a day in advance, but assemble it only an hour or 2 before serving time. If the sauce is too thick, beat it with a whisk and add enough milk or cream to give it the proper consistency. Give the chicken about an hour to return to room temperature if it has been refrigerated.

Circassian Chicken
(Chicken with Walnut Sauce)

(SERVES 6)

4 pounds chicken parts or 2 small chickens
4 cups chicken stock, canned or homemade, p. 72
1–2 tablespoons paprika
2 cups walnut meats
3 slices white bread, soaked in a little chicken stock and squeezed
   dry

GARNISH
walnut meats
black Greek olives

Cook the chicken in the stock. The chicken need not be covered by the stock; just bring it to a boil, turn the heat to medium and steam the chicken until it is done, 15-20 minutes for parts, about ½ hour for a small chicken. Remove the meat from the bones and cut it into bite-sized pieces. Boil the stock until it is reduced to 2 cups, add the paprika and let it cool until it is lukewarm.

To make the sauce by hand. Grind the nuts in a blender or put them through a grinder twice. In a bowl, blend the nuts with the soaked bread, using a wooden spoon. Gradually add the stock to the mixture, beating it first with the wooden spoon, then with a whisk, until it has the consistency of heavy cream. Taste the sauce and add salt, pepper and/or paprika if necessary.

To make the sauce in a food processor. Grind the nuts with the metal blade, add the soaked bread and blend them together. Gradually add the stock through the tube until the sauce has the consistency of heavy cream. Correct the seasoning with salt, pepper and/or paprika.

Mix the chicken with about ⅔ of the sauce, put it in a serving dish and cover it with the rest of the sauce. Garnish it with whole nut meats and black Greek olives.

If the chicken has been refrigerated, be sure to allow it to come to room temperature before serving (about 1 hour).

Fried Chicken Balls

(30 WALNUT-SIZED BALLS)

These chicken balls are wonderful for a picnic, on a buffet table or at a party. You can make them tiny, if you wish. They are also excellent made with turkey, or half-and-half with ham. Substitute different herbs or spices for the parsley, but be sure to season them highly, especially if you intend to serve them at room temperature.

2 cups cooked chicken
¼ cup milk
2 slices white bread
1 egg
1 heaping tablespoon chicken fat or softened butter
1 large clove garlic, minced
2 heaping tablespoons chopped parsley
juice of ½ lemon (about 2 tablespoons)
salt and freshly ground pepper
flour
oil for frying

Chop the chicken in a food processor or by hand, or put it through the fine blade of a meat grinder. Put it in a mixing bowl. Pour the milk over the bread, squeeze it dry and combine it with the egg and chicken fat or butter in the food processor or blender. Add the bread-egg mixture to the chicken. Add the chopped garlic and parsley, the lemon juice and about a teaspoon of salt and a few grindings of pepper. Using your fingers, combine everything thoroughly. Taste and adjust the season-

ing with salt, pepper and/or lemon juice. Form the chicken mixture
into walnut-sized balls and roll them in flour. Put about an inch of
vegetable oil into a heavy skillet. Let it get hot, then brown the chicken
balls over medium-high heat a few at a time, rolling them around in the
oil to brown them all over. Drain them on paper towels, put them on a
serving dish, garnish with parsley and lemon wedges. Serve hot or at
room temperature.

Stir-Fried Chicken Bits

(SERVES 6)

This is one of my favorite ways of cooking chicken. It is delicious hot
or cold and is a wonderful stuffing for raw tomatoes.

The secret of the dish is to sauté the chicken, not to stew it. If the
chicken is crowded in the pan, the juices will come out of it instead of
being sealed in by the hot oil, and the chicken will stew in its own juice.
If you want to cook this for more than 4 people, it's a good idea to cook
it in 2 batches, unless you have an enormous frying pan. Since it takes
only 5 minutes to cook, it's no great hardship to do it twice. Be sure to
have all the ingredients cut up and ready before you start cooking.

4–6 tablespoons olive oil
2 pounds boneless chicken, cut into bite-size pieces
2 large cloves garlic, minced
¾ cup chopped parsley   *mixed together*
¾ cup sliced scallions, including green tops
juice of 1 small lemon (2–3 tablespoons)
salt and plenty of freshly ground pepper

Get 4 tablespoons of oil good and hot in your largest frying pan. Put
in the chicken and immediately stir it all around to sear as many surfaces as possible. Keep the heat very high. Push the chicken aside a little
and stir the garlic, parsley and scallions into the oil. Stir everything
together well, squeeze the lemon over it and add a good teaspoon of salt
and plenty of freshly ground pepper. Stir again. The chicken should be
done by the time everything has been mixed together, and the parsley
and scallions should be just wilted and a bright green. Take out a piece
of chicken and cut into it. If it is not done, cook the chicken for 2 or 3

minutes more, and next time, make the pieces smaller. The faster it cooks, the better.

Sautéed Chicken

(SERVES 6)

Sautéed Chicken is one of those quickly cooked, simple, inexpensive dishes that can be varied endlessly. Deglaze the chicken pan with wine or cream, lemon juice or tomato sauce or add some vegetables to the pan to cook with the chicken, and each time you have an entirely different dish. The usual words of caution: don't combine too many flavors in any one dish, and don't overcook the chicken. Cook it only until its juices run clear yellow when it is pierced with a fork or sharp knife. The cooking time will be shorter for white meat (about 15 minutes) than for dark meat (20–25 minutes). Brown the pieces of white meat first and remove them from the pan. Then brown the dark pieces and cook them for a few minutes before returning the white meat to the pan. Use both butter and oil when you brown the chicken; the oil will keep the butter from burning.

    3–4 pounds chicken parts
    2 tablespoons butter
    2 tablespoons olive oil
    salt and freshly ground pepper
    3–4 tablespoons seasonings: chopped scallions, herbs and/or garlic
    1 cup wine or cream or a combination or 1 cup tomato sauce
        (Tomato Sauce with Cream and Tarragon, p. 249, is especially
        good)

Wipe the pieces of chicken dry with paper towels. Heat the butter and oil in a large frying pan or Dutch oven over medium-high heat. Put a few pieces of white meat into the hot fat, turn the heat to medium and brown the chicken for 2–3 minutes on each side, or until it is golden brown. When all the chicken has been browned, sprinkle it with salt and freshly ground pepper. Cook the dark meat over low heat, covered, for about 10 minutes, then add the white meat to the pan and cook it for 15 minutes more. Turn the chicken several times and baste it with the juice in the pan. Test the chicken to see if it is done and put it on a platter. Cover it loosely with foil and set it on a pan of simmering water if it will take you more than a few minutes to make the sauce.

Turn up the heat in the pan, cook the seasonings in the butter and oil for a couple of minutes, and add the liquid you have chosen. If you are using wine, boil it until it is reduced by about half, stirring any browned bits from the pan into the sauce. Pour this over the chicken or add some cream, if you wish, and again boil the sauce until it is slightly reduced. Taste, adjust the seasoning and pour the sauce over the chicken.

If you are using tomato sauce, add it to the butter and oil in the pan, scrape any browned bits into the sauce and pour it over the chicken as soon as it is hot.

You can add some cut-up peppers, onions or summer squash to the pan after the chicken has been browned and cook it along with the chicken. Remove it when you make the sauce and pour the sauce over all.

If it is convenient, you may brown the chicken in advance, but don't finish cooking it until about 15 minutes before serving (or enough time for a first course if you are having one).

Sautéed Chicken with Olives

(SERVES 6)

4 tablespoons olive oil
3–4 pounds chicken parts, cut into serving pieces
2 large cloves garlic, finely chopped
6 scallions including green tops or 1 small onion, finely chopped
6 anchovy fillets
3 large tomatoes, peeled and cut into pieces
1 teaspoon chopped fresh marjoram or ¼ teaspoon dried oregano
freshly ground pepper
½ pound (about 24) black, Greek oil-cured olives, pitted and cut in
    half

Heat the oil in a large skillet. Brown the chicken in the oil, a few pieces at a time, and set it aside. Add the garlic, scallions and anchovies to the oil in the pan and cook them over low heat for a few minutes, mashing the anchovies into the oil with a fork or a wooden spoon until they have dissolved. Raise the heat to medium and add the tomatoes and marjoram, stirring well to incorporate any brown bits stuck on the bottom of the pan. Taste the sauce and add salt if it is needed (remember that the olives will add a salty taste) and 7 or 8 grinds of pepper. Cook the sauce for about 5 minutes. Put the chicken pieces back in the pan, turning each one to flavor it with the sauce, cover the pan and cook the chicken over medium-low heat for about 15 minutes, or until it is tender and the juices run clear yellow, not pink, when you pierce a piece with a fork. Add the olives, push them down into the sauce and continue cooking another minute or 2 until the olives are hot. This is especially good served with green noodles. It is also excellent cold.

Variations

Sautéed Fish Steaks with Olives. Brown 6 fish steaks (any kind, about 1-inch thick) in the oil and set them aside until the sauce is made. Return the fish to the pan, cover it and cook it in the sauce for about 10 minutes, or until it is white throughout. Add the olives, heat them through and serve. Good with new potatoes. Also good cold.

Olive and Anchovy Sauce for Pasta. The sauce, made *without* the chicken or fish, is excellent on pasta, with a few changes. To make enough sauce for 1½ pounds of pasta, double the quantities of olive oil, anchovies and tomatoes. Add 2 or 3 tablespoons of chopped parsley just before pouring the sauce over freshly cooked pasta.

Chicken and Sausage Stew

(SERVES 6)

1 pound Italian sausage, hot and/or sweet, cut in 1-inch pieces
3–4 pounds chicken legs and thighs
olive oil
2 medium zucchini (about 2 pounds), cut in quarters lengthwise, then into 3-inch pieces
2 large onions, coarsely chopped
2–3 large tomatoes, coarsely chopped
2 large cloves garlic, coarsely chopped
plenty of salt and freshly ground pepper
½ cup chopped parsley

Brown the sausage in a Dutch oven over medium-high heat. When it is well browned, remove it from the pan to a large platter. Add the chicken pieces to the pan, a few at a time, and brown them in the sausage fat over medium heat, adding some olive oil if there is not enough fat. When all the chicken is well browned, remove it from the pan and add the zucchini. Cook the zucchini, tossing it constantly, for 6 or 7 minutes, until it is barely cooked, and remove it to a bowl. Pour off some fat, if necessary, leaving a thin film over the bottom of the pan. Put in the onions and cook them, stirring frequently, until they are golden, 10–15 minutes. Add the tomatoes and garlic and stir them well into the onions, scraping all the brown bits from the bottom of the pan into the sauce. The dish can be prepared several hours ahead up to this point. Refrigerate the chicken and sausage if it is a very warm day. Heat the tomato sauce before proceeding with the recipe.

Simmer the sauce for 5 minutes, return the sausage and chicken to the pan and spoon some of the sauce over the meat. Cover the pan and cook the meat over low heat for 15 or 20 minutes. Pierce a piece of chicken with a fork; if the juices are clear yellow, the chicken is done. If not, cover the pan and cook the chicken for another 5 minutes. *Do not overcook the chicken.* When the chicken is done, put it and the sausage on a platter. Turn the heat to high, stir the parsley into the sauce, taste it and season with salt and freshly ground pepper. Add the zucchini to the sauce, heat it through and arrange it on the platter. Pour the sauce over all and serve hot.

Chicken Scallopine

(SERVES 6)

Quick, easy, elegant and relatively inexpensive; what more could anyone ask of a summer dish? It does require a little last-minute cooking, so plan to serve it with other dishes that can be completed entirely in advance, such as Tomato Soubise, p. 36, Watercress and Potato Salad, p. 93, Peperonata, p. 128, or Eggplant with Yogurt, p. 116.

2 pounds boned chicken breasts (2 pounds after boning)
2 eggs
1 ½ cups unseasoned dry bread crumbs, preferably homemade

1 teaspoon salt
5 or 6 grinds of pepper
2–3 tablespoons butter
2–3 tablespoons olive oil
lemon wedges
chopped parsley

You should have 2 good-sized or 3 small pieces of chicken per serving. Cut the chicken into serving pieces and place the pieces, a few at a time, between 2 pieces of waxed paper. Pound them with a meat mallet or with the bottom of a heavy pan until they have spread and flattened, but be careful not to pound right through the chicken. Beat the eggs together on a dinner plate and spread the bread crumbs, seasoned with the salt and pepper, on a large piece of waxed paper. Dip the chicken into the egg, then into the bread crumbs, pressing the crumbs into the meat to be sure each piece is well covered. Put the prepared chicken on a platter, cover and refrigerate it until 15 minutes before serving time. The chicken can be prepared to this point up to 4 or 5 hours before serving.

Heat 2 tablespoons each of oil and butter in a large frying pan. When it is quite hot, put in as many pieces of chicken as will fit in the pan without touching each other. If you cook the chicken over moderately high heat and do not crowd the pieces, each batch should be crisp, golden brown, cooked through and still juicy in 5–7 minutes. Cut into a piece to be sure it is cooked through. You will have to cook the chicken in 2 or 3 batches, depending on the size of your pan, and you will probably have to add a little more oil and/or butter occasionally. If you prefer, use 2 pans. You will need almost twice as much butter and oil, but the cooking time will be very short.

Arrange the chicken on a platter, garnish it with lemon wedges and sprinkle the whole with parsley.

Paella

(SERVES 6–8)

This is a fine dish for a summer dinner party. It can be rather expensive or rather cheap, depending on what you put in it. If you have a source of free clams and/or mussels, use lots of them and do with fewer shrimp, or even none at all, though they do add both a delicious flavor and a delightful touch of color. If you add a lot more clams or mussels than this recipe calls for, decrease the chicken stock by about ½ cup because the shellfish will produce a lot of their own juice. You can stretch the paella by adding more rice (and a corresponding amount of stock—an extra 1½ cups of stock for a cup of rice, and a pinch more seasoning). Turmeric is an inexpensive substitute for saffron. It will color the rice properly but will not give it the very distinctive flavor it should have.

The texture of the rice is all important. Each grain must be firm and separate. Use converted rice and cook it in an *uncovered* pan, adding the liquid little by little as it is absorbed.

I would not recommend cooking paella for a group larger than 8. It is very unlikely that you will have a shallow pan large enough to hold any more food than this recipe calls for, and it is very difficult to control the texture of the rice in much larger quantities. If you have a *very* large, shallow pan and a lot of self-confidence, you might manage enough for 12.

4 tablespoons olive oil
3–4 pounds chicken, cut into small serving pieces
salt and freshly ground pepper
2 large cloves garlic, minced
1–2 cups sweet red pepper, seeded and cut in small pieces
3 or 4 chorizos (dry Spanish sausage) or hot or sweet Italian sausages
3 cups uncooked converted *white rice*
4 cups chicken stock
½ teaspoon saffron
¾ teaspoon dried oregano
1 cup shelled peas
1 pound shrimp, shelled
1½–2 dozen small hard-shelled clams or mussels, well scrubbed

Heat the oil in a large, wide, shallow frying pan or Dutch oven. Brown the chicken in the oil, in a few batches if necessary, and remove it from the pan, seasoning it well with salt and freshly ground pepper. While the chicken is browning, cut the chorizos into thin slices. If you are using Italian sausages instead, prick them several times and boil them for about 5 minutes to rid them of some of their fat, then cut into 1-inch slices. When all the chicken has been browned, add the garlic, red peppers and sausage to the oil in the pan, mix them well and cook over low heat for a minute or 2. Put the chicken back into the pan and cook it, covered, over low heat, until it is about half done, about 10 minutes. If your large pan does not have a lid, cover it with foil.

The paella may be prepared in advance to this point. Refrigerate it in the pan until about an hour before serving time. Before proceeding with the recipe, remove the chicken from the pan and warm the sausage mixture over low heat for 10 minutes.

Warm the chicken stock and add the saffron and oregano to it. Add the rice to the pan and cook it over medium heat, stirring frequently, for about 5 minutes. Add 1 cup of the hot stock and stir well, incorporating into the mixture any browned bits that have stuck to the bottom of the pan. Continue to stir until the stock has been absorbed, then add another cup of stock and continue to cook, stirring frequently, until it, too, has been absorbed. Continue to do this until all the stock has been added, and cook the rice, *uncovered*, for 5–10 minutes more. Taste a few grains every minute or so. When the rice is getting tender but not quite cooked, put the chicken back into the pan, add the peas, cover the pan and cook over medium heat for about 10 minutes (not more). Add the shrimp and clams or mussels, mix everything together, cover the pot again and cook over medium high heat for about 5 more minutes, until the shrimps are pink and the clam or mussel shells have opened. Turn off the heat immediately. The shellfish will be cooked perfectly and the grains of rice will be firm and separate. Serve hot.

Cold Duck with Rice Salad

(SERVES 4–6)

A cold, braised duck is an easy dish to prepare. Sliced with care and served with its own delicious jellied sauce and a cold rice salad, it is a splendid dinner for 4. Cut in small pieces, mixed into the rice salad and granished with crisp, raw vegetables, it will easily serve 6 for dinner; used as a stuffing for raw green pepper halves, it will serve 8 for lunch.

BRAISED DUCK
5-pound duck
duck fat
1 large onion, peeled and coarsely chopped
2 large cloves garlic, coarsely chopped
2 large stalks celery with leaves, cut into 1-inch pieces
3 or 4 leaves lovage, chopped or some extra celery leaves
4 or 5 sprigs parsley
4 or 5 sprigs thyme or ¼ teaspoon dried thyme
duck giblets
juice and grated rind of 1 orange
juice and grated rind of 1 lemon
1–2 cups chicken stock
1 cup dry white wine
salt and freshly ground pepper

RICE SALAD
1½ cups raw rice, preferably converted rice
2 or 3 scallions including green tops, chopped
½ cup chopped parsley or fresh coriander or a mixture of the 2
3 tablespoons olive oil
salt and freshly ground pepper
1 cup sauce from the duck

Cut the duck into quarters and remove any loose fat. Heat a piece of this fat in a heavy Dutch oven until there is a thin film of fat on the bottom of the pan. Remove and discard the piece of fat and add the onions, garlic, celery, herbs and the duck's giblets to the pan. Cook slowly, stirring occasionally, for about 10 minutes. Mix the juice of the orange and the lemon with enough chicken stock to make 2 cups, and add it and the wine to the pan. Add a teaspoon of salt and 7 or 8 grinds of pepper, cover the pan and cook over medium heat for about 15 minutes. Add the pieces of duck, skin-side down, and, after the liquid has returned to the boil, turn down the heat and cook the duck over very low heat for about 40 minutes, turning it once during the cooking.

While the duck is cooking, cook the rice by your usual method or follow the package directions. Converted rice makes a nice, firm-textured rice for a salad. Drain the rice and mix it with the scallions, the parsley or coriander, the oil and salt and pepper to taste.

Prick the duck with a fork; it is done when it is tender and the juices run clear yellow. Remove the duck from the pan and let it cool. Remove and discard the skin as soon as the duck is cool enough to handle. Strain the sauce through several layers of cheesecloth, stir in the grated orange and lemon rind, taste and adjust the seasoning. Add a cup of the sauce to the rice mixture and combine them well. Put the rest of the sauce in the refrigerator or freezer until the fat has risen to the top and congealed. Remove the fat from the sauce. When the sauce is thoroughly chilled, it will set into a very light aspic.

If you are serving the meat separately. Carve the meat into neat serving pieces and arrange it on a platter. Cover and refrigerate. Shortly before serving, spoon a thin layer of sauce over the duck, garnish the platter with parsley or watercress and serve the rest of the sauce on the side.

If you are serving the duck as a salad. Cut the meat into bite-sized pieces and add it to the rice mixture. Add about half the remaining sauce and combine thoroughly. Taste and adjust the seasoning. Serve the salad in a salad bowl or on top of a bed of lettuce. Garnish it with assorted raw vegetables. Serve the remaining aspic on the side.

Sautéed Kidneys

(SERVES 4)

4 veal kidneys or 10–12 lamb kidneys
2 tablespoons butter
2 tablespoons olive oil
2–3 teaspoons dry mustard, depending on how hot you like it
1 cup heavy cream
salt and freshly ground pepper

Remove the cores and fat from the kidneys and cut them into thin slices. Combine the powdered mustard with a few tablespoons of cream until the mixture is smooth, then stir it into the rest of the cream. Heat the butter and oil in a large frying pan until they are very hot. Put the sliced kidneys in the pan and cook them *very rapidly* in the hot fat, turning the slices once with a spatula. The kidneys should cook only *2–3 minutes*. Remove them to a serving dish with a slotted spoon and immediately pour in the mustard-cream mixture. Boil it in the pan for a minute or 2, scraping any browned bits into the sauce. Taste the sauce and season it with plenty of salt and freshly ground pepper. Put the kidneys (and their juice) back in the pan, turn off the heat, stir them well in the sauce, return them to the serving dish and serve immediately.

PORK

Pork Steaks in Vinegar Sauce

(SERVES 6)

6 pork steaks or 12 eyes of loin chops
4 tablespoons olive oil
¼ teaspoon fennel seeds or anise seeds
6 juniper berries, crushed   } mixed together
2 bay leaves, broken into small pieces
salt and freshly ground pepper
4 tablespoons good wine vinegar
    (sherry wine vinegar is especially good)

Rub the meat with the seasoned oil and let it marinate for 3 or 4 hours or overnight, turning it from time to time. Remove the bay leaves. Heat a large, heavy skillet and put in the meat and the seasoned oil. Brown the meat very well on both sides over medium-high heat. Season it with a little salt and freshly ground pepper. When the meat is nicely browned, push it to one side and deglaze the pan with the vinegar, scraping up all the browned bits on the bottom. Turn the meat in these juices, turn the heat low, partially cover the pan and cook for 20–30 minutes, until the meat is done and the juices have been reduced to a few teaspoonfuls. Put the meat on a platter and pour the juice over it, adding a few drops of water to the pan if it is necessary to detach all the browned bits.

Pork Braised in Milk

(SERVES 6)

Pork cooked this way has a particularly sweet and delicious flavor.

*3–4 pounds boned pork loin or shoulder (weight after boning), rolled
    and tied*
salt and freshly ground pepper
2 cloves garlic, minced
cooking oil, optional
3 cups milk, heated to the boiling point

Rub the pork all over with the salt, pepper and garlic and let it stand at room temperature for half an hour or more. Put the meat fat side down in a Dutch oven just large enough to hold it, and brown the meat on all sides over medium heat. If the meat is very lean, film the pan with oil before browning. Pour off the fat or oil and add the hot milk; it should come about halfway up the sides of the meat. If it does not, the pot is too big. Move the meat to a smaller pot if you have one, or add another cup of hot milk. With the cover just a little askew, simmer the meat very slowly in the milk for about 2 hours, turning it once, after an hour. Pierce it with a fork to be sure it is tender, and let the meat cool in the juices.

Remove the meat from the pot and put the gravy in a bowl in the refrigerator. Remove the fat from the surface when it solidifies. Refrigerate the meat until about an hour before serving. Slice it and pour the gravy over it.

Pork Paprikash

(SERVES 6)

This is a rich dish. Serve it with steamed green beans and a plain cucumber salad.

pork fat
6 pork steaks or 12 eyes of loin chops
salt

1 large onion, chopped
1 large clove garlic, chopped
1 medium green pepper, seeded and finely chopped, optional
1 tablespoon good paprika
1 cup sour cream
1 tablespoon flour
1 cup beef broth

Trim the fat from the pork. Heat some of the fat in a large, heavy skillet until there is a thin film of melted fat on the bottom of the pan. Remove the pieces of fat and discard them. Sprinkle the meat with salt and sear it on both sides in the hot fat. Remove it to a platter and add the onion and garlic and green pepper, if you are using it, to the pan. Cook them, stirring frequently, until they are soft, about 10 minutes, then stir in the paprika. Return the meat to the pan, cover, and cook the meat with the onions over low heat, turning once, until it is cooked through, 20–30 minutes.

While the meat is cooking, mix the flour with 2 or 3 tablespoons of the sour cream until it is smooth. When the meat is done, remove it to the platter again and add the stock to the pan. Raise the heat and boil the stock to reduce it a bit, scraping the browned bits from the pan into the stock. After about 5 minutes, lower the heat and stir the sour cream mixture into the pan. Gradually stir in the remaining sour cream. Keep the heat low, stir the sauce until it thickens and let it simmer gently for 5 minutes or so. Taste the sauce and adjust the seasoning. Return the meat to the pan and heat it through in the sauce. Serve hot.

Pork Stuffed with Spinach and Salami

(SERVES 6–8)

This is as handsome a dish as you could put on a summer dinner table. It must be cooked in advance and can be arranged on its platter 3 or 4 hours before serving, so there's absolutely nothing to be done at dinner time. A simple soup first (also made in advance) and cheese and fruit to follow would make what I consider an ideal summer dinner.

3–4 pounds boneless roast of pork (weight after boning), loin or
    shoulder

SPINACH AND SALAMI STUFFING
1 pound fresh spinach, washed and trimmed of tough stems
2 tablespoons olive oil
2 large cloves garlic, coarsely chopped
6–8 scallions including green tops, chopped
¼ pound Genoa salami, cut into small pieces
1 cup chopped parsley
2 tablespoons chopped fennel leaves or ¼ teaspoon anise seeds
salt and freshly ground pepper

string for tying the meat
2 tablespoons olive oil
1 large onion, sliced
2 large cloves garlic, chopped
1 cup dry white wine
2 cups meat or chicken stock
pork bones
1 pig's foot, cut in half
1 bay leaf
¼ teaspoon anise seeds
6 carrots, peeled and cut into thick slices

Have the meat boned (save the bones) but not rolled and tied; it should be a fairly flat piece. You can easily roll and tie it yourself after stuffing; directions are given at the appropriate point in the recipe.

Blanch the spinach according to the directions on p. 100. Chop it coarse and set it aside.

Heat the olive oil in a large skillet. Add the garlic, scallions and Genoa salami and stir them for a minute or so. Stir in the parsley and fennel leaves (or anise), then the bread crumbs. Turn off the heat. Add the chopped spinach, about half a teaspoon of salt and some freshly ground pepper and stir to combine well.

Lay the meat out flat and pile the stuffing down the center. Fold the sides of the meat over the stuffing, making sure they overlap by about an inch to prevent the stuffing from leaking out. Cut some string into 10-inch lengths and tie the roast every 2 inches into a roll. Tie the string firmly but not so tight that the stuffing comes out the ends of the roast. Sprinkle the meat generously with salt and pepper.

You will need a Dutch oven large enough to hold the rolled roast, its bones and the pig's foot. Heat the oil in the Dutch oven, brown the meat on all sides and remove it to a platter. Add the onion and garlic and cook them for 5 minutes or so. Add the wine, the stock, bay leaf and anise seeds and about 1 teaspoonful of salt and bring the liquid to a boil. Add the pork bones and the pig's foot, cover the pot and cook over medium heat for 20–30 minutes. Push the bones to the sides of the pot and add the meat, making sure that the liquid comes about halfway up the sides of the meat. If it does not, the pan is too big. Do not add more liquid, but move everything to a smaller pot if you have one. Bring the liquid back to the boil, cover the pot, lower the heat and cook the meat over very low heat, with the liquid barely simmering, for 1 hour. Turn the meat and continue to cook for another hour. Add the carrots to the pot and continue to cook very slowly until the carrots are tender, about ½ hour. Remove the carrots from the pot and set them aside. Let the meat cool in the juices. Then remove it, wrap it well and refrigerate it. Strain the juices through several layers of cheesecloth, taste and add salt if necessary, and refrigerate. When the juices are cold, the fat will congeal on the surface and can be removed easily, and the juice will jell into a delicious aspic.

The meat should be arranged on a platter several hours before serving. Cut the strings off the meat and very carefully cut it into thin slices. Each slice will have a beautiful green and pink center. Put a thick layer of the aspic on the platter and arrange the meat on top of it. Decorate the platter with the cooked carrots. An excellent additional garnish is the Spinach and Parsley Salad, p. 96 . If you intend to make this salad, cook the spinach for the stuffing and the salad at the same time.

If there is any extra aspic, put it in a bowl and pass it as a sauce.

This dish should be made 1 or 2 days in advance.

Smoked Ham or Tongue

(SERVES 6–8)

To cook a delicious ham or smoked tongue with an unusual flavor, use the recipe for Meats Roasted on Top of the Stove, p. 177 . The quantities of vegetables will be enough to season half a smoked ham, a smoked butt or a tongue. There's no need to brown the meat in oil. Just put it in the pot with the vegetables and add 2 cups of white wine and 2 cups of water. Bring the liquid to a boil, turn down the heat, cover the pot and simmer gently, about 2 hours for ham, about 3 hours or until tender for tongue. Turn the meat once during cooking. Skin the tongue while it is still warm.

The bonus will be a pot of very rich stock. Strain it and use it instead of water to cook lentils for Lentils with Sorrel, p. 131 , to make Chicken Mousse, p. 189 , to steam cabbage to eat hot or use in a Cooked Cabbage Salad, p. 82 .   Or put it in the freezer and use it to make pea or bean soup when the cold weather comes.

Pâté-Stuffed Veal

(SERVES 6–8)

This is a very elegant dish for a dinner or buffet table. The pale veal slices with their spiral pattern of chicken-liver pâté are so tender you can cut them with a fork. Add a Swiss Chard Salad, p. 97, sliced tomatoes sprinkled with chopped basil, and Stuffed Squash Blossoms, p. 147 (all made well in advance) for a glorious August dinner.

3–4 pounds boneless veal (weight after boning) breast or shoulder

PÂTÉ STUFFING
½ cup (1 stick) butter, at room temperature
½ pound chicken livers, trimmed
2 or 3 scallions including green tops, chopped
1 large clove garlic, chopped
*1 heaping teaspoon chopped fresh rosemary or ½ teaspoon dried
    rosemary, crushed to a powder*
½ cup chopped parsley
¼ cup unseasoned, dry bread crumbs
salt and freshly ground pepper

string for tying the meat
2 tablespoons olive oil
3 scallions including green tops, chopped
1 large clove garlic, chopped
1½ cup white wine mixed with 1½ cups water
small sprig rosemary
a small pig's foot, split
½ cup chopped parsley

Have the meat boned and well trimmed by the butcher into a flat, rectangular piece. Save the bones. If you buy a rolled and tied roast, unroll it to stuff it and buy a couple of pounds of veal bones or a calf's or pig's foot so that the sauce will jell into a richly flavored aspic.

To make the stuffing. Melt 2 tablespoons butter in a frying pan and sauté the chicken livers over medium heat until they are just cooked through, about 5 minutes. Remove them from the pan with a slotted spoon and add the scallions and garlic to the butter in the pan. Sauté them for a minute or 2, stir in the rosemary, parsley and bread crumbs and remove the pan from the heat.

Chop the chicken livers and combine them with 4 tablespoons butter. Add the herb-bread crumb mixture, combine well and season to taste with salt and freshly ground pepper. Spread this mixture evenly over the entire surface of the veal. Cut the string into 6 or 8 10-inch lengths. Roll the meat up, jelly-roll fashion, and tie it every 2 inches. The string should be tight enough to hold the meat together, but not so tight that it forces the stuffing out the ends of the roll. Sprinkle the meat with salt and pepper.

Heat 2 tablespoons olive oil in a Dutch oven just large enough to hold the meat and the bones. Brown the meat on all sides over medium heat. Remove it from the pan, add the scallions and garlic, cook them for a minute or so in the oil and add the wine and water, the sprig of rosemary, the pig's foot and the bones. Bring the liquid to a boil, cover the pot and cook over medium heat for about half an hour.

To cook the meat. Push the bones aside and put the meat into the pot. The liquid should come about halfway up the sides of the meat. If it doesn't, do not add more liquid, but transfer everything to a smaller pot if you have one. Cook the meat over very low heat, with the liquid barely simmering, for 2–2½ hours, turning it once. Stick a fork into an end of the roll to be sure it is very tender. Let the meat cool in the juice. Then remove it, wrap it well and refrigerate. Strain the juice through several layers of cheesecloth and refrigerate it. When the juice is cold it will have jelled into a delicious aspic. Remove the congealed fat from the surface and mix ½ cup of chopped parsley into the aspic.

A few hours before serving, remove the string and carefully cut the meat into thin slices. Put a thick layer of aspic on the platter and arrange the meat on top of it. Garnish the platter with parsley and serve the remaining aspic in a bowl.

This dish should be made 1 or 2 days in advance.

Veal Chops or Scallopine in Tarragon Sauce

(SERVES 6)

6 large veal chops or 12 veal scallopine, flattened between 2 pieces
    of waxed paper with a mallet or heavy pan
2 cloves garlic, peeled and cut
½ cup flour mixed with 1 teaspoon salt
4 tablespoons butter
2 scallions including green tops, finely sliced
4 tablespoons dry white wine or vermouth
½ cup heavy cream   heated slowly together
2 teaspoons finely chopped tarragon
2 tablespoons chopped chervil or parsley

Rub the meat well on both sides with the cut sides of the garlic
cloves. Discard the garlic. Flour the meat well on both sides. Melt 3
tablespoons of the butter in a large skillet and brown the veal on one
side over medium heat. Turn the meat and cook it over medium-low
heat, covered, for 25–30 minutes for chops, 10–15 minutes for
scallopine, or until the meat is tender and the juices run clear yellow
when it is pierced with a fork. While the meat is cooking, combine the
cream and tarragon in a small pot and warm them together. When the
meat is done, remove it to a platter and cover it.

Add the remaining tablespoon of butter to the pan and when it has
melted, add the scallions. Sauté them for a minute or 2, then deglaze the
pan with the wine, raising the heat a little and scraping all the brown
bits from the pan into the wine. Add the tarragon cream and chervil or
parsley, boil the sauce for a minute, stirring constantly, and pour it over
the meat.

Vitello Tonnato

(SERVES 6)

This Italian classic is one of the best summer dishes. It should be
made 24 hours in advance.

2 tablespoons olive oil
1 large onion, sliced

1 medium carrot, sliced
2 large cloves garlic, sliced
6 flat anchovy fillets, drained
2 cups chicken or meat stock
1 bay leaf
6 peppercorns, bruised
2–3 pounds boneless veal shoulder, rolled and tied

SAUCE
1 (6½-ounce) can tuna, drained
6 anchovy fillets, drained
3 egg yolks
4 tablespoons lemon juice
½ cup olive oil
about ½ cup of the veal cooking liquid
2–3 tablespoons capers

GARNISH
lemons and parsley

Heat the oil in a Dutch oven and cook the onion, carrot, garlic and anchovies over medium heat for 5 minutes or so. Add the stock, the bay leaf and peppercorns and bring it to a boil. Put the veal in the pot, cover it and turn the heat low. Cook the meat for about 1½ hours, turning it once. It should be tender when pierced with a fork and the juices should be yellow, not pink. Let the meat cool in the stock.

To make the sauce, put the tuna, anchovies, egg yolks and lemon juice in the container of a blender or food processor and process until you have a smooth puree. Gradually add the olive oil, as if you were making mayonnaise. Scrape the sauce into a bowl and gradually mix in some veal stock until the sauce has the consistency of heavy cream. Add about ½ cup of stock—the sauce will thicken a little as it stands. Stir in the capers.

Cut the veal into thin slices and put it in a dish just big enough to hold it. Spread a little sauce between the slices and spoon some over the top. Save at least half the sauce to spread over the meat shortly before serving. Let the meat stand at room temperature for at least a half hour before serving. Garnish the platter with thin slices of lemon and sprigs of parsley.

Strain the stock and save it to use in soups or sauces.

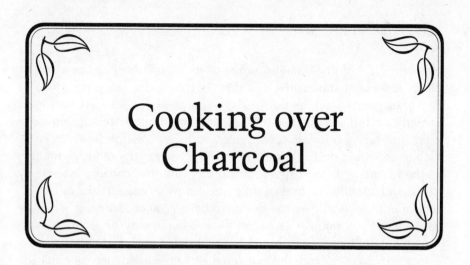

Cooking over Charcoal

COOKING OVER CHARCOAL

Our ancestors originally cooked over glowing coals and many people in the world still do. In the summer, even those of us who have convenient, modern kitchens sometimes choose to cook over a charcoal fire both for the pleasure of cooking and eating outdoors and because food cooked this way has a distinctive, delicious taste.

Almost everyone knows that meats and fish, cooked over charcoal, have a flavor, crispness and juiciness that never seem to be matched by other methods. But not everyone realizes how much more can be done once the fire is going. All kinds of vegetables can be broiled along with the meat. Or they can be wrapped in foil with bits of butter and a sprinkling of herbs and put on the grill to stew in their juices. Bread can be brushed with garlic-flavored olive oil and toasted on the grill. It's sensible to cook a whole meal over charcoal, using all of the heat of the fire and not just the few prime minutes it takes to grill a steak; it's also easier than running back and forth between the kitchen and the grill.

Cooking over Perforated Foil. Meats that are neither too lean nor too fat can be broiled to perfection on a grill directly over the coals.

Hamburgers, hot dogs, steaks, cubes of marinated beef or lamb, lamb chops and a lean, butterflied loin of pork fall into this category.

Other meats, such as pork chops, spareribs and various sausages (usually too fat) and chicken (too lean) are more successfully broiled on a layer of heavy duty aluminum foil which has been perforated every inch or so with a sharp fork or skewer. This arrangement keeps the fat or the marinade from dripping down onto the fire, causing it to flare and scorch the food or to send up gusts of ashy steam onto the meat. At the same time, it allows the hot charcoal to flavor the meat while it cooks it. I have found this to be a very simple way of getting crisp, brown but not burnt, juicy but not fatty, broiled pork and chicken. It is also a good way of cooking skewered bits of things, such as chicken livers, pieces of kidney or chunks of fish that have a tendency to fall off the skewers and into the fire, or that would be dried up by more direct heat.

Charcoal-Broiled Steak or Chops

If you have a good charcoal grill, a good butcher and a good tarragon plant, you can eat and entertain beautifully all summer: master the recipe for Béarnaise Sauce, p.238 and learn to grill hamburgers, steaks and chops to perfection.

Light your fire well in advance of cooking, especially if you use lighter fluid to start it. The lighter fluid will certainly have disappeared in half an hour or so, but the coals will probably not be ready to use for another 20 minutes, when they will have burned down slightly and are covered with a layer of white ash.

Only experience will teach you how to time the meat so that it will be crisp and brown on the outside and as pink and juicy as you like on the inside. If the fire is very hot and your grill is adjustable, you can sear the meat rapidly over a hot fire, then move it a little farther from the coals to complete the cooking if the surface seems to be cooking too fast. If you like your steak rare, you may find it easier to cook it that way if you start with a chilled steak. For more evenly cooked meat, bring it to room temperature first. Try to turn the meat only once during the cooking, to avoid losing the juice that collects on the surface of the meat as the second side cooks. Turn meat with tongs or a spatula (or stick a fork into the very edge of it) to avoid piercing it, and salt the meat only after it is cooked or, better still, let people salt their own.

Have the sauce for the meat ready before you cook it and plan the menu so that there is a minimum of last-minute preparation. Serve the meat with several cold vegetable dishes or salads, or cook some vegetables over the coals before you put the meat on. Prepare the platter for the meat, with herb butter or a garnish, and set it in a convenient place. Hamburgers and chops should be served immediately if you want them to be hot; thick steaks should sit for 5–10 minutes before you slice them.

Remember that charcoal-broiled steak is just as good cold as it is hot. If it is convenient, cook an extra piece of meat while the coals are hot, to be served any time within the next 2 or 3 days.

Sauces that are good with broiled meats are:

Hot Sauce, p. 240 .
Onion-Vinegar Sauce, p. 246 .
Green Peppercorn Sauce, p. 234 .
Herb Butters, p. 235 .

The finest cuts of meat need no marinating or seasoning before cooking. Shoulder, round or flank steaks (London broil) can be marinated or not, as you wish (see Marinades, p. 218), but they should always be sliced by holding a very sharp knife almost parallel with the meat and cutting it into thin slices.

MARINADES

Lemon-Garlic Marinade

⅔ cup olive oil
6 tablespoons lemon juice (2 medium lemons)
2 cloves garlic, chopped
4–6 tablespoons chopped herbs
} mixed together
with a fork

Choose herbs appropriate to the food you are marinating. Mint and rosemary are especially good with lamb, thyme with beef and pork. All the fragrant herbs are good with chicken.

Oil and Vinegar Marinade

½ cup olive oil
½ cup wine vinegar
½ cup dry red wine
2 cloves garlic, chopped
1 bay leaf
2–3 tablespoons chopped herbs
} mixed together with a fork

Hot Oil Marinade

Hot oil is a condiment the Chinese always have on hand. It's a snap to make and very useful to have for pepping up a marinade, sauce, stew or even, occasionally, a salad. It keeps indefinitely in a closed jar.

MARINADE
½ cup hot oil
¼ cup soy sauce   } mixed together with a fork
1 large or 2 small cloves garlic, chopped)

HOT OIL FOR THE MARINADE
1 cup peanut oil
2 or 3 tablespoons hot red pepper flakes

Heat the oil and pepper flakes very slowly for ½–1 hour. Let the oil cool and strain it into a small bottle or cruet. Close tightly.

Grilled Lamb Chops

(SERVES 6)

Lamb is delicious grilled over coals. Tender lamb chops need no seasoning, but it is a nice change to marinate them sometimes. Follow the recipe below, or use the Hot Oil Marinade, above, and serve the chops without sauce.

12 loin lamb chops
Lemon-Garlic Marinade, p. 218
Parsley Butter, p. 236, made with half chopped parsley, half
    chopped mint or rosemary
half a lemon

Rub the chops with the marinade and let them sit in the refrigerator for about 4 hours, turning them once. Wipe them off with paper towels and grill them close to very hot coals for 4 or 5 minutes on each side.

Cut the herb butter into small pieces and put it on a platter. Squeeze the lemon over it. Set the platter on one side of the grill to warm, if there is room. Put the hot chops on top of the platter and hurry it to the table. The butter will melt. Spoon some of it over each chop.

Shish Kebab

(SERVES 6)

3 pounds boned leg of lamb, cut into 1½-inch cubes
Lemon-Garlic or Oil and Vinegar Marinade, p. 218
lots of bay leaves
Rice Salad with Rosemary, p. 95

Marinate the lamb for 3–4 hours, mixing it from time to time. Thread the meat on skewers with a bay leaf between each 2 pieces. Grill the lamb about 6 inches from hot coals, turning it several times. It should cook in 10 minutes. Serve with Rice Salad with Rosemary.

If you want to cook vegetables on skewers, marinate them with the meat, but thread them onto skewers and cook them before you put the meat on the fire. Keep them warm at the side of the fire, if there is room, or wrap them in foil for the few minutes it takes the meat to cook.

Broiled Butterflied Pork Loin

(SERVES 6–8)

3 pounds boneless pork loin (weight after boning)
Hot Oil Marinade, p. 218

Have the butcher trim the meat, if possible, so that you have the eye of the loin—a solid piece of meat. If you trim it yourself, cut away as much of the fat as you can, and trim the meat itself into a compact, solid piece. (Save the trimmings and make *Rillettes de Porc*, p. 21, or a Veal and Pork Pâté, p. 19.) Cut a gash down the length of the meat, about ⅔ of the way through its thickness, and spread it out as flat as possible. Marinate it for 4 or 5 hours in Hot Oil Marinade.

Broil the meat 6–8 inches above medium hot coals. If dripping fat causes the fire to flare too much, put a piece of heavy duty foil, perforated every inch or so with a sharp fork or skewer, between the meat and the grill, after the meat is well browned on both sides. Grill the meat until it is cooked through, 12–15 minutes on each side. Be careful not to overcook the pork. After 25–30 minutes, the meat should still be tender and juicy and quite sufficiently cooked. Put the meat on a platter and pour some of the marinade over it—it makes an excellent sauce.

Country-Style Spareribs

(SERVES 6)

"Country-style spareribs," thick slices from the ends of the loin, are much better for cooking over charcoal than their bonier version. They are usually available in supermarket meat cases.

4–5 *pounds country-style spareribs, trimmed of as much fat as*
    possible
½ *cup soy sauce*
3 *large cloves garlic*

Mix the soy sauce and garlic together in a large, shallow pan or dish and turn each piece of meat in it. Let the meat marinate for a couple of hours, turning it once in a while. Put a layer of heavy duty foil, perforated every inch or so with a sharp fork or skewer, on the grill, 6–8 inches above hot coals. Put the meat on the foil and cook it for about 20 minutes on each side, sprinkling it with a little of the marinade from time to time.

Grilled Sausages

All kinds of sausages are good grilled over charcoal. Hot dogs, *knockwurst* and *kielbasa* can be broiled over direct heat. The more delicate German sausages, such as *bratwurst* and *weisswurst*, should be broiled slowly on a layer of heavy duty foil, perforated every inch or so with a sharp fork or skewer.

Italian sausages can be cooked over direct heat if they are pricked and parboiled for about 5 minutes to rid them of some of their fat. If the parboiled sausages are put on skewers with chunks of raw peppers and onions, they will be cooked through in 10–15 minutes and the vegetables will be half cooked—a delicious combination. Run the skewers through the sausages the long way for easy handling, or cut them in 2-inch chunks.

If you don't want to parboil the sausages, cook them on perforated foil as far above the coals as possible. Turn them frequently while they are cooking. Cut into a sausage after 20 minutes or so to see if it is cooked through.

Grilled Chicken

Marinate chicken pieces in one of the marinades for an hour or 2. Put a piece of heavy duty foil, perforated every inch or so with a sharp fork or skewer, on the grill, 6–8 inches above the coals, and cook the chicken for about 15 minutes on each side, or until the juice runs clear yellow when you pierce a piece of dark meat with a fork. Put pieces of dark meat toward the hotter center of the fire and the breasts closer to the edges.

Pork and Veal on a Skewer

(SERVES 6–8)

MARINADE
½ cup olive oil
1 large onion, finely chopped   } mixed together with a fork
6 bay leaves, broken in pieces

1 ½ pounds boneless, lean pork, cut in 1 ½-inch cubes
1 ½ pounds boneless leg of veal, cut in 1 ½-inch cubes
1 large sweet onion, cut in eighths and separated into layers

Marinate the pork and veal for at least 6 hours (even overnight, if it is more convenient), mixing it from time to time. Alternate pieces of pork, veal and raw onion on each skewer. Put a piece of perforated foil on the grill, 6–8 inches from moderately hot coals, and grill the meat from 20–30 minutes, turning it frequently and basting it from time to time with a little of the marinade if it seems dry.

Chicken Breasts and Livers on a Skewer

(SERVES 6)

1 pound boned chicken breasts
1 pound chicken livers
6 tablespoons olive oil
1 clove garlic, crushed
1 tablespoon chopped thyme, tarragon or rosemary
cherry tomatoes

} mixed together

Cut the chicken into pieces about 1½-inches square. Trim the livers and cut each one in half. Put the meat in a bowl, pour the flavored oil over it and mix thoroughly. Alternate pieces of chicken and pieces of liver on skewers, adding cherry tomatoes as often as you like. Put a piece of perforated foil on a very hot charcoal fire, as close to the coals as possible. Put the skewers on the foil and cook the meat rapidly, turning the skewers several times and basting with the flavored oil left in the bowl. If the fire is hot enough, 10–15 minutes should be enough time to cook the meat. Serve at once.

FISH COOKED OVER CHARCOAL

It is easy to cook fish over the charcoal grill, using one of the methods described below. Small fish are preferable, I think, because it is very difficult to handle and to time a large fish unless you have one of those wonderful fish-shaped grills. If you want to cook a large fish outdoors, season it, wrap it in foil and cook it on the grill (recipe below).

Grilled Whole Small Fish

(SERVES 6)

6 small whole fish (1–1 ½ pounds each) whatever variety is freshest
       or 6 fish steaks (about ¾ -inch thick)
3 tablespoons soy sauce   ⎫
3 tablespoons vegetable oil   ⎬   *mixed together*
lemons   ⎭

Have the fish cleaned and the heads removed. Wash the fish, dry them well and rub some of the soy sauce and oil mixture into all the exposed surfaces. Put the fish in a hamburger turner and cook it over a hot charcoal fire for 7 or 8 minutes on each side, until the skin is brown and crisp and the flesh is cooked through. A total cooking time of 15 minutes should be enough; stick a knife through to the bone to make sure the fish is opaque throughout, and remove it from the fire the minute it is done. Serve hot with lemon wedges.

Grilled Fish Fillets

(SERVES 4)

Fish cooked this way has crisp, delicious skin and tender, juicy meat. Use any kind of fish.

2 whole, 2-pound fish
4 tablespoons Herb Butter, p. 235
salt and freshly ground pepper
lemons

Have the fish filleted but the skin left on. You will grill them *on one side only.* (Save the trimmings; freeze them to make stock.)

Brush the grill with oil and put it about 6 inches above medium-hot coals. Dot the tops of the fillets with herb butter and sprinkle them with salt, pepper and lemon juice. Put the fillets on the grill, skin side down, and grill them until the flesh is opaque and the butter melts, 10–15 minutes. Loosen the fillets from the grill and remove them very carefully, using 2 spatulas. Serve immediately with lemon wedges.

Clams on the Grill

A wonderful way to cook clams. They can be cooked as a first course while the coals are reaching the right stage for cooking meat.

Put hard-shelled clams on the grill over hot coals. When they have opened, remove them from the fire and eat them while they are hot. They are good without any seasoning, or with a squeeze of lemon and/or some melted butter. It's hard to predict how long they will take to open—it depends on their size and temperature and on how hot the coals are.

Fish Wrapped in Foil

(SERVES 4)

If you want to cook fish this way for more than 4 people, cook 2 fish, each wrapped separately.

4 tablespoons butter, cut in small pieces
2 large tomatoes, sliced
4 scallions including green tops, chopped
4 tablespoons chopped parsley   } mixed together
4 tablespoons chopped basil
salt and freshly ground pepper
a 2½–3 pound fish (bass, sea trout or bluefish, for example), cleaned
    and with head removed

Spread out a large, double-layered piece of heavy duty foil. Put small pieces of butter in a row down the middle of the foil, place on it a row of tomato slices as long as the fish and sprinkle the tomatoes with half the scallion-herb mixture. Sprinkle on about a teaspoon of salt and a few grinds of pepper. Lay the fish on top of the tomatoes. Season its cavity with salt, pepper, a tablespoon or so of the scallion mixture and a few pieces of butter. Sprinkle the top of the fish with salt and pepper, lay the remaining tomato slices along it, sprinkle on the rest of the scallions and herbs and dot with the rest of the butter.

Hold the 2 large edges of the foil together and roll them up to form a tight seal. Roll up the ends of the foil to seal them. Place the package of fish on a grill about 10 inches above hot coals. It will take about 45 minutes to cook. Serve it right out of the foil, spooning the buttery juices over the fish as a sauce.

Variations. The seasonings and vegetables used in this package of fish can be varied endlessly. Tarragon and summer squash make a lovely combination of flavors. Fennel is especially good with fish: use chopped fennel stalks, fennel leaves or anise seeds. If you make the package a little bigger, you can put in some half-cooked potatoes and some zucchini wedges and make a whole meal of it.

VEGETABLES

Vegetables often cook more slowly than meat on a charcoal fire and need a less intense heat, so it's a good idea to cook them before the coals have reached their highest temperature. Then set them along the edges of the fire to keep warm while the meat cooks. I have never had a single morsel of charcoal-cooked vegetables left over; people love them.

Zucchini on a Skewer

1 zucchini per person (as much as you think they will eat)
lots of basil leaves

Cut each zucchini in quarters lengthwise, then into 2-inch pieces. Alternate pieces of zucchini and basil leaves on skewers. Broil over low-medium heat for 25–30 minutes, turning from time to time, until the zucchini is cooked but still a little crisp.

Eggplant is good this way, too. Cook it until it is quite soft.

Mixed Vegetables on a Skewer

Oil and Vinegar Marinade, p. 218
small zucchini, quartered lengthwise and cut into 2-inch pieces
green peppers, seeded and cut into 2-inch squares
sweet onion, peeled and cut in sixths or eighths and separated into
*   layers*
eggplant, cut into 2-inch cubes

Marinate the vegetables for an hour or so, turning them from time to time. Thread them on skewers, in whatever order you like. Cook over a rather slow charcoal fire for about half an hour, or until the eggplant is nice and soft and the other vegetables are crisp-tender. If the vegetables are cooking too fast, put a piece of perforated foil between them and the grill.

Foil Packages of Vegetables

Cook portion-sized packages of vegetables. Put any mixture of vegetables you like in each package. Put the vegetables in the middle of a 12-inch square piece of heavy duty foil, season them with salt, freshly ground pepper and herbs and be generous with the butter. Bring the edges of the foil together and roll them to make a leakproof package. Put the packages on the grill, about 4–6 inches above fairly hot coals. It's a good idea to put in a piece of tomato for its juice, or a few drops of lemon juice or water.

Here are a few suggestions, to give you an idea of ingredients and timing. Add salt and freshly ground pepper to each mixture.

Variations.
Green beans with half a tomato, butter and thyme (about 15
    minutes).
Sliced summer squash, 3 or 4 cherry tomatoes, tarragon and butter
    (about 15 minutes).
A thinly sliced, raw potato, half a tomato, a chopped anchovy, some
    basil and butter (20–25 minutes).
A raw tomato, stuffed with a cooked rice salad or some minced,
    cooked vegetables (10–15 minutes).

Roasted Corn on the Cob

If you're cooking outdoors and want to cook your corn on the grill, here's a way to do it. Shuck the corn shortly before cooking it. Put each ear of corn on a piece of heavy duty foil large enough to wrap it up.

Sprinkle the corn with a few drops of water and some salt and add about a tablespoon of butter to each package. Bring the ends of the foil together and roll them to form a sealed package. Put the packages of corn on top of a hot charcoal fire for 10–15 minutes. Remove the corn and keep it wrapped until ready to serve.

Broiled Peaches with Raspberry Sauce

(SERVES 6)

6 large peaches, cut in half lengthwise, with stones removed
about 1 cup raspberries
sugar
Kirsch

Prick the peach cavities with a fork in several places. Put the peaches, cut side up, on a piece of well-perforated, heavy duty foil. Mash the raspberries and flavor them to taste with sugar and Kirsch. Spoon some of this mixture into each peach half. Put the foil and peaches on the charcoal grill, quite near the coals, and cook for 15–20 minutes, until the peaches and sauce are very hot.

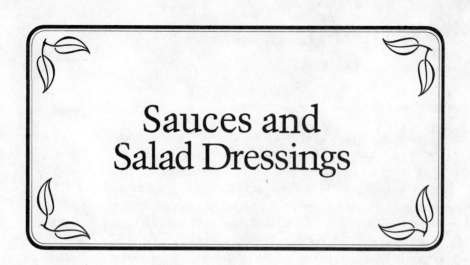

Sauces and Salad Dressings

Anchovy Sauce

(¾ CUP)

This sauce is one that is good to have in the refrigerator. It will keep for a week or so and seems to improve with age.

1 can (2 ounces) flat anchovy fillets with their oil
juice of 1 large lemon
½ cup olive oil
1 large clove garlic, peeled
about ½ cup chopped parsley

Put all the ingredients in the container of a blender or food processor and blend until the sauce is smooth, with small flecks of parsley. Add lots of freshly ground pepper and more chopped parsley if you wish. If you plan to use this sauce as a salad dressing, you may want to add more olive oil. If you add more oil, check to make sure that the sauce is still properly seasoned.

Basil Puree

This is not a sauce. It is the basis for many sauces and adds its fragrance to many foods of all kinds. Everyone can think of new uses for basil puree. Some people like just to spread it on buttered toast or English muffins. Others like to dip things into it: breadsticks, bits of cold meat, raw vegetables, fingers. Spread it on bread, then make your tuna, tomato, cucumber, onion or cold roast beef sandwich. Put a spoonful of it on top of your hot, buttered baked potato. Stir some into a dish of rice or a pot of soup that tastes uninteresting. Try to keep it around the kitchen; it disappears into everything. It freezes perfectly; you can have the flavor of fresh basil all year.

To make basil puree, use 2 cups of loosely packed, coarsely chopped basil leaves to ¼ cup good olive oil. Chop the basil with the oil in a food processor or puree it in a blender. This will give you 4–5 ounces of basil puree. Four-ounce plastic cups, tightly covered with foil and packed in plastic bags, are perfect containers for freezing basil. One of these cupfuls will give you enough basil puree to make the glorious sauce, Pesto, p. 44, for 1 pound of pasta. Some other dishes you need basil puree for are: Basil Crêpes, p. 37, Basil *Gnocchi*, p. 34, and *Pistou*, p. 54.

Cucumber Sauce

(ABOUT 2 CUPS)

1 large cucumber, peeled and seeded
1 cup sour cream
½ cup mayonnaise
¼ cup chopped chives
2 tablespoons chopped mint, optional
salt and freshly ground pepper
lemon juice or vinegar, optional

Shred the cucumber in a food processor or cut it by hand into very small dice. Sprinkle it with 2 teaspoons of salt and put it in a sieve to drain for at least a half hour. Mix the sour cream, mayonnaise, chives and mint together. Pat the cucumbers dry with paper towels and combine them with the sour cream mixture. Taste the sauce and season it with freshly ground pepper and more salt if necessary. If the sauce tastes too bland to you, add a little lemon juice or vinegar.

Egg-Lemon Sauce for Fish

(ABOUT 2½ CUPS)

This versatile Greek sauce is good on fish, chicken and vegetables. Substitute chicken stock for the fish stock to serve with chicken or vegetables.

2 cups fish stock from poaching fish or see p. 69
1 tablespoon cornstarch dissolved in ¼ cup of the cold fish stock
3 egg yolks
juice of ½–1 lemon
salt and freshly ground pepper
1 medium clove garlic, minced, optional

Heat the fish stock in a small saucepan. Whisk the yolks with the juice of half the lemon and the minced garlic, if you are using it. Whisk about a cup of the hot stock into the yolks, then pour the mixture into the hot stock, stirring constantly. Cook, stirring, for about 5 minutes, then stir in the cornstarch. Continue to stir the sauce; it will thicken in a short time. Remove it from the heat and correct the seasoning with salt, pepper and more lemon juice. Serve hot or cold with poached or steamed fish.

This sauce is sensational when made with the liquid from *Moules Marinière*, p. 172. It is the perfect sauce to use for steamed fish which produces no stock of its own. The mussels can be served vinaigrette, p. 174, or on the half shell with Horseradish Sauce, p. 174. Do not use the garlic when making the sauce with mussel juice—it is already quite garlicky enough.

Green Peppercorn Sauce

(ABOUT 1 CUP)

This is a very concentrated sauce, meant to be served cold or hot on cold steak or roast beef. It will seem very thin and salty when it is hot, but when cold it will be a thick, delicious essence with the distinctive flavor of green peppercorns. Don't strain the sauce—the peppercorns are delicious, too.

1 cup good beef broth, either homemade or College Inn
2 tablespoons green peppercorns
1 cup heavy cream

Put the beef broth in a small saucepan and add the green peppercorns and a tablespoon or 2 of their liquid. Bring it to a boil and cook it over medium heat until it is reduced in half (measure it and return it to the pot). Add the cream, bring to a boil, lower the heat and simmer the sauce until it is reduced to 1 cup. Add no salt; the concentrated beef stock will be salty enough. Chill the sauce and serve it cold, with hot or cold meat. This sauce will keep for about a week if it is well refrigerated.

HERB BUTTERS

These are an all purpose, useful, delicate seasoning. Use a dollop to garnish grilled meat, melt a little in a soup, cook eggs in it, spread it on sandwiches or hamburger rolls. Split a loaf of French bread lengthwise, spread it with herb butter and heat it on the charcoal fire.

You can make herb butters in any flavor or strength you like. For a stick of butter (½ cup), use at least 2 tablespoons and not more than 6 tablespoons of chopped herbs—one kind or a mixture of several. The method is the same for all flavors, but let the strength of the herb determine the amount you use.

Let the butter come to room temperature. Mash it in a bowl with the finely chopped herbs and any other seasoning you want to add: a dash of lemon, Tabasco, salt or pepper, an anchovy or a little garlic.

If you have a food processor, you don't even have to chop up the herbs. Cut the butter and the herbs into 1-inch pieces, put them in the container and process them with the metal blade until the butter and herbs are well blended and the herbs are very finely chopped.

Herb butters can be frozen for a short time, but they lose their fresh flavor after a few weeks. Here are some classic combinations. Make up your own, using whatever herbs are available.

Snail Butter
(the classic French seasoning for snails)

1 stick (½ cup) unsalted butter
2 tablespoons chopped scallions, chives or shallots
2 cloves garlic, minced
4 tablespoons minced parsley

Parsley Butter (called Beurre Maître d'Hotel)

1 stick (½ cup) unsalted butter
4 tablespoons very finely chopped parsley
a squeeze of lemon juice

Garlic Butter

1 stick (½ cup) unsalted butter
1–2 cloves garlic, minced

HOLLANDAISE AND ITS VARIATIONS

Hollandaise and Béarnaise are the most famous members of this family. Hollandaise is unmatched for its delicacy and its versatility, Béarnaise for the wonderful combination of suavity and intense flavor. A couple of variations follow each recipe. Both sauces are to be served tepid, not hot. They can be kept at the proper temperature in the top of a double boiler over warm, not hot, water.

These sauces can be made in two different ways: mixing unmelted or melted butter with the yolks. I have given one method for the Hollandaise, the other for Béarnaise—try them both and choose the one you prefer. There are also directions for making both sauces in the blender or food processor—a very simple alternative.

Hollandaise Sauce

(ABOUT 1½ CUPS)

4 egg yolks
¾ cup (1½ sticks) butter, preferably unsalted, cut into small pieces
½ lemon
pinch of salt

Heat some water in the bottom of a double boiler, but do not let it boil. Put the egg yolks in the top of the double boiler and beat them vigorously with a wire whisk for a minute or 2. Put the pot over the hot water and continue to beat. Add a few pieces of the butter, continuing to beat, and as the butter melts and the sauce begins to thicken, continue to add the butter a few pieces at a time. Be sure that the water does not boil. If the sauce seems to be getting very thick at the bottom, remove the pan from the hot water and beat in a few pieces of butter off the heat. When all the butter has been absorbed and the sauce is creamy, remove it from the heat and whisk in a squeeze of lemon juice and a little salt. Taste the sauce and adjust the seasoning with salt and/or lemon juice.

Mousseline Sauce

Whip ½ cup of heavy cream and fold it into the Hollandaise Sauce just before serving. Heavenly with asparagus or broccoli.

Sour Cream Hollandaise

This is an interesting variation. Because it is made with sour cream instead of butter, it is excellent cold and can be made a day in advance. It is even better if you add some chopped fresh dill (dried will not do).

3 egg yolks
1 tablespoon lemon juice
salt
1 cup sour cream
2 tablespoons chopped fresh dill

Whisk the yolks, lemon juice and salt over hot but not boiling water in the top of a double boiler. When the yolks have just begun to thicken, whisk in the sour cream 1 tablespoon at a time, stirring constantly. The sauce is done when it is thick and smooth. Remove it from the heat, stir in the dill and add more salt if necessary. Good with fish and boiled potatoes.

Béarnaise Sauce

(ABOUT 1½ CUPS)

¼ cup tarragon vinegar
¼ cup dry white wine
2 tablespoons minced shallots or the white parts of scallions

2 or 3 1-inch sprigs of fresh tarragon or 1 teaspoon dried tarragon
4 egg yolks
¾ cup (1½ sticks) butter, preferably unsalted
salt
1 tablespoon chopped fresh tarragon or chervil or parsley

Put the vinegar, wine, shallots and tarragon in the top of a double boiler. Over direct heat, boil the mixture vigorously until almost all the liquid has evaporated and there is about 2 tablespoons of shallot slush left in the pan. Remove and discard the sprigs of tarragon.

Heat some water in the bottom of the double boiler but do not let it boil. Melt the butter in a small saucepan. Add the egg yolks to the shallot mixture and beat vigorously with a whisk. Put the yolks over the hot water and continue to beat until they begin to thicken. Do not let the water come to a boil, and beat the yolks constantly or they will cook on the bottom of the pot and the sauce will be ruined.

When the yolks have thickened slightly, begin to pour in the butter very gradually, about a teaspoonful at a time, beating constantly to amalgamate it with the yolks as they thicken. If the sauce seems to be thickening too much or too fast, remove it from the hot water and keep beating it until it cools down a bit. It should be a little thicker than heavy cream. Don't worry if the sauce seems a little thin; it will thicken as it cools. The sauce is done when all the butter has been added. Taste it and add salt. You can strain the sauce or not at this point—I like it with the little bits of shallot left in. Add a good tablespoon of fresh chopped tarragon or chervil leaves. If you have neither of these, add some chopped parsley; do *not* add dried tarragon.

Béarnaise is also good made with herbs other than tarragon. Use plain wine vinegar instead of tarragon vinegar. Thyme and parsley make a good sauce: cook 8 or 10 sprigs of thyme with the shallots, then remove them. Add chopped parsley to the finished sauce. Basil makes a delicious addition to a Béarnaise made without tarragon: stir 2 tablespoons Basil Puree, p. 232, or ¼ cup finely chopped basil leaves into the finished sauce.

Choron Sauce calls for the addition of 2 or 3 tablespoons of tomato puree to a Béarnaise sauce. This is particularly good when the sauce has been made with basil.

Another interesting way to vary both Hollandaise and Béarnaise sauces is to substitute one of the Herb Butters, p. 235, for some or all of the butter in the recipe. Snail Butter is a particularly good one for garlic lovers.

Blender Hollandaise or Béarnaise

Put the yolks and seasonings (lemon juice and salt for Hollandaise, shallot-vinegar slush for Béarnaise) in the container of a blender or food processor. Melt the butter in a small pan until it is bubbling hot (but not brown). Turn on the blender and spin the yolks for a few seconds. Without stopping the motor, pour in the hot butter in a slow but steady stream. Transfer the sauce to the top of a double boiler, put it over warm (not hot) water, and adjust the seasonings. Herbs can be added at this point.

Horseradish Sauce

(1 CUP)

A simple but excellent sauce for cold fish, fish salad and cooked mussels on the half shell.

1 cup sour cream
1–2 tablespoons freshly grated horseradish or prepared horseradish,
    well drained
salt

Combine the sour cream and horseradish and add salt to taste. Let the sauce stand for about half an hour, then taste and adjust the seasoning with salt and/or horseradish.

Hot Sauce for Meat

(ABOUT 1 CUP)

This is a version of the Latin American *salsa cruda* which is always served with grilled meat. It takes about 2 minutes to make—1 minute if you have a food processor. Excellent with any plain meat, hot or cold.

3 very hot red peppers, finely chopped (about 3 tablespoons)
¼ sweet red onion, finely chopped (1–2 tablespoons)
1 large ripe tomato, pureed or finely chopped
½ teaspoon salt

If you have a food processor. Put all the vegetables into the container and process, using the metal blade, until they are fairly finely chopped.

If you use a blender. Puree the tomato first, then add the other vegetables and blend only until they are chopped; the sauce is better if it's a bit crunchy.

If you make the sauce by hand. Here's a word of warning: protect your hands while chopping hot peppers. I always wear an old pair of white cotton gloves (it's the best use you can find for them these days) to keep the fiery juice both from hands and any other parts of the body (especially eyes and lips) you might touch with those peppery fingers.

MAYONNAISE AND ITS VARIATIONS

Homemade mayonnaise is so easy to make that there is really no reason not to use it all the time. People who have gotten into the habit of making their own don't even think of it as a chore; it takes less than 10 minutes to make a pint of it by hand, 3 or 4 minutes in a blender or food processor. The only problem might be that homemade mayonnaise is so good that you eat a lot more of it.

The sauce is an emulsion of egg yolks and oil; the higher the proportion of yolks to oil, the easier it is to make the sauce. Use 2 yolks to 1–1½ cups of oil. Mayonnaise can be made using olive oil, a combination of olive and salad or peanut oil, or all salad oil. All olive oil gives it a very distinctive flavor which is sometimes just what you want, sometimes a bit overpowering. I often use a half-and-half mixture. A small amount of seasoning is usually mixed with the yolks before the oil is added; salt, pepper, lemon juice or vinegar and a pinch of dry mustard are the classic seasonings. Other flavorings are listed at the end of this recipe.

If you follow these directions to the letter you should have no difficulty making mayonnaise. A hand-held electric beater is the most convenient tool to use. If I didn't have one, I'd make mayonnaise in a blender. A wire whisk combined with a lot of energy will also make a fine mayonnaise.

Basic Mayonnaise

(1½ CUPS)

2 egg yolks, at room temperature
salt
2 teaspoons lemon juice or wine vinegar
1½ cups olive oil or half olive oil, half salad oil

Put the egg yolks, the lemon juice or vinegar and a little salt in a small bowl and beat with an electric beater at medium speed until the yolks are thick and sticky. Beating constantly, add the first ½ cup of oil *a drop or two at a time*, making sure that each addition has been completely absorbed by the yolks before adding more. The very gradual addition of the oil makes the difference between the success or failure of this sauce. Do not become impatient and add too much oil at the beginning. By the time the first ½ cup has been added, the mayonnaise will begin to thicken. Add the rest of the oil in a thin stream, beating constantly and moving the beaters around in the bowl to be sure all the oil is beaten into the sauce. As the mayonnaise becomes thick, reduce the speed of the beater. When all the oil has been added, the mayonnaise will be very thick and glossy. If you prefer it a little creamier, beat in a tablespoon or so of boiling water at the very end. Taste the mayonnaise and adjust the seasoning.

Mustard Mayonnaise

Add up to a teaspoon of dry mustard to the yolks before adding the oil, or stir in prepared mustard to taste after the sauce is made. Especially good with cold pork or on ham sandwiches.

Herb or Green Mayonnaise

There are two ways to make this. One is simply to stir a little or a lot of chopped herbs, either one kind or a mixture of several, into the mayonnaise.

The other method is a little more trouble but makes a smoother and beautifully green sauce. Blanch ½–1 cup of herb leaves (include some spinach and/or watercress) in boiling water for a minute or so. Drain the herbs and squeeze them dry in a paper towel. If you are making the mayonnaise in a blender or food processor, add the herbs with the egg. If you are making the mayonnaise by hand, puree the herbs in the blender or chop them very fine by hand and mix the puree with the finished mayonnaise. Wonderful with cold poached or steamed fish or in chicken salads.

Tuna Mayonnaise

Puree half of a 6½-ounce can of tuna in the blender with 1 egg, an extra yolk, the juice of half a lemon and 2 anchovies or ½ teaspoon of salt. Keep the motor going and very gradually add a cup of oil. Especially good as a filling for hard-cooked eggs, mashed with the yolks, or as a dip for raw vegetables.

Very Light Mayonnaise

This can be made by folding ½ cup of heavy cream, whipped, or the beaten white of an egg *very* carefully into the mayonnaise just before serving.

Aioli

Aioli is a *very* garlicky mayonnaise. Push 3, 4, 5 or even 6 cloves of garlic through the garlic press and beat them for several minutes with the yolks before adding the oil to a hand-beaten mayonnaise. *Aioli* should be made only with olive oil. I never make *aioli* in the blender; for some reason, the garlic never seems to taste quite right. But if you add a lot of crushed garlic to Blender Mayonnaise, p. 245 , you will have something very like *aioli*.

Aioli is best served as the centerpiece of a cold meal consisting of cooked fish and/or shellfish, hard-cooked eggs, boiled new potatoes, and an assortment of raw and/or lightly blanched vegetables, each dipped into the *aioli* before eating. It is one of the best meals in the world. For 6 people you will need at least 2 cups of *aioli*.

Skordalía

A Greek version of *aioli*, this is made using less oil and adding bread, ground almonds and parsley. It is very easy to make in a blender or food processor and is especially good with cold fish and raw vegetables.

2 slices white bread
¼ cup blanched almonds
2 egg yolks
lemon juice
salt
½ cup olive oil
5–6 large sprigs parsley
4–6 cloves garlic, crushed

Soak the bread in a little water and squeeze it dry. Grind the almonds in the blender or food processor, then add the bread, broken into small pieces, the egg yolks, a good squeeze of lemon juice and a little salt. Process or blend until everything is combined, then very gradually add the oil until the sauce has the consistency of thick mayonnaise. Add the parsley and blend until it is chopped. Put the sauce in a bowl and squeeze in the garlic, blending it in one clove at a time, until you have added as much as you like. Taste the sauce and adjust the seasoning with salt and/or lemon juice.

Blender Mayonnaise

(1 CUP)

Put 1 whole egg, 2 teaspoons of lemon juice or vinegar and a little salt in the container of a blender or food processor. Blend for a few seconds. Continuing to blend, add 1 cup of oil *in a very thin stream.* The mayonnaise will begin to thicken after about half the oil has been added. Put the mayonnaise in a bowl, taste and adjust the seasoning.

Onion-Vinegar Sauce

(ABOUT 1 CUP)

An excellent vinegar is essential for this sauce—sherry wine vinegar is my favorite. Use for roasted or grilled meat.

2 large sweet onions, finely chopped
½ cup excellent quality vinegar
½ cup water
freshly ground pepper
2 tablespoons butter, optional

Cook the onions in the vinegar and ½ cup water over low heat until the onions are very soft and the mixture is reduced to about a cup. Remove it from the heat and add 8–10 grinds of pepper. If you are serving the sauce hot, put the butter in the hot sauce, off the heat, and tip the pot from side to side until the butter has melted and amalgamated with the sauce. You can make the sauce in advance and reheat it before adding the butter.

Omit the butter if you are serving the sauce cold.

TOMATO SAUCES

Homemade tomato sauce is one of the staples of the summer kitchen, and the winter one too, because it freezes very well. It's well worth the trouble of making a lot of tomato sauce when the big tomato crop comes in. I usually freeze the sauce in plastic cocktail glasses, a convenient 1-cup size, and defrost as many as I need. The tomatoes retain an absolutely fresh flavor and the sauce is incomparably better than anything you can buy. It is also very convenient to keep a jar of the sauce in the refrigerator during the summer to use in soups, rice, pasta, for cooking fish or chicken or flavoring stuffed vegetables.

Tomato Sauce with Butter

(ABOUT 3 CUPS)

This sauce is cooked a short time so it retains its fresh flavor and a pleasantly chunky texture. It is a delicate sauce, excellent just as it is on pasta, or used as a last-minute addition to other dishes when it will not be cooked very long.

4 tablespoons butter
1 medium onion, finely chopped (about ½ cup)
about 2 pounds ripe tomatoes, preferably Italian plum tomatoes or
*   6–8 large ripe tomatoes, peeled and coarsely chopped*
6 large leaves fresh basil, chopped (about 2 tablespoons)
2 tablespoons chopped parsley
½–1 teaspoon salt
freshly ground pepper
sugar (not more than ½ teaspoon)

It is best to make this sauce in a pan with a large surface so that the liquid will evaporate rapidly and the tomatoes will cook in a short time.

Melt the butter in a large skillet, add the onion and cook slowly, without browning, 5–10 minutes, until the onion is soft. Stir in the tomatoes, the herbs and about a teaspoon of salt. Cook the sauce rapidly, stirring frequently, until most of the juice from the tomatoes has evaporated. This should not take more than 5–10 minutes. Taste the sauce and add a little sugar if necessary. The addition of even a very little bit of sugar makes an amazing difference in the mellowness of the flavor; the amount needed will depend on the acidity of the tomatoes, which varies considerably. Add more salt if necessary, and 3 or 4 grinds of pepper.

Pour the sauce immediately over freshly cooked pasta (this is enough for 1½ pounds), add it to a pan of half-cooked, sautéed fish steaks, stir it into some cooked rice to serve with grilled meat or put it in a jar and refrigerate it for future use. The sauce will keep in the refrigerator for about 2 weeks.

Tomato Sauce with Olive Oil

(ABOUT 3 CUPS)

This sauce is cooked until it is smooth and a little concentrated. Since it is made with olive oil, which will not congeal when it is cold, it can be used equally well in hot or cold dishes.

> 4 tablespoons olive oil
> 1 medium onion, finely chopped (about ½ cup)
> 1 large clove garlic, finely chopped
> about ½ cup of a combination of chopped herbs such as parsley,
>   thyme, summer savory and oregano, marjoram, basil or
>   rosemary (but never basil and rosemary together)
> about 2 pounds ripe tomatoes, preferably Italian plum tomatoes or
>   6–8 large ripe tomatoes, peeled and coarsely chopped
> ½–1 teaspoon salt
> freshly ground pepper
> a little sugar

Heat the olive oil in a large skillet, add the onion and cook it slowly, without browning, until it is soft, 5–10 minutes. Add the garlic, stir it in well, then add the tomatoes, the herbs and some salt. Cook the sauce over medium low heat, stirring from time to time, for about 30 minutes, until it is thick and quite smooth. Cook a little longer if it is still too liquid. Taste the sauce and add as much sugar as is needed to take the edge off the acidity of the tomatoes. Add more salt if necessary, and a few grinds of pepper. If you like a more garlicky flavor, stir in another clove of finely chopped garlic at this point. Use the sauce immediately, refrigerate it up to 2 weeks, or freeze it.

Tomato Sauce with Cream and Tarragon
(ABOUT 3 CUPS)

4 tablespoons butter
4 scallions including green tops, thinly sliced
6–8 ripe tomatoes (about 2 pounds), peeled, seeded and coarsely
    chopped
1 heaping tablespoon chopped fresh tarragon
1 cup heavy cream
salt and freshly ground pepper
a little sugar

Melt the butter in a saucepan and add the scallions. Cook them over medium heat for 2 or 3 minutes, add the tomatoes and the tarragon, mix well and simmer the sauce over medium heat for 20–30 minutes, until it is reduced by about a third. Add the cream and a little salt and pepper and simmer the sauce for another 5–10 minutes. Taste the sauce and correct the seasoning, adding a little sugar if the tomatoes are too tart. Serve over freshly cooked pasta (this is enough for 1½ pounds), with Sautéed Chicken, p. 195 or Chicken Liver Custard, p. 33.

This sauce can be used to make an exquisite Cream of Tomato with Tarragon soup, p. 62.

Cooked Basil-Tomato Sauce
(ABOUT 1 CUP)

4 tablespoons butter
2 cups ripe tomatoes, peeled and chopped
8–10 large leaves of basil, very finely chopped or 1 tablespoon Basil
    Puree, p. 232
salt

Melt the butter in a small saucepan, add the tomatoes and cook over medium-high heat, stirring from time to time, until the tomatoes are reduced to 1 cup. Stir in the chopped basil or the basil puree, add salt to taste, and keep the sauce warm over very low heat or over hot water until it is needed. Good cold, too.

This sauce is especially good with the Fish Mousse, p. 163, hot or cold, or in stuffing for zucchini. Sauces for fish are listed in the index.

SALAD DRESSINGS

Basic Vinaigrette Dressing

(ABOUT 1 CUP)

Vinaigrette is as basic to good eating as each of the very simple elements that go into it. Good olive oil, fresh lemon juice or wine vinegar, fresh garlic, salt and freshly ground pepper should always be found in any kitchen, however modestly equipped. Mix them together, in proportions to suit your taste, and you have a Vinaigrette Dressing, useful not only as a salad dressing but for cooked vegetables, chicken, meat and fish, rice, dried beans and lentils. Add small amounts of chopped herbs or substitute herb vinegar or walnut oil to vary the flavor.

juice of ½ a small lemon (2–3 teaspoons)
or 2–3 teaspoons wine vinegar
4 tablespoons olive oil
1 medium clove garlic, minced
salt and freshly ground pepper

} *beaten together with a fork*

Arugula Vinaigrette

(ABOUT 1 CUP)

Arugula and vegetables in the cabbage family have an affinity for one another. This dressing is especially good with raw or cooked cabbage (red or green), kohlrabi, broccoli and cauliflower.

½ cup finely chopped arugula leaves
⅔ cup olive oil
3 tablespoons wine vinegar
1 clove garlic, peeled
salt and freshly ground pepper

Puree in the blender or food processor. Taste and adjust the seasoning.

Garlicky Mayonnaise Dressing

(ABOUT 1 CUP)

This dressing is good with fish, chicken and potato salads.

1 cup mayonnaise, preferably homemade
2 or 3 large cloves garlic, crushed
2 or 3 tablespoons vinegar
salt and plenty of freshly ground pepper

Combine all the ingredients and use in a salad or over hard-cooked eggs.

TO MAKE YOGURT

(2 CUPS)

Bring 2 cups of milk to a boil, let it simmer for a minute, then turn it off and let it cool until you can hold your finger in it to a count of 10 (105–110 degrees). Put 2 teaspoons of plain yogurt in a jar or dish which has a good cover. Stir a little of the warm milk into the yogurt, then add the rest of the milk and mix very thoroughly. Cover the dish, wrap it in a large terry towel and put it in a sheltered place for 8 hours or overnight. The turned-off oven is a good place; so is a Styrofoam food carrier. Chill the yogurt when it has thickened, and save a little bit to start the next batch.

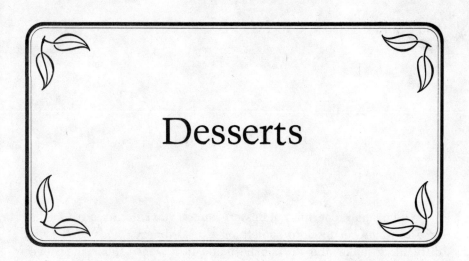

Desserts

SUMMER FRUITS

Summer fruits are luscious, irresistible. Nothing is better than eating them just as they are—ripe, juicy, fragrant, unadorned. What could be more seductive than a sun-warmed peach, more luxurious than a bowl of just picked raspberries?

There are also exquisite desserts that can be made with summer fruits. The secret, as usual, is simplicity and purity. A fine, buttery crust complements blueberries. Gooseberry Fool, made of nothing but fruit, cream and sugar, is enough to make a summer meal memorable. Wild black raspberries, picked by the side of the road in July, can be turned into a celestial ice cream, one of the few acceptable ways of freezing summer fruits.

All of these dessert recipes use summer fruits as their main ingredient. Some cream or fresh cheese, eggs, a little wine or liqueur, and sugar used with great discretion almost completes the list of other ingredients used in this chapter.

DESSERT SAUCES

With a small repertoire of dessert sauces, you can turn a fruit salad or a bowl of berries into something extraordinary. None of these is difficult to make and all can be made in advance. Pour them over berries or cut-up fruit. A bowl of Zabaglione Sauce is a wonderful dip for handsome, unhulled strawberries. Custard Sauce is especially good with stewed plums or peaches. The Kirsch and Strawberry Sauces are both excellent on fruit salads made with peaches, nectarines and melons. *Crème Fraîche*, homemade sour cream, is good on almost everything: raw fruit, cooked fruit and fruit tarts.

Zabaglione Sauce

(ABOUT 2 CUPS)

6 egg yolks
3 tablespoons sugar
½ cup Marsala wine
½ cup heavy cream, whipped, optional

Fill a large bowl with ice and a little water. Bring some water to a boil in the bottom of a double boiler. Beat the egg yolks for 2 or 3 minutes in the top of the double boiler, gradually beat in the sugar and Marsala and place the pot over the just boiling water. Use an electric hand beater if you have one, a whisk if you don't. Continue to beat, without stopping, until the sauce is thick and foaming, 5–10 minutes. When the sauce has thickened, immediately put the pot into the bowl of ice and continue to beat *until the sauce is cool*. If you stop too soon, the sauce will separate. If this happens, beat it again just before serving. Fold the whipped cream into the finished sauce, if you wish.

Kirsch Sauce

(ABOUT 1 CUP)

3 egg yolks
¼ cup sugar
¼ cup Kirsch or other unsweetened fruit brandy or whiskey
½ cup heavy cream, whipped

Beat the yolks with the sugar until they are thick, 3 or 4 minutes. Gradually beat in the Kirsch. Fold in the whipped cream and chill the sauce.

Custard Sauce

(ABOUT 2½ CUPS)

4 egg yolks
¼ cup sugar
a pinch of salt
2 cups milk, brought to the boiling point
1 teaspoon vanilla or 1–2 tablespoons brandy or liqueur

Beat the yolks with the sugar and salt in the top of a double boiler, over hot but not boiling water, for a minute or 2. Gradually whisk in the hot milk and cook the sauce over the hot water, whisking constantly, until it is thick and smooth—about 5 minutes. Add the vanilla or other flavoring and chill the sauce.

Strawberry Sauce

(ABOUT 1 CUP)

1 pint strawberries
¼ cup sugar
¼ cup Grand Marnier, Curaçao or Cointreau

Wash and hull the berries and chop them in a food processor or slice them by hand. Put the berries in a small saucepan, stir in the sugar and bring them to a boil. Turn down the heat and simmer for 2 minutes—not more, or the fruit will lose its fresh flavor. Add the liqueur and taste the sauce. Add a little more sugar if necessary. Serve chilled or at room temperature.

Crème Fraîche

(1 CUP)

Pour 1 cup of unsterilized heavy sweet cream into a jar, stir in 1 teaspoon of buttermilk, cover the jar, shake well and let it stand at room temperature for 24 hours, or until the cream has thickened. Refrigerate. *Crème Fraîche* will keep for several weeks in the refrigerator.

Blueberry Tart

(ONE 8-INCH TART)

PASTRY
½ cup butter, at room temperature
½ cup cream cheese, at room temperature
1 cup flour

FILLING
4 cups blueberries or raspberries, washed and stemmed
about ¼ cup honey (more or less, depending on the sweetness of the
    berries)

GARNISH
½ cup Crème Fraîche, above

To make the pastry, mash the butter and cream cheese together. Blend in the flour, using your fingers, and form the dough into a ball. Chill it for about an hour.

Preheat the oven to 375°.

Roll out the dough on a well-floured board and press it into an 8-inch flan ring or pie plate or 6 small individual tart pans. Prick the bottom of the pastry several times with a fork and put the pan on the middle shelf of the oven. After 5 minutes, prick the shell again to keep it from bubbling up from the bottom of the pan and continue to bake a few more minutes, until the crust is lightly browned. Let it cool.

To prepare the filling, put the honey, 2 tablespoons of water and 1 cup of the berries in a small saucepan over medium heat. Bring them to a boil, turn down the heat and cook the berries, stirring frequently, for about 10 minutes, or until they form a slightly syrupy jam. Let the cooked fruit cool for a few minutes, then mix it with the uncooked berries. Pour the berries into the baked tart shell just before serving, and top each portion with a dollop of *Crème Fraîche*.

Raspberry and Currant Tarts

(ONE 8-INCH TART)

2 cups raspberries
2 cups currants, stemmed
sugar to taste

Put the raspberries and currants in a small saucepan with 2 tablespoons of water and ½ cup of sugar. Mix them together and bring the fruit very gradually to the boil. Turn down the heat and simmer it for 5 minutes. Turn off the heat and taste the fruit. Add sugar to taste while the fruit is hot. Let it cool and use it to fill the tart shell(s), adding it at the last minute so it does not make the pastry soggy.

Gooseberry Tarts

(ONE 8-INCH TART)

4 cups gooseberries
sugar to taste

Follow the directions for cooking the fruit in the preceding recipe. The gooseberries may need considerably more sugar than the raspberries and currants. Add it gradually, tasting after each addition. Gooseberry tarts must be very tart.

Sweet and Sour Cherry Soup (Kisselitza)

(3–4 QUARTS)

Beautiful and delicious, this clear red fruit soup tastes like the essence of summer.

This is an excellent way to use less-than-perfect fruit (but be sure to cut away the soft parts). Only the cherries have to be perfect. *Kisselitza* freezes very well.

2 pounds sour cherries, stemmed
2 pounds sweet cherries, stemmed
4 pounds mixed plums, peaches, apricots and nectarines, cut in half
    and pitted
sugar to taste

Put the fruit in a large pot, add 6 cups of water and bring it to a boil. Lower the heat, cover the pot and simmer until the fruit is soft but not mushy, 15–20 minutes. Remove the pot from the heat and add just enough sugar to make the tartness of the fruit bearable. Stir until the sugar is dissolved and chill the soup. Serve cold.

Coeur à la Crème

(SERVES 6–8)

Fresh cheese and sweet cream molded in a basket makes a lovely summer dessert. If you have the traditional heart-shaped mold it's very pretty, but any ordinary, small, un-dyed basket works perfectly well as a mold. I prefer *Coeur à la Crème* unsweetened, made with ricotta and served with whatever fruit is at its peak; strawberries, raspberries, juicy peaches or nectarines are all good, and it is especially good with tart, homemade currant jelly. For those who like a somewhat firmer, richer dish, there's an alternate mixture given, and you may add a little sugar if you like.

1 pound cottage cheese
1 pound ricotta or 1 pound cream cheese, at room temperature

1 cup heavy cream, whipped
2 egg whites, stiffly beaten
1–2 tablespoons sugar, optional
fresh fruit, sliced and slightly sweetened

Line a 1 ½ –2-quart basket with dampened cheesecloth.

Put the cottage cheese and ricotta or cream cheese in a large mixing bowl. Beat them together until they are smooth with an electric beater or mixer. You can mix the cheeses in a food processor but be careful not to overprocess or the cheese will become quite liquid. Fold in the whipped cream and, when it is thoroughly blended, fold in the beaten egg whites.

Scrape the mixture into the prepared mold. Put the mold on a rack on a plate (2 crossed sticks or pieces of silverware will serve as a rack), cover with plastic wrap and let the cheese drain at least 6–8 hours, preferably overnight. You can make this dish 24 hours in advance if it is very well refrigerated.

Turn the cheese out of the basket onto a serving plate and peel off the cheesecloth. Decorate the platter with whole berries, leaves or flowers. Serve cold with fruit.

Crème Brûlée *with Blueberries*

(SERVES 6–8)

The tart berries, the bland, smooth, cold cream and the crisp, sweet crust of sugar make an incomparable combination. This is a first-rate dessert. It is worth lighting the broiler and getting down on your knees to tend it for a couple of minutes.

2 cups (1 pint) blueberries, washed, dried and stemmed
1 ½ cups heavy cream
½ cup milk   } mixed together and heated
1 tablespoon sugar   to the boiling point
a pinch of salt
8 egg yolks
1 teaspoon vanilla
½–1 cup granulated brown sugar or plain brown sugar, sifted

Put the blueberries in a 9- or 10-inch glass pie plate or shallow, heat-proof serving dish of a similar capacity (about 4 cups). Whisk the egg yolks in the top of a double boiler over hot but not boiling water. Very gradually whisk the hot cream into the egg yolks. Do not let the water in the bottom of the double boiler come to a boil, and do not stop whisking. The cream and egg yolks will thicken into a light custard in a very short time—5 minutes at the most. It is not necessary to continue cooking the custard once it has thickened. Stir in the vanilla and pour the custard over the berries. Put the dish in the refrigerator.

When the custard is thoroughly chilled, in 1–2 hours, remove it from the refrigerator. Light the broiler. Sprinkle the brown sugar in an even layer over the top of the custard, covering it completely. Slide the plate under the broiler to melt the sugar. The plate should be 2–3 inches from the element. Watch it carefully; move it if necessary to be sure the sugar melts evenly. As soon as all the sugar has melted, and before it burns, remove the plate from the broiler. The sugar will have turned into a brittle crust. The melting of the sugar can be a tricky business. It is better to have a little unmelted sugar than a black, inedible mess, so err on the side of caution the first time you make this.

Return the custard to the refrigerator until serving time. If the crust is very hard, it may be necessary to tap it with the side of a spoon to divide it into portions.

You can make *Crème Brûlée* in individual custard cups or soufflé dishes—it is attractive and easy to serve.

FRUIT SALADS

All summer fruits can be cut up and combined to make fruit salads. This is an especially good way to use fruit that is slightly bruised or otherwise imperfect, but only if it is perfectly ripe. If a piece of fruit doesn't taste good enough to eat out of hand, putting it in a salad won't improve it.

When putting together a fruit salad, aim for contrasts in color, texture and flavor. A tart citrus or yogurt dressing is good to use on melons or other sweet fruit; a sweetened berry puree makes a lovely sauce for peaches or nectarines that are a little tart. Whole berries of all kinds add a good contrast of texture to most sliced fruits.

A perfect fruit salad is a big bowl of all kinds of summer fruits: peaches, plums, melons, nectarines, apricots—cut in large chunks, sprinkled with an assortment of berries and served with a few sauces (pp. 256-258) for dipping.

Melons are one of the glories of summer, to be enjoyed every day during the height of the season. Ripe melons are at their best slightly chilled (too much chilling kills their flavor), cut into wedges and eaten with a spoon. For a pleasant contrast in tastes, try a squeeze of lime juice on cantaloupe, a discreet sprinkling of salt on watermelon, of powdered ginger on honeydew.

A fruit salad consisting only of different kinds of melon, cut into chunks and dressed generously with fresh orange or lime juice, is a beautiful and refreshing summer dessert. The melon chunks can be served individually in the shells of cantaloupes or in one big watermelon bowl. Berries are an excellent and attractive addition to a melon salad.

Fruit Salad with Yogurt

(SERVES 6)

This salad makes an excellent summer breakfast. This combination of fruits happens to be especially good, but of course you can vary it with what's choice and available. If you add plums, put them in at the last minute so they don't make the dressing too liquid.

> 1 *cantaloupe, very ripe*
> 2 *large peaches*
> 1 *cup blueberries*
> 1 *cup plain yogurt, preferably homemade, p. 253* ⎱
> ½ *cup brown sugar*   ⎬ *mixed together*
> *juice of ½ lemon*   ⎰

Peel and seed the cantaloupe, cut it into bite-sized pieces and put it in a serving bowl. Cut up the peaches and add them to the melon; there's no need to peel them unless you want to. Add the berries. Gently fold in the yogurt mixture, taking care not to bruise the fruit. Refrigerate for a few hours. Leave the fruit at room temperature for about half an hour before serving, and stir it up again to make sure it is well combined.

Gooseberry Fool

(SERVES 6–8)

> 4 *cups gooseberries*
> ½–1 *cup sugar*
> 1 *cup heavy cream*

Wash the gooseberries. There is no need to top and tail them. Put the berries and ½ cup of sugar in a heavy saucepan and cook very gently until the sugar melts and the berries have given up some of their juice. Then raise the heat slightly and cook the berries, stirring frequently, until they are soft. Put the berries through a food mill or sieve (not the blender). Taste the puree and add sugar if you wish. Whip the cream and fold it thoroughly into the fruit. Chill the fool for several hours in the refrigerator or in the freezer. It is very good slightly frozen, but don't let it get hard. Serve small portions—it's powerful stuff!

The gooseberry puree freezes perfectly. Thaw, fold in the cream, and serve on some special winter occasion.

GRANITE *(ITALIAN WATER ICES)*

(SERVES 6–8)

Granite are the most refreshing of summer desserts and provide a fine way to capture the flavor of summer fruits and save them for winter (actually, they are so good they rarely last beyond autumn). Try making coffee *granita* too—just brew 3 cups of extra strong, lightly sweetened espresso and follow the directions for freezing it.

The food processor has revolutionized the making of *granita*; it can pulverize cubes of flavored ice in a couple of minutes to make a smooth-textured sherbet. The old-fashioned, handmade *granita* has large, slightly crunchy ice crystals. I prefer it and give directions for both methods.

Strawberry Granita

1 quart strawberries
½ cup sugar
1 cup water } *boiled together for 5 minutes and cooled*
juice of 1 orange or ⅓ cup orange juice

Wash and hull the strawberries and puree them, in the blender with the sugar water and orange juice or in the food processor with the juice, and mix them into the sugar water. Taste the mixture and add more sugar if you like.

To make granita *by hand.* Put the puree in a metal bowl in the coldest part of the freezer. After about an hour, when the *granita* starts to solidify, stir it with a large fork, scraping the frozen puree from the bottom and sides of the bowl and mashing it in well. Repeat this every half-hour or so, using a fork or potato masher, until the *granita* has completely crystalized. There should be no large lumps—only crystals of flavored ice. If it is lumpy, take it out of the freezer for a few minutes and chop it up with a fork. Once it has crystalized, the *granita* will keep for quite a while in a tightly covered container. If it should solidify, thaw it slightly, chop it and mash it again and put it back in the freezer.

To make granita *in the food processor.* Freeze the fruit puree, using 2 ice-cube trays. When it is frozen solid, just before serving, process as many cubes as you need. Put the cubes into the processor (not more than one ice tray at a time) and, using the metal blade, process the ice until it is fine, smooth and free of lumps. You will have to turn the motor on and off a number of times—do this rapidly or you will soon have a liquid puree again. Serve the ice immediately and store the unused cubes in plastic bags.

Watermelon Granita

4 pounds watermelon
juice of 1 large lemon (3–4 tablespoons) or more
2 tablespoons sugar
½ teaspoon salt

Make this ice only with delicious, ripe melon. Cut the melon from the rind and remove the seeds. Cut it into 1-inch chunks and puree it in the food processor or blender. If you are using a blender, press the watermelon down in the container with your fingers to make enough juice to puree the melon. Put the puree in a metal bowl and season it to taste with lemon juice, sugar and salt. Remember that its flavor will be much less intense when it is frozen, so don't be afraid to use plenty of lemon juice and salt. Freeze the Watermelon *Granita*, following the directions in the preceding recipe.

ICE CREAM

(SERVES 6–8)

Fresh fruit ice creams—or vanilla ice cream with fresh fruit—are wonderful in summer. If you have an ice cream freezer, you probably have a favorite basic mixture. Follow the directions for freezing that come with your freezer.

Basic Ice Cream Mixture

3 cups heavy cream
2 cups half-and-half
¾ cups sugar
2 teaspoons vanilla
a pinch of salt

This makes a creamy, not-too-sweet ice cream. Our best fruit ice cream is made with the wild black raspberries, called blackcaps, which ripen near us in early July. (They are also very good in *Crème Brûlée*, p. 261.) But other fruits are good, too. To make *fresh fruit ice cream*, add 2 cups of fruit puree to the basic mixture and omit the vanilla. Adjust the sugar to taste.

FRESH FRUIT PIES

Summer fruit pies can be made with peaches, apricots, plums, nectarines, summer apples, green tomatoes, sweet and/or sour cherries, blueberries or gooseberries. Peaches and apricots should be peeled before slicing; plums need not be peeled unless you object to the very tart flavor of their skins. Cherries must be pitted, blueberries stemmed, gooseberries topped and tailed. You will need about 5 cups of sliced fruit or 4 cups of cherries or berries for a 9-inch pie. The amount of sugar you need depends upon how tart the fruit is and how sweet you like it. The flavor of brown sugar is especially good in fruit pies. If you use a lattice crust, you can add more sugar during baking if the fruit tastes too tart.

The considerable amount of juice produced by baking fruits should be thickened *a little bit* to help it cling to the fruit. Always add less thickening than you think you need; a very runny pie is still delicious and there's no remedy for the sticky mess produced by too much flour or corn starch. Add about 2 tablespoons of flour to the fruit before putting it in the crust or pour a small amount of an egg yolk-cream mixture over the fruit to combine with the juices into a delicious, thin custard.

In the recipes that follow, the Green Tomato and Apple Pie filling is thickened with flour. Add another tablespoon or so of flour to juicier fruits such as plums, cherries or blueberries.

The custard used to thicken the filling in the peach pie is equally good with nectarines, apricots and plums. Add a dash of powdered cinnamon to the custard for a plum pie.

Green Tomato and Apple Pie

(9-INCH PIE)

This pie tastes best when it is made with the early autumn apples that ripen at just about the end of tomato season. Look for apples with a very apple-like taste; the green tomatoes will supply the tartness.

PASTRY
1 ½ cups flour mixed with a dash of salt
¾ cup cold butter, cut into small pieces
1 egg

FILLING
4 or 5 apples
4 or 5 green tomatoes
juice of ½ lemon
¾ cup brown sugar
2 tablespoons flour
½ teaspoon salt

Prepare the pie dough by working the butter into the flour, using a pastry blender, 2 knives or your fingers, until it has the consistency of meal. Stir in the egg with a fork and work the dough into a ball. Roll a little more than ½ the dough into a bottom crust or press it into a 9-inch pie plate with your fingers. Refrigerate the pie plate and the remaining dough while you prepare the filling.

Preheat the oven to 375°.

Peel and core the apples and cut them into thin wedges. Cut the tomatoes into thin wedges and put them in a bowl with the apples. Squeeze the lemon over the fruit, then sprinkle on the sugar, flour and salt. Mix the filling thoroughly, using your hands, and put it into the pie plate. Roll out the rest of the dough and cover the pie. Dip your finger in water and run it along the pie plate between the two crusts, then press the edges together with a fork and trim the crust. Slash the top to allow the steam to escape and bake the pie on the bottom shelf of the oven for about 45 minutes, or until the crust is browned and the fruit is tender (stick a knife into it through the slash in the crust to see if it is done). Serve warm or cool.

Peach Pie

1 recipe Pastry, p. 269
6 or 7 large peaches or about 2 pounds nectarines, apricots or plums
2 egg yolks
½ cup heavy cream
½ cup brown sugar

Preheat the oven to 375°.

Make the dough for the piecrust and line a 9-inch pie plate with it. Put the pie plate and the remaining dough in the refrigerator while you prepare the peaches.

Dip the peaches briefly into boiling water to loosen their skins, and peel them. Cut them, over a bowl, into thin wedges and put the fruit in the bowl. Beat the egg yolks, the cream and brown sugar together with a fork. Remove the unused piece of dough from the refrigerator and roll it out, ⅛-inch thick. Cut the dough into inch-wide strips to be used for a lattice crust.

Spoon the peaches into the bottom crust, using a slotted spoon, combine the juice left in the bowl with the egg yolk mixture and pour the mixture over the peaches. Put the lattice crust on the pie and put it on the bottom shelf of the oven. After half an hour, move the pie to the middle of the oven. Taste a little of the juice—if it is too tart, spoon a little brown sugar onto the fruit between the strips of crust. Bake 10 or 15 minutes more. Serve warm or cool.

Brandied Peach Mousse

2 pounds fresh, ripe peaches or nectarines or apricots
2 tablespoons sugar
2–3 tablespoons brandy
a generous squeeze of lemon juice
1 envelope unflavored gelatin
½ cup heavy cream
3 egg whites

Drop the peaches into a pan of boiling water for a minute to loosen the skins. Peel and slice them; you should have about 3 cups. Put the peaches in a bowl, sprinkle them with the sugar, brandy and lemon juice and let them marinate for about 15 minutes, stirring gently from time to time.

Sprinkle the gelatin into ½ cup of cold water in a small saucepan. Let it soften for 5 minutes, then heat it until the gelatin is thoroughly dissolved.

Set aside 1 cup of the peaches. Put the remaining peaches, the peach juice and the dissolved gelatin into the container of a blender or food processor and blend to a fine puree. Pour the puree into a large bowl. Taste, and adjust the seasoning with sugar and/or brandy.

Whip the cream and fold it into the peach puree. Beat the egg whites in a separate bowl until they are stiff but not dry, and fold them into the peach mixture. Pour half the mixture into a 1½-quart soufflé dish or serving dish. Cover it with the reserved peach slices and add the remaining mousse. Chill for 3 or 4 hours until set.

Decorate the mousse with peaches, berries or just some fresh green leaves before serving.

Plum Compote

(SERVES 6–8)

Stewed fresh plums are nothing like canned ones. Add just as much sugar as you have to, and serve plain or with a Custard Sauce, p. 257. Peaches are good this way, too.

2 cups red or white wine (sweet wine is fine, but use less sugar)
½ cup sugar
a 2-inch piece of cinnamon bark or ½ teaspoon powdered cinnamon
2 pounds plums

Put the wine in a 2–3 quart saucepan, mix in the sugar, add the cinnamon and bring the wine to a boil. Let it simmer slowly while you cut the plums in half and pit them. Put the plums in the wine and simmer them, partially covered, for about 10 minutes. Taste the juice and add more sugar to taste. Cook the plums for 5 more minutes and let them cool in the juice. Serve cold, with Custard Sauce if you wish.

Plumpernickel

(SERVES 6–8)

3 pounds plums, pitted and cut in half
½ cup water
5 or 6 tablespoons brown sugar
1 twelve-ounce package square, dark, thinly sliced pumpernickel
½ cup heavy cream, whipped or Crème Fraiche, p. 258

Cook the plums in the water until they are soft but not mushy. Add the brown sugar while they are cooking, sweetening the plums until they are only slightly tart.

While the fruit is cooking, butter a 1-quart soufflé dish or mold. Cut the crusts from the pumpernickel and use the slices to line the mold on the bottom and the sides. Cut the bread so that it fits exactly, in one layer, without overlapping the slices.

After the fruit has cooked, spoon most of the hot juice all over the bread, then fill the lined dish with the fruit. Cover the fruit with a single layer of bread slices, and spoon the remaining juice over the top. Cover the mold with a double layer of foil and place a plate on top. Choose a plate slightly smaller than the mold, so it will fit inside it. Weight the mold with a heavy can or stone and refrigerate it for about 24 hours. Unmold the Plumpernickel and serve it with whipped cream or Crème Fraîche.

Tart Strawberry Mousse

(SERVES 6)

¼ cup orange juice
1 envelope unflavored gelatin
1 pint strawberries
4 tablespoons sugar or to taste
1 cup sour cream

Put the orange juice in your smallest saucepan (a metal measuring cup is fine) and sprinkle the gelatin over it. Wash and hull the strawberries and put them in the container of a food processor or press them down hard in a blender container until they form a little juice in the bottom of the container. Sprinkle them with the sugar. Heat the orange juice-gelatin mixture until the gelatin has melted and the juice is clear. Puree the strawberries, then add the gelatin and continue to process or blend until it is well blended in. Add the sour cream and blend it in well. Taste the mixture and blend in more sugar if you wish.

Pour the mousse into 6 individual soufflé dishes or into stemmed wine glasses and refrigerate it for at least 3 hours before serving.

Zucchini Bread

(1 LARGE LOAF)

2 cups grated zucchini (2 medium zucchini, about 1 ½ pounds)
1 teaspoon salt
3 eggs
1 cup brown sugar
1 cup (2 sticks) melted butter
3 cups white flour or 2 cups white flour mixed
    with 1 cup whole wheat flour
½ teaspoon baking soda   } mixed together
1 teaspoon baking powder
½ teaspoon cinnamon
½ teaspoon nutmeg
1 teaspoon vanilla
1 cup chopped nuts

Preheat the oven to 350° and butter a 9 x 5-inch loaf pan.

Put the grated zucchini in a colander, sprinkle it with the salt and let it drain while you prepare the batter. Beat the eggs in a large bowl and beat in the sugar, butter, flour mixture and vanilla, beating after each addition until the batter is well mixed. Squeeze as much juice as you can from the zucchini, press it dry with paper towels and mix it into the batter. Stir in the chopped nuts and pour the batter into the pan. Bake for about an hour and 20 minutes, or until a toothpick inserted into the center comes out clean. Let the loaf cool. Cut it into thin slices and serve as a snack or dessert.

Menus for a
Summer Feast

Each of the following menus offers a variety of dishes for every course of your meal. Each is a masterplan with dozens of possible combinations. With a bit of ingenuity you can create a different meal for every day of the summer. All the menus are designed to keep last-minute cooking to a minimum; some can be prepared entirely in advance.

Lunch Menus

SALAD LUNCH

Hard-cooked Eggs: Butter Stuffed or with Anchovy Sauce or with Dill
Mayonnaise

Chicken and Spinach Salad or Mussel Salad with Rice or Tuna and
Watercress Salad

Fruit Salad with Yogurt or Sweet and Sour Cherry Soup or Peaches with
Strawberry Sauce

SOUP AND MOUSSE

Beet Borsch or Cucumber Soup with Buttermilk or Jellied Chicken Soup
with Lemon and Herbs

Chicken Mousse or Chicken Liver Custard or Fish Mousse with
Basil-Tomato Sauce

Melon Salad or Strawberry Granita or Plum Compote

Dinner Menus

HOT SOUP AND COLD MEAT

Raw Vegetables with Sardine-Anchovy Dip or Arugula Dip or Tapénade

Hot Tomato Soup with Peppers or Swiss Chard or Cream and Tarragon

Fried Chicken Balls or Pork Braised in Milk or Pâté-Stuffed Veal

Potato and Watercress Salad

Fruit Pie

COOL STUFFED PEPPERS AND HOT MEAT

Stuffed Peppers with Tomato and Herb Stuffing or Anchovy and Caper Stuffing or Hot Sausage Stuffing

Steak alla Pizzaiola or Veal Chops in Tarragon Sauce or Stir-Fried Chicken Bits

Swiss Chard Salad

Bread with Herb Butter

Coeur à la Crème

CHARCOAL-GRILLED MEAT, VEGETABLES, DESSERT

Eggplant with Yogurt

Grilled Steak or Butterflied Pork Loin or Shish Kebab

Zucchini on a Skewer

Lentils with Sorrel or Rice Salad with Rosemary or Bulgur Salad

Broiled Peaches with Raspberry Sauce

COLD FISH DINNER

Hot or Cold Lettuce Soup

Large Whole Steamed or Poached Fish with Aïoli or Skordalía or Herb
   Mayonnaise

Boiled New Potatoes with Herb Butter

Cucumber, Fennel and Radish Salad or Carrot and Radish Salad or Hot
   and Sweet Pepper Salad

Blueberry Tart

CHARCOAL-GRILLED FISH DINNER

Grilled Clams on the Half-Shell

Small Whole Grilled Fish or Fillets

Foil Packages of Vegetables

Green Beans with Yogurt or Peperonata or Potato Salad with Horseradish

Gooseberry Fool or Peach Mousse or Berries with Crème Fraîche

COLD ROAST BEEF BUFFET

Fish Pâté

Cold Roast Beef

Assorted Stuffed Vegetables
   (eggplant, zucchini, tomatoes, summer squash, cucumbers, squash
   blossoms, peppers)

Tomato Bavarian Cream or Beets with Their Greens or Spinach and
   Parsley Salad

Summer Fruits with Zabaglione Sauce

VEGETARIAN FEAST

Fried Green Tomatoes or Butter-Steamed Green Beans or Sautéed
 Radishes

Gazpacho

Summer's Best Basil Crêpes or Stuffed Eggplant or Zucchini Flan

Lettuce Salad with Cheese

Watermelon Granita

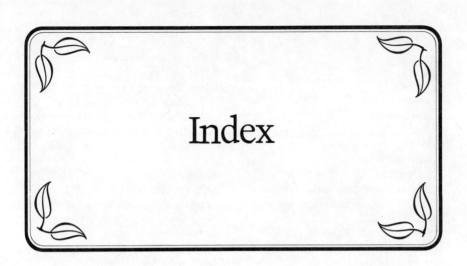

Index